Y0-BRW-722

National Safety Council

INJURY FACTS®

2001 Edition

FORMERLY
ACCIDENT FACTS®

LIBRARY
WITHDRAWN
DULUTH, MINNESOTA 55811

2001

The National Safety Council, chartered by an act of Congress, is a nongovernmental, not-for-profit, public service organization devoted solely to educating and influencing society to adopt safety, health, and environmental policies, practices, and procedures that prevent and mitigate human suffering and economic losses arising from preventable causes.

Injury Facts®, the Council's annual statistical report on unintentional injuries and their characteristics and costs, was prepared by:

Research and Statistics Department
Mei-Li Lin, Director
Alan F. Hoskin, Manager
Kevin T. Fearn
Kathleen T. Porretta, Production Manager
Jaime D. Vaeth

Fleet accident rates were prepared by:

Carolanne Haase

Questions or comments about the content of *Injury Facts*® should be directed to the Research and Statistics Department, National Safety Council, 1121 Spring Lake Drive, Itasca, IL 60143, or telephone 630-775-2322, or fax 630-285-0242, or E-mail rssdept@nsc.org.

For price and ordering information, write Customer Relations, National Safety Council, 1121 Spring Lake Drive, Itasca, IL 60143, or telephone 1-800-621-7619, or fax 630-285-0797.

Acknowledgments
The information presented in *Injury Facts*® was made possible by the cooperation of many organizations and individuals, including state vital and health statistics authorities, state traffic authorities, state workers' compensation authorities, state and local safety councils, trade associations, Bureau of the Census, Bureau of Labor Statistics, Consumer Product Safety Commission, Federal Highway Administration, Federal Railroad Administration, National Center for Health Statistics, National Fire Protection Association, National Highway Traffic Safety Administration, National Transportation Safety Board, National Weather Service, and Mine Safety and Health Administration. Specific contributions are acknowledged in footnotes and source notes throughout the book.

Visit the National Safety Council's website:

http://www.nsc.org

Copyright © 2001, National Safety Council.

All rights reserved.

The copyrighting of *Injury Facts*® is not intended to prevent use of the material for injury prevention purposes. The information may be used (except where copyright is held by another organization), with credit to the National Safety Council—the only restriction being that the original meaning shall be preserved.

Suggested citation: National Safety Council. (2001). *Injury Facts*®, *2001 Edition.* Itasca, IL: Author.

Library of Congress Catalog Card Number: 99-74142

Printed in U.S.A.   ISBN 0–87912–231–5   NSC Press Product No. 02301–0000

TABLE OF CONTENTS

FOREWORD

Summary and Trends

Unintentional-injury deaths were unchanged in 2000 compared to the revised 1999 total. Unintentional-injury deaths were estimated to total 97,300 in both years. The 2000 estimate is less than 1% lower than the 1998 final count of 97,835. The 2000 figure is 12% greater than the 1992 total of 86,777 (the lowest annual total since 1924) but 16% below the 1969 peak of 116,385 deaths.

The death rate in 2000 was 35.3 per 100,000 population—4% greater than the lowest rate on record, which was 34.0 in 1992.

According to the latest final data (1998), unintentional injuries continued to be the fifth leading cause of death, exceeded only by heart disease, cancer, stroke, and chronic obstructive pulmonary diseases. Preliminary death certificate data for 1999 indicate that unintentional injuries will remain in fifth place.

Nonfatal injuries also affect millions of Americans. In 1999, about 2.6 million people were hospitalized for injuries; about 37.6 million people were treated in hospital emergency departments and about 9.3 million in outpatient departments; and about 86.9 million visits to physicians' offices were due to injuries. In 1997, about 34.4 million people—more than one in eight—sought medical attention because of an injury.

The economic impact of these fatal and nonfatal unintentional injuries amounted to $512.4 billion in 2000. This is equivalent to about $1,900 per capita, or about $5,000 per household. These are costs that every individual and household pays whether directly out of pocket, through higher prices for goods and services, or through higher taxes.

The graph on the opposite page shows one of the reasons that unintentional-injury deaths are of such great concern even though they account for only about 4.2% of all deaths. The average age at death for the four leading causes of death varies from 70.3 years for cancer to 78.9 years for stroke. For unintentional injuries, however, the average age at death is only 50.0 years old. People who die from unintentional injuries may still be raising families and be employed full time. They also may look forward to an average of 29.8 years of remaining lifetime whereas those who die from heart disease, cancer, stroke, or chronic obstructive pulmonary disease have, on average, 9.6 to 14.3 years of life remaining.

Changes in the 2001 Edition

For the second year in a row, eight pages have been added to *Injury Facts*® to provide more usable information to readers. The book has grown from 108 pages to 170 pages over the past 10 years.

The Work section has been expanded and reorganized to provide more detailed information for each industry division. The occupational injury and illness incidence rates of reporters to the National Safety Council are no longer available because the award program from which they were obtained was restructured. The incidence rates from the Bureau of Labor Statistics annual survey may still be found on pages 58–63.

The Home and Public sections were consolidated into a single Home and Community section so that more special topics could be covered.

Also look for *new* data on...

- Falls
- Confined spaces
- Part of body (work)
- Carpal tunnel syndrome
- Illness and productivity
- Graduated licensing
- School violence

and *updated* data on...

- Occupational injury and illness incidence rates
- Workers' compensation claims and costs
- Highway work zones
- Sports injuries
- Home fires
- Environmental health issues
- State-level injury mortality

AVERAGE AGE AT DEATH AND REMAINING LIFETIME, UNITED STATES, 1998

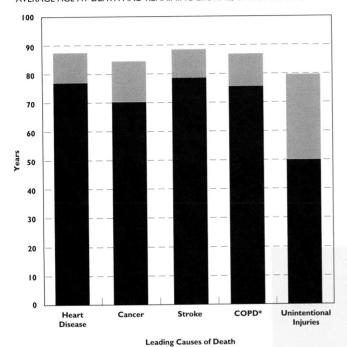

*Chronic obstructive pulmonary disease.

ALL UNINTENTIONAL
INJURIES

ALL UNINTENTIONAL INJURIES, 2000

Unintentional-injury deaths were unchanged in 2000 compared to 1999 following a decrease in 1999 compared to 1998. The 2000 estimated death total was 97,300.

The population death rate for all unintentional injuries decreased slightly. The 2000 death rate of 35.3 per 100,000 population was 1% lower than the 1999 revised rate of 35.7. The 1992 rate, 34.0, was the lowest on record.

Comparing 2000 to 1999, home deaths increased and public deaths decreased, while work and motor-vehicle deaths were virtually unchanged. The population death rate in the motor-vehicle and public classes declined, work was unchanged, and home increased.

The motor-vehicle death total was unchanged in 2000. The motor-vehicle death rate per 100,000,000 vehicle-miles was 1.60 in 2000, unchanged from the 1999 revised rate and down 3% from the 1998 revised rate of 1.65.

ALL UNINTENTIONAL INJURIES, 2000

Class	2000 Deaths	Change from 1999	Deaths per 100,000 Persons	Disabling Injuries[a]
All Classes[b]	**97,300**	0%	35.3	20,500,000
Motor-vehicle	43,000	0%	15.6	2,300,000
Public nonwork	*40,600*			*2,200,000*
Work	*2,200*			*100,000*
Home	*200*			*([c])*
Work	5,200	+1%	1.9	3,900,000
Nonmotor-vehicle	*3,000*			*3,800,000*
Motor-vehicle	*2,200*			*100,000*
Home	29,500	+5%	10.7	7,100,000
Nonmotor-vehicle	*29,300*			*7,100,000*
Motor-vehicle	*200*			*([c])*
Public	22,000	−6%	8.0	7,300,000

Source: National Safety Council estimates (rounded) based on data from the National Center for Health Statistics, Bureau of Labor Statistics, state departments of health, state traffic authorities, and state industrial commissions. The National Safety Council adopted the Bureau of Labor Statistics' Census of Fatal Occupational Injuries count for work-related unintentional injuries retroactive to 1992 data. See the Glossary for definitions and the Technical Appendix for revised estimating procedures.

[a] Disabling beyond the day of injury. Disabling injuries are not reported on a national basis, so the totals shown are approximations based on ratios of disabling injuries to deaths developed by the National Safety Council. The totals are the best estimates for the current year. They should not, however, be compared with totals shown in previous editions of this book to indicate year-to-year changes or trends. See the Glossary for definitions and the Technical Appendix for estimating procedures.

[b] Deaths and injuries above for the four separate classes add to more than the All Classes figures due to rounding and because some deaths and injuries are included in more than one class. For example, 2,200 work deaths involved motor vehicles in transport and are in both the work and motor-vehicle totals and 200 motor-vehicle deaths occurred on home premises and are in both home and motor-vehicle. The total of such duplication amounted to about 2,400 deaths and 100,000 injuries in 2000.

[c] Less than 10,000.

UNINTENTIONAL-INJURY DEATHS BY CLASS, UNITED STATES, 1996–2000

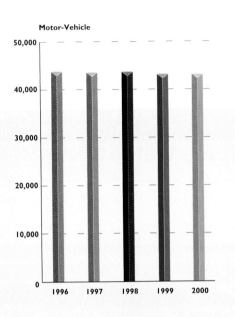

Motor-Vehicle

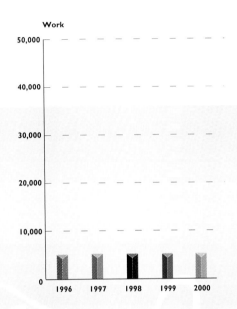

Work

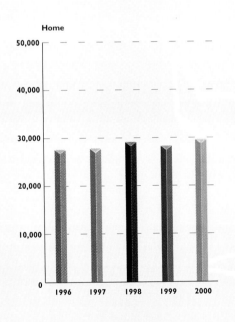

Home

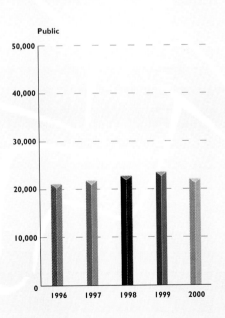

Public

COSTS OF UNINTENTIONAL INJURIES BY CLASS, 2000

The total cost of unintentional injuries in 2000, $512.4 billion, includes estimates of economic costs of fatal and nonfatal unintentional injuries together with employer costs, vehicle damage costs, and fire losses. Wage and productivity losses, medical expenses, administrative expenses, and employer costs are included in all four classes of injuries. Cost components unique to each class are identified below.

Motor-vehicle costs include property damage from motor-vehicle accidents. Work costs include the value of property damage in on-the-job motor-vehicle accidents and fires. Home and public costs include estimated fire losses, but do not include other property damage costs.

Besides the estimated $512.4 billion in economic losses from unintentional injuries in 2000, lost quality of life from those injuries is valued at an additional $1,158.7 billion, making the comprehensive cost $1,671.1 billion in 2000.

Cost estimating procedures were revised extensively for the 1993 edition of *Accident Facts*®. New components were added, new benchmarks adopted, and a new discount rate assumed (see the Technical Appendix). In general, cost estimates are not comparable from year to year. As additional or more precise data become available, they are used from that point forward. Previously estimated figures are not revised.

CERTAIN COSTS OF UNINTENTIONAL INJURIES BY CLASS, 2000 ($ BILLIONS)

Cost	Total[a]	Motor-Vehicle	Work	Home	Public Nonmotor-Vehicle
Total	**$512.4**	**$201.5**	**$131.2**	**$111.9**	**$82.6**
Wage and productivity losses	259.8	71.5	67.6	70.9	53.6
Medical expenses	93.5	24.6	24.2	26.4	19.6
Administrative expenses[b]	72.6	48.0	22.3	4.9	4.5
Motor-vehicle damage	55.5	55.5	2.2	(c)	(c)
Employer cost	20.9	1.9	11.5	4.4	3.5
Fire loss	10.1	(c)	3.4	5.3	1.4

Source: National Safety Council estimates. See the Technical Appendix.
[a] Duplication between work and motor-vehicle, which amounted to $14.8 billion, was eliminated from the total.
[b] Home and public insurance administration costs may include costs of administering medical treatment claims for some motor-vehicle injuries filed through health insurance plans.
[c] Not included, see comments above.

COST OF UNINTENTIONAL INJURIES BY CLASS, 2000

TOTAL COST $512.4 BILLION

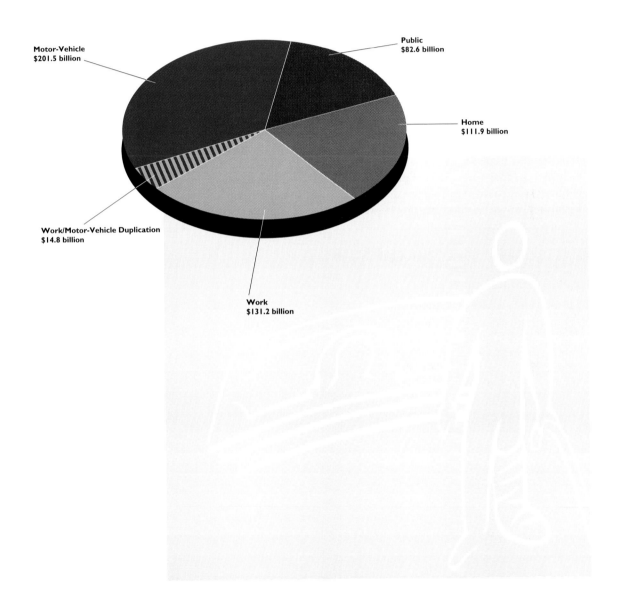

Motor-Vehicle
$201.5 billion

Public
$82.6 billion

Home
$111.9 billion

Work/Motor-Vehicle Duplication
$14.8 billion

Work
$131.2 billion

COSTS OF UNINTENTIONAL INJURIES BY COMPONENT

Wage and Productivity Losses

A person's contribution to the wealth of the nation usually is measured in terms of wages and household production. The total of wages and fringe benefits together with an estimate of the replacement-cost value of household services provides an estimate of this lost productivity. Also included is travel delay for motor-vehicle accidents.

Medical Expenses

Doctor fees, hospital charges, the cost of medicines, future medical costs, and ambulance, helicopter, and other emergency medical services are included.

Administrative Expenses

Includes the administrative cost of public and private insurance, and police and legal costs. Private insurance administrative costs are the difference between premiums paid to insurance companies and claims paid out by them. It is their cost of doing business and is a part of the cost total. Claims paid by insurance companies are not identified separately, as every claim is compensation for losses such as wages, medical expenses, property damage, etc.

Motor-Vehicle Damage

Includes the value of property damage to vehicles from motor-vehicle accidents. The cost of normal wear and tear to vehicles is not included.

Employer Costs

This is an estimate of the uninsured costs incurred by employers, representing the dollar value of time lost by uninjured workers. It includes time spent investigating and reporting injuries, giving first aid, hiring and training of replacement workers, and the extra cost of overtime for uninjured workers.

Fire Loss

Includes losses from both structure fires and nonstructure fires such as vehicles, outside storage, crops, and timber.

Work–Motor-Vehicle Duplication

The cost of motor-vehicle crashes that involve persons in the course of their work is included in both classes but the duplication is eliminated from the total. The duplication in 2000 amounted to $14.8 billion and was made up of $3.8 billion in wage and productivity losses, $1.3 billion in medical expenses, $7.1 billion in administrative expenses, $2.2 billion in vehicle damage, and $0.4 billion in uninsured employer costs.

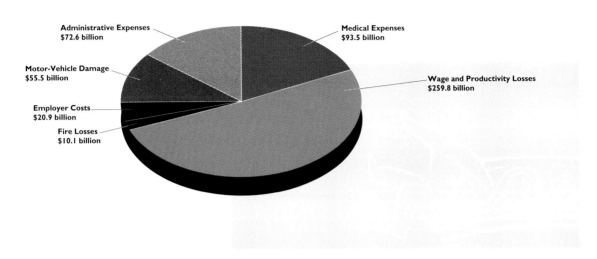

TOTAL COST $512.4 BILLION

Administrative Expenses
$72.6 billion

Medical Expenses
$93.5 billion

Motor-Vehicle Damage
$55.5 billion

Wage and Productivity Losses
$259.8 billion

Employer Costs
$20.9 billion

Fire Losses
$10.1 billion

COST EQUIVALENTS

The costs of unintentional injuries are immense—
billions of dollars. Since figures this large can be
difficult to comprehend, it is sometimes useful to
reduce the numbers to a more understandable scale by
relating them to quantities encountered in daily life.

The table below shows how the costs of unintentional
injuries compare to common quantities such as taxes,
corporate profits, or stock dividends.

COST EQUIVALENTS, 2000

The Cost of ...	Is Equivalent to ...
...All Injuries ($512.4 billion)	...51 cents of every dollar paid in federal personal income taxes, **or** ...54 cents of every dollar spent on food in the United States.
...Motor-Vehicle Crashes ($201.5 billion)	...purchasing 610 gallons of gasoline for each registered vehicle in the United States, **or** ...almost $1,100 per licensed driver, **or** ...more than 25 times greater than the combined profits reported by Ford and General Motors.
...Work Injuries ($131.2 billion)	...33 cents of every dollar of corporate dividends to stockholders, **or** ...14 cents of every dollar of pre-tax corporate profits, **or** ...exceeds the combined profits reported by the top thirteen Fortune 500 companies.
...Home Injuries ($111.9 billion)	...a $90,900 rebate on each new single-family home built, **or** ...45 cents of every dollar of property taxes paid.
...Public Injuries ($82.6 billion)	...an $8.4 million grant to each public library in the United States, **or** ...a $104,200 bonus for each police officer and firefighter.

Source: National Safety Council estimates.

DEATHS DUE TO UNINTENTIONAL INJURIES, 2000

All Unintentional Injuries

The term "unintentional" covers most deaths from injury and poisoning. Excluded are homicides (including legal intervention), suicides, deaths for which none of these categories can be determined, and war deaths.

	Total	Change from 1999	Death Rate[a]
Deaths	97,300	0%	35.3

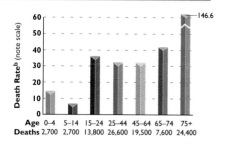

Motor-Vehicle Accidents

Includes deaths involving mechanically or electrically powered highway-transport vehicles in motion (except those on rails), both on and off the highway or street.

	Total	Change from 1999	Death Rate[a]
Deaths	43,000	0%	15.6

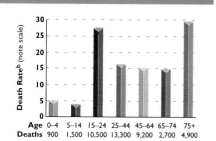

Falls

Includes deaths from falls from one level to another or on the same level. Excludes falls in or from transport vehicles, or while boarding or alighting from them.

	Total	Change from 1999	Death Rate[a]
Deaths	16,200	+1%	5.9

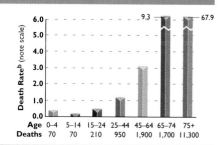

Poisoning by solids and liquids

Includes deaths from drugs, medicines, mushrooms, and shellfish, as well as commonly recognized poisons. Excludes poisonings from spoiled foods, salmonella, etc., which are classified as disease deaths.

	Total	Change from 1999	Death Rate[a]
Deaths	11,700	+6%	4.2

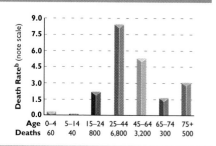

Drowning

Includes all drownings (work and nonwork) in boat accidents and those resulting from swimming, playing in the water, or falling in. Excludes drownings in floods and other cataclysms, which are classified to the cataclysm.

	Total	Change from 1999	Death Rate[a]
Deaths	3,900	-3%	1.4

See footnotes on page 9.

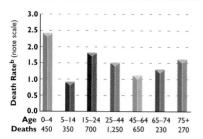

Fires, Burns, and Deaths Associated with Fires

Includes deaths from fires, burns, and from injuries in conflagrations—such as asphyxiation, falls, and struck by falling objects. Excludes burns from hot objects or liquids.

	Total	Change from 1999	Death Rate[a]
Deaths	3,600	+16%	1.3

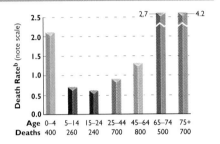

Age	0–4	5–14	15–24	25–44	45–64	65–74	75+
Deaths	400	260	240	700	800	500	700

Suffocation by Ingested Object

Includes deaths from unintentional ingestion or inhalation of food or other objects resulting in the obstruction of respiratory passages.

	Total	Change from 1999	Death Rate[a]
Deaths	3,400	+10%	1.2

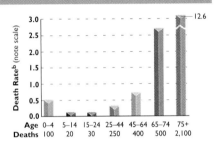

Age	0–4	5–14	15–24	25–44	45–64	65–74	75+
Deaths	100	20	30	250	400	500	2,100

Firearms

Includes unintentional deaths from firearms injuries principally in recreational activities or on home premises. Excludes deaths from explosive material or in war operations.

	Total	Change from 1999	Death Rate[a]
Deaths	600	-25%	0.2

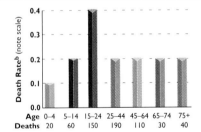

Age	0–4	5–14	15–24	25–44	45–64	65–74	75+
Deaths	20	60	150	190	110	30	40

Poisoning by Gases and Vapors

Mostly carbon monoxide due to incomplete combustion, involving cooking and heating equipment and standing motor vehicles. Excludes deaths in conflagrations, or associated with transport vehicles in motion.

	Total	Change from 1999	Death Rate[a]
Deaths	400	0%	0.1

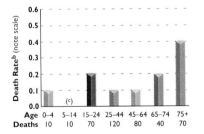

Age	0–4	5–14	15–24	25–44	45–64	65–74	75+
Deaths	10	10	70	120	80	40	70

All Other Types

Most important types included are: medical and surgical complications and misadventures, machinery, air transport, water transport (except drownings), mechanical suffocation, and excessive cold.

	Total	Change from 1999	Death Rate[a]
Deaths	14,500	-9%	5.3

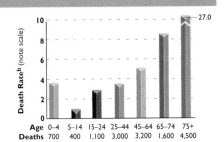

Age	0–4	5–14	15–24	25–44	45–64	65–74	75+
Deaths	700	400	1,100	3,000	3,200	1,600	4,500

[a]Deaths per 100,000 population.
[b]Deaths per 100,000 population in each age group.
[c]Rate less than 0.05.

LEADING CAUSES OF DEATH

Unintentional injuries are the leading cause of death among persons in age groups from 1 to 34. Among persons of all ages, unintentional injuries are the fifth leading cause of death. For children in the 5 to 14 year age group, unintentional injuries claim more than three times as many lives as the next leading cause of death, accounting for almost 42% of the 7,791 total deaths of these persons in 1998. Approximately 60% of the victims in this age group are males.

DEATHS AND DEATH RATES BY AGE AND SEX, 1998

Cause	Number of Deaths			Death Rates[a]		
	Total	Male	Female	Total	Male	Female
All Ages						
All Causes	**2,337,256**	**1,157,260**	**1,179,996**	**864.9**	**876.5**	**853.7**
Heart disease	724,859	353,897	370,962	268.2	268.0	268.4
Cancer	541,532	282,065	259,467	200.4	213.6	187.7
Stroke (cerebrovascular disease)	158,448	61,145	97,303	58.6	46.3	70.4
Chronic obstructive pulmonary diseases	112,584	57,018	55,566	41.7	43.2	40.2
Unintentional Injuries	**97,835**	**63,042**	**34,793**	**36.2**	**47.7**	**25.2**
Motor-vehicle	43,501	28,990	14,511	16.1	22.0	10.5
Falls	16,274	8,035	8,239	6.0	6.1	6.0
Poison (solid, liquid)	10,255	7,497	2,758	3.8	5.7	2.0
Drowning	4,406	3,575	831	1.6	2.7	0.6
Ingestion of food, object	3,515	1,735	1,780	1.3	1.3	1.3
All other unintentional injuries	19,884	13,210	6,674	7.4	10.0	4.8
Pneumonia and influenza	91,871	40,979	50,892	34.0	31.0	36.8
Diabetes mellitus	64,751	29,584	35,167	24.0	22.4	25.4
Suicide	30,575	24,538	6,037	11.3	18.6	4.4
Nephritis and nephrosis	26,182	12,561	13,621	9.7	9.5	9.9
Chronic liver disease, cirrhosis	25,192	16,343	8,849	9.3	12.4	6.4
Septicemia	23,731	10,225	13,506	8.8	7.7	9.8
Alzheimer's disease	22,725	7,054	15,671	8.4	5.3	11.3
Homicide and legal intervention	18,272	14,023	4,249	6.8	10.6	3.1
Atherosclerosis	15,279	5,719	9,560	5.7	4.3	6.9
Hypertension	14,308	5,526	8,782	5.3	4.2	6.4
Under 1 Year						
All Causes	**28,371**	**15,786**	**12,585**	**748.4**	**814.7**	**679.2**
Certain conditions originating in perinatal period	13,294	7,429	5,865	350.7	383.4	316.5
Congenital anomalies	6,212	3,282	2,930	163.9	169.4	158.1
Sudden infant death syndrome	2,882	1,698	1,124	76.0	87.6	60.7
Unintentional Injuries	**754**	**433**	**321**	**19.9**	**22.3**	**17.3**
Mechanical suffocation	312	178	134	8.2	9.2	7.2
Motor-vehicle	162	88	74	4.3	4.5	4.0
Ingestion of food, object	64	34	30	1.7	1.8	1.6
Drowning	63	37	26	1.7	1.9	1.4
Fires, burns	41	24	17	1.1	1.2	0.9
All other unintentional injuries	112	72	40	3.0	3.7	2.2
Heart disease	609	312	297	11.6	12.3	10.9
Homicide	322	172	150	8.5	8.9	8.1
Stroke	296	174	122	6.0	7.0	5.0
Septicemia	216	111	105	5.7	5.7	5.7
Nephritis and nephrosis	138	69	69	2.8	3.1	2.5
Viral diseases	98	50	48	2.6	2.6	2.6
Diseases of blood and blood forming organs	94	53	41	2.5	2.7	2.2
Malignant neoplasms	78	43	35	2.1	2.2	1.9
1 to 4 Years						
All Causes	**5,251**	**2,920**	**2,331**	**34.5**	**37.6**	**31.4**
Unintentional Injuries	**1,935**	**1,155**	**780**	**12.7**	**14.9**	**10.5**
Motor-vehicle	759	416	343	5.0	5.4	4.6
Drowning	496	326	170	3.3	4.2	2.3
Fires, burns	258	148	110	1.7	1.9	1.5
Ingestion of food, object	78	51	27	0.5	0.7	0.4
Mechanical suffocation	74	43	31	0.5	0.6	0.4
All other unintentional injuries	270	171	99	1.8	2.2	1.3
Congenital anomalies	564	287	277	3.7	3.7	3.7
Homicide and legal intervention	399	223	176	2.6	2.9	2.4
Cancer	365	189	176	2.4	2.4	2.4
Heart disease	214	114	100	1.4	1.5	1.3
Pneumonia and influenza	146	73	73	1.0	0.9	1.0
Septicemia	89	54	35	0.6	0.7	0.5
Certain conditions originating in the perinatal period	75	37	38	0.5	0.5	0.5
Stroke	57	25	32	0.4	0.3	0.4
Benign neoplasms	53	28	25	0.3	0.4	0.3

See source and footnotes on page 12.

DEATHS AND DEATH RATES BY AGE AND SEX, 1998, Cont.

Cause	Number of Deaths			Death Rates[a]		
	Total	Male	Female	Total	Male	Female
5 to 14 Years						
All Causes	**7,791**	**4,686**	**3,105**	**19.9**	**23.4**	**16.2**
Unintentional injuries	**3,254**	**2,086**	**1,168**	**8.3**	**10.4**	**6.1**
Motor-vehicle	1,868	1,144	724	4.8	5.7	3.8
Drowning	444	337	107	1.1	1.7	0.6
Fires, burns	300	164	136	0.8	0.8	0.7
Firearms	102	81	21	0.3	0.4	0.1
Mechanical suffocation	91	74	17	0.2	0.4	0.1
All other unintentional injuries	449	286	163	1.1	1.4	0.9
Cancer	1,013	582	431	2.6	2.9	2.3
Homicide and legal intervention	460	257	203	1.2	1.3	1.1
Congenital anomalies	371	197	174	0.9	1.0	0.9
Heart disease	326	191	135	0.8	1.0	0.7
Suicide	324	241	83	0.8	1.2	0.4
Chronic obstructive pulmonary diseases	152	88	64	0.4	0.4	0.3
Pneumonia and influenza	121	57	64	0.3	0.3	0.3
Benign neoplasms	84	46	38	0.2	0.2	0.2
Stroke (cerebrovascular disease)	82	48	34	0.2	0.2	0.2
15 to 24 Years						
All Causes	**30,627**	**22,717**	**7,910**	**82.3**	**119.3**	**43.5**
Unintentional injuries	**13,349**	**9,887**	**3,462**	**35.9**	**51.9**	**19.0**
Motor-vehicle	10,026	7,109	2,917	26.9	37.3	16.0
Drowning	821	738	83	2.2	3.9	0.5
Poison (solid, liquid)	779	627	152	2.1	3.3	0.8
Firearms	260	243	17	0.7	1.3	0.1
Falls	236	193	43	0.6	1.0	0.2
All other unintentional injuries	1,227	977	250	3.3	5.1	1.4
Homicide and legal intervention	5,506	4,720	786	14.8	24.8	4.3
Suicide	4,135	3,532	603	11.1	18.5	3.3
Cancer	1,699	1,029	670	4.6	5.4	3.7
Heart disease	1,057	672	385	2.8	3.5	2.1
Congenital anomalies	450	256	194	1.2	1.3	1.1
Chronic obstructive pulmonary diseases	239	149	90	0.6	0.8	0.5
Pneumonia and influenza	215	109	106	0.6	0.6	0.6
Human immunodeficiency virus infection	194	93	101	0.5	0.5	0.6
Stroke (cerebrovascular disease)	178	109	69	0.5	0.6	0.4
25 to 34 Years						
All Causes	**42,516**	**29,215**	**13,301**	**109.7**	**151.8**	**68.2**
Unintentional injuries	**12,045**	**9,154**	**2,891**	**31.1**	**47.6**	**14.8**
Motor-vehicle	7,132	5,203	1,929	18.4	27.0	9.9
Poison (solid, liquid)	2,078	1,590	488	5.4	8.3	2.5
Drowning	637	557	80	1.6	2.9	0.4
Falls	351	295	56	0.9	1.5	0.3
Fires, burns	254	177	77	0.7	0.9	0.4
All other unintentional injuries	1,593	1,332	261	4.1	6.9	1.3
Suicide	5,365	4,404	961	13.8	22.9	4.9
Homicide and legal intervention	4,565	3,611	954	11.8	18.8	4.9
Cancer	4,385	2,092	2,293	11.3	10.9	11.8
Heart disease	3,207	2,071	1,136	8.3	10.8	5.8
Human immunodeficiency virus infection	2,912	2,056	856	7.5	10.7	4.4
Stroke (cerebrovascular disease)	670	327	343	1.7	1.7	1.8
Diabetes mellitus	636	356	280	1.6	1.9	1.4
Pneumonia and influenza	531	308	223	1.4	1.6	1.1
Chronic liver disease, cirrhosis	506	332	174	1.3	1.7	0.9
35 to 44 Years						
All Causes	**88,866**	**57,139**	**31,727**	**199.7**	**258.7**	**141.6**
Cancer	17,022	7,592	9,430	38.3	34.4	42.1
Unintentional injuries	**15,127**	**11,078**	**4,049**	**34.0**	**50.1**	**18.1**
Motor-vehicle	6,963	4,791	2,172	15.6	21.7	9.7
Poison (solid, liquid)	4,146	3,077	1,069	9.3	13.9	4.8
Falls	695	574	121	1.6	2.6	0.5
Drowning	686	588	98	1.5	2.7	0.4
Fires, burns	421	297	124	0.9	1.3	0.6
All other unintentional injuries	2,216	1,751	465	5.0	7.9	2.1
Heart disease	13,593	9,725	3,868	30.5	44.0	17.3
Suicide	6,837	5,296	1,541	15.4	24.0	6.9
Human immunodeficiency virus infection	5,746	4,453	1,293	12.9	20.2	5.8
Homicide and legal intervention	3,567	2,599	968	8.0	11.8	4.3
Chronic liver disease, cirrhosis	3,370	2,338	1,032	7.6	10.6	4.6
Stroke (cerebrovascular disease)	2,650	1,376	1,274	6.0	6.2	5.7
Diabetes mellitus	1,885	1,151	734	4.2	5.2	3.3
Pneumonia and influenza	1,400	810	590	3.1	3.7	2.6

See source and footnote on page 12.

DEATHS AND DEATH RATES BY AGE AND SEX, 1998, Cont.

Cause	Number of Deaths			Death Rates[a]		
	Total	Male	Female	Total	Male	Female
45 to 54 Years						
All Causes	**146,479**	**91,727**	**54,752**	**423.7**	**542.9**	**309.7**
Cancer	45,747	23,071	22,676	132.3	136.6	128.3
Heart disease	35,056	25,715	9,341	101.4	152.2	52.8
Unintentional injuries	**10,946**	**7,983**	**2,963**	**31.7**	**47.3**	**16.8**
Motor-vehicle	4,996	3,439	1,557	14.4	20.4	8.8
Poison (solid, liquid)	2,159	1,615	544	6.2	9.6	3.1
Falls	844	665	179	2.4	3.9	1.0
Drowning	445	379	66	1.3	2.2	0.4
Fires, burns	361	243	118	1.0	1.4	0.7
All other unintentional injuries	2,141	1,642	499	6.2	9.7	2.8
Chronic liver disease, cirrhosis	5,744	4,296	1,448	16.6	25.4	8.2
Stroke (cerebrovascular disease)	5,709	3,121	2,588	16.5	18.5	14.6
Suicide	5,131	3,896	1,235	14.8	23.1	7.0
Diabetes mellitus	4,386	2,488	1,898	12.7	14.7	10.7
Human immunodeficiency virus infection	3,120	2,563	557	9.0	15.2	3.2
Chronic obstructive pulmonary diseases	2,828	1,380	1,448	8.2	8.2	8.2
Pneumonia and influenza	2,167	1,302	865	6.3	7.7	4.9
55 to 64 Years						
All causes	**233,724**	**140,134**	**93,590**	**1,031.2**	**1,297.3**	**788.9**
Cancer	87,024	47,665	39,359	383.9	441.3	331.8
Heart disease	65,068	44,423	20,645	287.1	411.3	174.0
Chronic obstructive pulmonary diseases	10,162	5,357	4,805	44.8	49.6	40.5
Stroke (cerebrovascular disease)	9,653	5,345	4,308	42.6	49.5	36.3
Diabetes mellitus	8,705	4,651	4,054	38.4	43.1	34.2
Unintentional injuries	**7,340**	**4,988**	**2,352**	**32.4**	**46.2**	**19.8**
Motor-vehicle	3,420	2,219	1,201	15.1	20.5	10.1
Falls	896	647	249	4.0	6.0	2.1
Poison (solid, liquid)	491	316	175	2.2	2.9	1.5
Surgical, medical complications	370	190	180	1.6	1.8	1.5
Fires, burns	308	186	122	1.4	1.7	1.0
All other unintentional injuries	1,855	1,430	425	8.2	13.2	3.6
Chronic liver disease, cirrhosis	5,279	3,735	1,544	23.3	34.6	13.0
Pneumonia and influenza	3,856	2,287	1,569	17.0	21.2	13.2
Suicide	2,963	2,305	658	13.07	21.34	5.6
Nephritis and nephrosis	1,812	983	829	8.0	9.1	7.0
65 to 74 Years						
All Causes	**458,982**	**259,343**	**199,639**	**2,495.8**	**3,144.3**	**1,968.6**
Cancer	154,753	86,247	68,506	841.5	1,045.7	675.5
Heart disease	135,295	82,275	53,020	735.7	997.5	522.8
Chronic obstructive pulmonary diseases	31,102	16,597	14,505	169.1	201.2	143.0
Stroke (cerebrovascular disease)	23,912	12,017	11,895	130.0	145.7	117.3
Diabetes mellitus	16,490	8,160	8,330	89.7	98.9	82.1
Pneumonia and influenza	11,005	6,376	4,629	59.8	77.3	45.6
Unintentional injuries	**8,892**	**5,286**	**3,606**	**48.4**	**64.1**	**35.6**
Motor-vehicle	3,410	1,938	1,472	18.5	23.5	14.5
Falls	1,884	1,095	789	10.2	13.3	7.8
Surgical, medical complications	714	360	354	3.9	4.4	3.5
Ingestion of food, object	530	313	217	2.9	3.8	2.1
Fires, burns	397	241	156	2.2	2.9	1.5
All other unintentional injuries	1,957	1,339	618	10.6	16.2	6.1
Chronic liver disease, cirrhosis	5,655	3,396	2,259	30.8	41.2	22.3
Nephritis and nephrosis	4,778	2,505	2,273	26.0	30.4	22.4
Septicemia	4,474	2,238	2,236	24.3	27.1	22.0
75 years and over[b]						
All Causes	**1,294,649**	**533,593**	**761,056**	**8,093.1**	**8,972.5**	**7,572.7**
Heart disease	470,434	188,399	282,035	2,940.8	3,168.0	2,806.3
Cancer	229,446	113,555	115,891	1,434.3	1,909.5	1,153.1
Stroke (cerebrovascular disease)	115,241	38,603	76,638	720.4	649.1	762.6
Pneumonia and influenza	71,989	29,418	42,571	450.0	494.7	423.6
Chronic obstructive pulmonary diseases	66,801	32,786	34,015	417.6	551.3	338.5
Diabetes mellitus	32,484	12,702	19,782	203.1	213.6	196.8
Unintentional injuries	**24,193**	**10,992**	**13,201**	**151.2**	**184.8**	**131.4**
Falls	11,247	4,472	6,775	70.3	75.2	67.4
Motor-vehicle	4,765	2,643	2,122	29.8	44.4	21.1
Ingestion of food, object	2,010	836	1,174	12.6	14.1	11.7
Surgical, medical complications	1,545	651	894	9.7	10.9	8.9
Fires, burns	721	336	385	4.5	5.6	3.8
All other unintentional injuries	3,905	2,054	1,851	24.4	34.5	18.4
Alzheimer's Disease	20,510	6,080	14,430	128.2	102.2	143.6
Nephritis and nephrosis	17,862	8,028	9,834	111.7	135.0	97.9
Septicemia	14,540	5,449	9,091	90.9	91.6	90.5

Source: Deaths are latest figures from National Center for Health Statistics. Rates are National Safety Council calculations. The "all causes" total for each age group includes deaths not shown separately.
[a]*Deaths per 100,000 population in each age group.*
[b]*Category includes deaths where the age is unknown.*

LEADING CAUSES OF DEATH BY AGE GROUP, UNITED STATES, 1998

Rank	Age Group							
	All Ages	**Under 1**	**1–4**	**5–14**	**15–24**	**25–44**	**45–64**	**65 & Over**
1	Heart disease 724,859	Congenital anomalies 6,212	Unintentional injuries 1,935	Unintentional injuries 3,254	Unintentional injuries 13,349	Unintentional injuries 27,172	Malignant neoplasms 132,771	Heart disease 605,673
2	Malignant neoplasms 541,532	Short gestation[a] 4,101	Congenital anomalies 564	Malignant neoplasms 1,013	Homicide 5,506	Malignant neoplasms 21,407	Heart disease 100,124	Malignant neoplasms 384,186
3	Cerebrovascular diseases 158,448	SIDS[b] 2,822	Homicide 399	Homicide 460	Suicide 4,135	Heart disease 16,800	Unintentional injuries 18,286	Cerebrovascular diseases 139,144
4	COPD[c] 112,584	Maternal complications[a] 1,343	Malignant neoplasms 365	Congenital anomalies 371	Malignant neoplasms 1,699	Suicide 12,202	Cerebrovascular diseases 15,362	COPD[c] 97,896
5	Unintentional injuries 97,835	Respiratory distress[a] 1,295	Heart disease 214	Heart disease 326	Heart disease 1,057	HIV[d] 8,658	Diabetes mellitus 13,091	Pneumonia & Influenza 82,989
6	Pneumonia & Influenza 91,871	Placenta, cord, membranes[a] 961	Pneumonia & Influenza 146	Suicide 324	Congenital anomalies 450	Homicide 8,132	COPD[c] 12,990	Diabetes mellitus 48,974
7	Diabetes mellitus 64,751	Perinatal infections[a] 815	Septicemia 89	COPD[c] 152	COPD[c] 239	Liver disease 3,876	Liver disease 11,023	Unintentional injuries 32,975
8	Suicide 30,575	Unintentional injuries 754	Perinatal conditions 75	Pneumonia & Influenza 121	Pneumonia & Influenza 215	Cerebrovascular diseases 3,320	Suicide 8,094	Nephritis[e] 22,640
9	Nephritis[e] 26,182	Intrauterine hypoxia[a] 461	Cerebrovascular diseases 57	Benign neoplasms 84	HIV[d] 194	Diabetes mellitus 2,521	Pneumonia & Influenza 6,023	Alzheimer's disease 22,416
10	Liver disease 25,192	Pneumonia & Influenza 441	Benign neoplasms 53	Cerebrovascular diseases 82	Cerebrovascular diseases 178	Pneumonia & Influenza 1,931	HIV[d] 4,099	Septicemia 19,012

Source: National Center for Injury Prevention and Control, CDC, tabulations of National Center for Health Statistics mortality data.
[a] Included in "Certain conditions originating in perinatal period" on p. 10.
[b] Sudden infant death syndrome.
[c] Chronic obstructive pulmonary disease.
[d] Human immunodeficiency virus infection.
[e] Including nephrotic syndrome and nephrosis.

Heart disease, cancer, stroke, chronic obstructive pulmonary disease, and unintentional injuries were the leading causes of death in the United States in 1998. The graph below depicts the number of deaths attributed to these causes by single years of age.

Unintentional injuries were the leading cause of death of individuals aged 1 to 38 in 1998. The pattern of 1998 unintentional-injury fatalities shows that a substantial increase in fatalities occurred to persons between ages 15 and 18, rising from 639 for 15-year-olds to 1,765 for 18-year-olds. This trend can be attributed to the sharp increase in motor-vehicle deaths for persons of the same age range. Persons age 18 fell victim to the most unintentional-injury fatalities with motor-vehicle crashes accounting for a majority of the death total. Fatalities gradually decreased and remained relatively stable thereafter with the exception of a slight increase in unintentional-injury deaths for persons between ages 30 and 42. From ages 1 to 33, deaths from motor-vehicle crashes alone exceeded those for any other cause.

Heart disease, the leading cause of death overall, was also the leading cause of death of persons aged 74 and over in 1998. Heart disease fatalities peaked at 25,507 for persons 84 years of age. Cancer, the second leading cause of death overall, was the leading cause of death of persons from ages 39 to 73 in 1998. Cancer deaths peaked at 18,317 for individuals aged 76. Human immunodeficiency virus (HIV) deaths peaked at 615 for persons aged 37, compared to the high in 1996 of 1,508 for 37-year-olds.

The third leading cause of death in the United States in 1998 was stroke, which was the second leading cause of death of persons aged 91 and over. Stroke deaths peaked at 6,629 for persons age 85. The next leading cause of death was chronic obstructive pulmonary disease, which was the third leading cause of death of persons aged 60 to 75. Chronic obstructive pulmonary disease deaths reached a high at 4,692 deaths for persons 77 years of age.

Source: National Safety Council tabulations of National Center for Health Statistics data. ICD–9 codes are 390–398, 402, 404–429 for heart disease; 140–208 for cancer; 430–438 for stroke; 490–496 for chronic obstructive pulmonary disease; E800–E949 for unintentional-injuries; E810–E825 for motor-vehicle fatalities.

LEADING CAUSES OF DEATH BY AGE, UNITED STATES, 1998

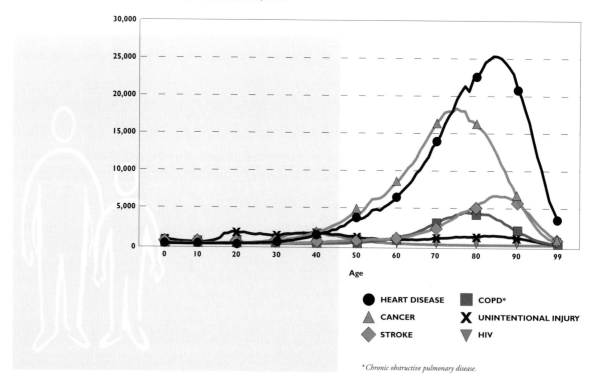

Chronic obstructive pulmonary disease.

LEADING CAUSES OF UNINTENTIONAL-INJURY DEATH BY AGE, 1998

Motor-vehicle crashes, falls, poisoning by solids and liquids, drownings, and choking were the leading causes of unintentional-injury death in the United States in 1998. The graph below depicts the number of deaths attributed to these causes by single years of age.

Motor-vehicle crashes were the leading cause of unintentional-injury death overall and the leading cause of unintentional-injury death from age 1 to 77 in 1998. The distribution of 1998 motor-vehicle fatalities shows a sharp increase for persons aged 13 to 18, rising from 222 for 13-year-olds to 1,400 for 18-year-olds. The greatest number of motor-vehicle fatalities occurred to persons aged 18 in 1998.

The second leading cause of unintentional-injury death overall in 1998 was falls. Falls were the leading cause of unintentional-injury death of persons aged 78 and over; deaths resulting from falls peaked at 674 for individuals

age 87. Poisoning by solids and liquids was the third leading cause of unintentional-injury death in the United States in 1998. Solid and liquid poisoning fatalities reached a high of 448 for 40-year-old individuals and were the second leading cause of unintentional-injury death for persons aged 19 and 21 to 54.

Drownings were the fourth leading cause of unintentional-injury death in 1998. Drowning fatalities reached a high of 188 for 1-year-olds and were the second leading cause of unintentional-injury death for ages 1 to 4, 6 to 18, and 20. The fifth leading cause of unintentional-injury death was choking, which peaked at 126 for 84-year-olds.

Source: National Safety Council tabulations of National Center for Health Statistics data. ICD–9 codes are E810–E825 for motor-vehicle; E880–E888 for falls; E850–E866 for solid and liquid poisonings; E830, E832, E910 for drowning; E911–E912 for choking.

LEADING CAUSES OF UNINTENTIONAL-INJURY DEATH BY AGE, UNITED STATES, 1998

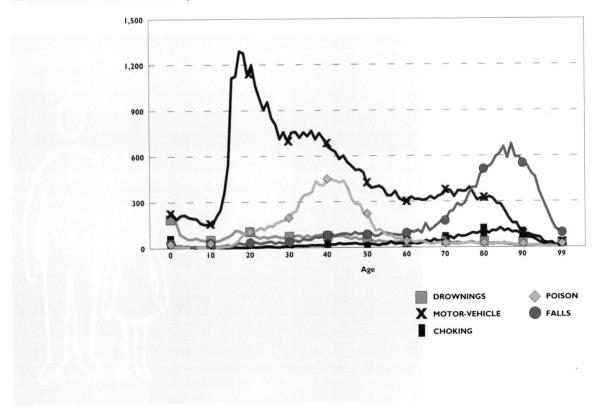

ALL DEATHS DUE TO INJURY

ALL DEATHS DUE TO INJURY, UNITED STATES, 1996–1998

Type of Accident or Manner of Injury	1998[a]	1997	1996
Total Deaths Due to Injuries, E800–E999[b]	**150,445**	**149,691**	**150,298**
All Accidental Deaths, E800–E949	**97,835**	**95,644**	**94,948**
Transport Accidents, E800–E848	**45,774**	**45,798**	**46,224**
Railway, E800–E807	515	527	565
Motor-vehicle, E810–E825	43,501	43,458	43,649
Other road vehicle, E826–E829	235	220	202
Water transport, E830–E838	692	758	675
Drowning (excluded from drowning below), E830, E832	*442*	*490*	*471*
Other water transport, E831, E833–E838	*250*	*268*	*204*
Air and space transport, E840–E845	692	734	1,061
Vehicle accidents not elsewhere classifiable, E846–E848	139	101	72
Poisoning by solids and liquids, E850–E866	10,255	9,587	8,872
Drugs, medicaments and biologicals, E850–E858	9,838	9,099	8,431
Analgesics, antipyretics, and antirheumatics, E850	*3,141*	*2,813*	*2,490*
Barbiturates, E851	*16*	*24*	*19*
Other sedatives and hypnotics, E852	*8*	*9*	*15*
Tranquilizers, E853	*107*	*94*	*82*
Other psychotropic agents, E854	*334*	*393*	*344*
Other drugs acting on central and autonomic nervous system, E855	*1,540*	*1,336*	*1,411*
Antibiotics, E856	*39*	*48*	*47*
Anti-infectives, E857	*4*	*8*	*6*
Other drugs, E858	*4,649*	*4,374*	*4,017*
Poisoning by other solids and liquids, E860–E866	417	488	441
Alcohol, E860	*300*	*342*	*308*
Cleansing, polishing agents, disinfectants, paints, varnishes, E861	*10*	*14*	*10*
Petroleum products, other solvents and their vapors, E862	*37*	*46*	*50*
Agricultural, horticultural chemical, pharmaceutical preparations, E863	*8*	*12*	*16*
Corrosives and caustics, E864	*5*	*8*	*9*
Foodstuffs and poisonous plants, E865	*3*	*11*	*6*
Other and unspecified solids and liquids, E866	*54*	*55*	*42*
Poisoning by gases and vapors, E867–E869	546	576	638
Gas distributed by pipeline, E867	15	13	23
Other utility gas and other carbon monoxide, E868	444	459	502
Motor-vehicle exhaust gas, E868.2	*190*	*208*	*219*
Others, not motor-vehicle exhaust gas, E868.0, E868.1, E868.3–E868.9	*254*	*251*	*283*
Other gases and vapors, E869	87	104	113
Complications, misadventures of surgical, medical care, E870–E879	3,228	3,043	2,919
Falls, E880–E888	**16,274**	**15,447**	**14,986**
Fall on or from stairs or steps, E880	1,389	1,295	1,239
Fall on or from ladders or scaffolding, E881	352	368	369
Fall from or out of building or other structure, E882	550	549	444
Fall into hole or other opening in surface, E883	95	70	88
Other fall from one level to another, E884	1,187	1,106	1,129
Fall on same level from slipping, tripping, or stumbling, E885	740	726	688
Fall on same level from collision, pushing, or shoving, E886	6	4	3
Fracture, cause unspecified, E887	3,679	3,589	3,694
Other and unspecified fall, E888	8,276	7,740	7,332
Fire and flames, E890–E899	**3,255**	**3,490**	**3,741**
Conflagration, E890–E892	2,687	2,927	3,165
Ignition of clothing, E893	171	165	160
Ignition of highly inflammable material, E894	55	52	54
Other and unspecified fire and flames, E895–E899	342	346	362
Natural and environmental factors, E900–E909	**1,521**	**1,316**	**1,550**
Excessive heat, E900	375	182	249
Excessive cold, E901	420	501	685
Hunger, thirst, exposure, and neglect, E904	252	224	224
Poisoning by and toxic reaction to venomous animals, plants, E905	64	68	68
Venomous snakes, lizards, and spiders, E905.0, E905.1	*5*	*12*	*13*
Hornets, wasps, and bees, E905.3	*46*	*43*	*45*
Other and unspecified animals, plants, E905.2, E905.4–E905.9	*13*	*13*	*10*
Other injury caused by animals, E906	93	102	107
Dog bite, E906.0	*15*	*19*	*23*
Other and unspecified injury by animal, E906.1–E906.9	*78*	*83*	*84*
Lightning, E907	63	58	63
Cataclysmic storms, and floods resulting from storms, E908	204	136	93
Cataclysmic earth surface movements and eruptions, E909	24	20	42
Other natural and environmental factors, E902, E903	26	25	19
Other accidents, E910–E928	**15,801**	**14,935**	**14,639**
Drowning, submersion (excluding water transport drownings above), E910	3,964	3,561	3,488
During sport or recreation, E910.0–E910.2	*685*	*648*	*645*
In bathtub, E910.4	*337*	*329*	*330*
Other, unspecified drowning, submersion, E910.3, E910.8, E910.9	*2,942*	*2,584*	*2,513*
Inhalation and ingestion of food, E911	1,147	1,095	1,126
Inhalation and ingestion of other object, E912	2,368	2,180	2,080

See source and footnotes on page 17.

Type of Accident or Manner of Injury	1998ᵃ	1997	1996
Mechanical suffocation, E913	1,070	1,145	1,114
In bed or cradle, E913.0	*247*	*236*	*219*
By plastic bag, E913.1	*27*	*44*	*40*
Due to lack of air (in refrigerator, other enclosed space), E913.2	*13*	*21*	*15*
By falling earth (noncataclysmic cave-in), E913.3	*55*	*54*	*57*
Other and unspecified mechanical suffocation, E913.8, E913.9	*728*	*790*	*783*
Struck by falling object, E916	723	727	732
Struck against or by objects or persons, E917	336	247	171
Caught in or between objects, E918	118	85	71
Machinery, E919	1,018	1,055	926
Agricultural machines, E919.0	*567*	*530*	*496*
Lifting machines and appliances, E919.2	*114*	*119*	*115*
Earth moving, scraping, and other excavating machines, E919.7	*79*	*85*	*73*
Other, unspecified machinery, E919.1, E919.3–E919.6, E919.8, E919.9	*258*	*321*	*242*
Cutting or piercing instruments or objects, E920	121	104	97
Firearm missile, E922	866	981	1,134
Handgun, E922.0	*140*	*161*	*187*
Shotgun (automatic), E922.1	*87*	*84*	*93*
Hunting rifle, E922.2	*50*	*65*	*50*
Other and unspecified firearm missile, E922.3–E922.9	*589*	*671*	*804*
Explosive material, E923	155	149	130
Fireworks, E923.0	*13*	*8*	*9*
Explosive gases, E923.2	*60*	*57*	*49*
Other and unspecified explosive material, E923.1, E923.8, E923.9	*82*	*84*	*72*
Hot substance or object, corrosive material and steam, E924	108	111	104
Electric current, E925	548	488	482
Domestic wiring and appliances, E925.0	*59*	*53*	*66*
Generating plants, distribution stations, transmission lines, E925.1	*144*	*139*	*135*
Industrial wiring, appliances, and electrical machinery, E925.2	*27*	*27*	*15*
Other and unspecified electric current, E925.8, E925.9	*318*	*269*	*266*
Radiation, E926	0	0	0
Other and unspecified, E914, E915, E921, E927, E928	3,259	3,007	2,984
Late effects (deaths more than one year after accident), E929	905	1,204	1,126
Adverse effects of drugs in therapeutic use, E930–E949	276	248	253
All Suicide Deaths, E950–E959	**30,575**	**30,535**	**30,903**
Poisoning by solid and liquid, E950	3,346	3,310	3,073
Poisoning by gases and vapors, E951, E952	1,726	1,818	2,007
Motor-vehicle exhaust gas, E952.0	*1,329*	*1,367*	*1,508*
Other and unspecified gases and vapors, E951, E952.1–E952.9	*397*	*451*	*499*
Hanging, strangulation, and suffocation, E953	5,726	5,413	5,330
Drowning, E954	375	384	361
Firearms, E955.0–E955.4	17,424	17,566	18,166
Handgun, E955.0	*3,541*	*3,519*	*3,675*
Shotgun, E955.1	*2,303*	*2,214*	*2,293*
Hunting rifle, E955.2	*849*	*865*	*945*
Other and unspecified firearm, E955.3, E955.4	*10,731*	*10,968*	*11,253*
Cutting and piercing instruments, E956	476	499	435
Jumping from high places, E957	621	600	645
Other, unspecified suicide and late effects, E955.5, E955.9, E958, E959	881	945	886
All Homicide Deaths, E960–E969	**17,893**	**19,491**	**20,634**
Assault by hanging and strangulation, E963	661	724	762
Assault by firearm, E965.0–E965.4	11,798	13,252	14,037
Handgun, E965.0	*1,047*	*1,307*	*1,256*
Shotgun, E965.1	*747*	*734*	*827*
Hunting rifle, E965.2	*141*	*163*	*138*
Other and unspecified firearm, E965.3, E965.4	*9,863*	*11,048*	*11,816*
Assault by cutting and piercing instrument, E966	2,087	2,246	2,619
Child battering and other maltreatment, E967	194	177	242
Other, unspecified assault and late effects, E960–E962, E964, E965.5–E965.9, E968, E969	3,153	3,092	2,974
Legal Intervention, E970–E978	**379**	**355**	**337**
Undetermined Whether Accidentally or Purposely Inflicted, E980–E989	**3,746**	**3,657**	**3,463**
Poisoning by solid and liquid, E980	2,351	2,254	1,910
Poisoning by gases and vapors, E981, E982	82	77	118
Motor-vehicle exhaust gas, E982.0	*42*	*41*	*61*
Other and unspecified gases and vapors, E981, E982.1–E982.9	*40*	*36*	*57*
Drowning, E984	249	231	242
Firearms, E985.0–E985.4	316	367	413
Other, unspecified undetermined deaths and late effects, E983, E985.5–E989	748	728	780
Deaths From Operations of War, E990–E999	**17**	**9**	**13**

Source: National Center for Health Statistics. Deaths are classified on the basis of the Ninth Revision of "The International Classification of Diseases" (ICD), which became effective in 1979.
ᵃ*Latest official figures.*
ᵇ*Numbers following titles refer to External Cause of Injury and Poisoning classifications in the ICD.*

DEATHS BY AGE, SEX, AND TYPE

Of the 97,835 unintentional-injury deaths in 1998, males accounted for 64% of all deaths. For women, the percentage was highest in the 75 and over age group.

By type of accident, men accounted for 88% of all firearm deaths, about seven times higher than the deaths for women.

UNINTENTIONAL-INJURY DEATHS BY AGE, SEX, AND TYPE, UNITED STATES, 1998[a]

Age & Sex	All Types[b]	Motor-Vehicle	Falls	Poison (Solid, Liquid)	Drowning[d]	Ingest. of Food, Object	Fires, Burns[c]	Firearms	Poison by Gas	% Male, All Types
All Ages	**97,835**	**43,501**	**16,274**	**10,255**	**4,406**	**3,515**	**3,255**	**866**	**546**	**64%**
Under 5	2,689	921	66	26	559	142	299	19	10	59%
5 to 14	3,254	1,868	55	20	444	42	300	102	13	64%
15 to 24	13,349	10,026	236	779	821	36	194	260	81	74%
25 to 44	27,172	14,095	1,046	6,224	1,323	270	675	280	169	75%
45 to 64	18,286	8,416	1,740	2,650	706	485	669	140	126	71%
65 to 74	8,892	3,410	1,884	223	241	530	397	34	62	59%
75 & over	24,193	4,765	11,247	333	312	2,010	721	31	85	45%
Male	**63,042**	**28,990**	**8,035**	**7,497**	**3,575**	**1,735**	**1,941**	**762**	**410**	
Female	34,793	14,511	8,239	2,758	831	1,780	1,314	104	136	
Percent male	64%	67%	49%	73%	81%	49%	60%	88%	75%	

See source and footnotes on page 19.

UNINTENTIONAL-INJURY DEATH RATES BY TYPE AND SEX, UNITED STATES, 1998

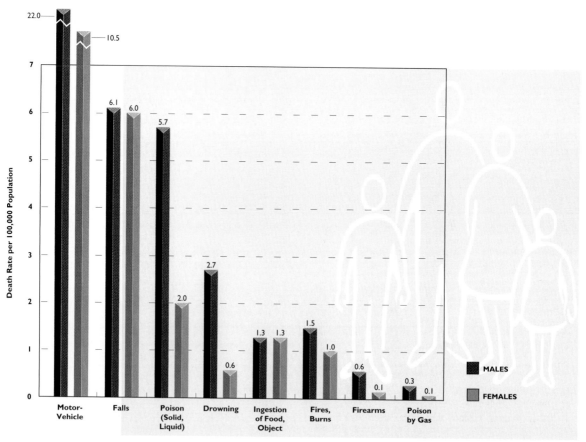

1998 Male Population = 132,030,000
1998 Female Population = 138,218,000

UNINTENTIONAL-INJURY DEATHS BY MONTH AND TYPE, UNITED STATES, 1998[a]

Month	All Types	Motor-Vehicle	Falls	Poison (Solid, Liquid)	Drowning[d]	Ingest. of Food, Object	Fires, Burns[c]	Firearms	Poison by Gas	All Other Types
All Months	**97,835**	**43,501**	**16,274**	**10,255**	**4,406**	**3,515**	**3,255**	**866**	**546**	**15,217**
January	8,072	3,265	1,534	903	184	361	409	100	80	1,236
February	7,136	2,956	1,353	783	186	305	333	67	54	1,099
March	7,716	3,229	1,371	858	228	302	338	61	55	1,274
April	7,413	3,216	1,192	825	313	289	279	54	38	1,207
May	8,165	3,625	1,319	850	530	267	194	76	31	1,273
June	8,390	3,733	1,204	910	710	263	178	62	25	1,305
July	9,122	4,079	1,371	864	776	282	186	65	38	1,461
August	8,968	4,216	1,359	863	595	309	179	68	27	1,352
September	8,114	3,741	1,292	853	352	261	199	52	32	1,332
October	8,284	3,867	1,447	808	214	292	239	68	47	1,302
November	7,997	3,728	1,406	848	162	268	309	97	44	1,135
December	8,458	3,846	1,426	890	156	316	412	96	75	1,241
Average	**8,153**	**3,625**	**1,356**	**855**	**367**	**293**	**271**	**72**	**46**	**1,268**

Source: National Safety Council tabulations of National Center for Health Statistics mortality data.
[a]*Latest official figures.*
[b]*Includes some deaths not shown separately.*
[c]*Includes deaths resulting from conflagration regardless of nature of injury.*
[d]*Includes drowning in water transport.*

UNINTENTIONAL-INJURY DEATHS BY MONTH, UNITED STATES, 1998

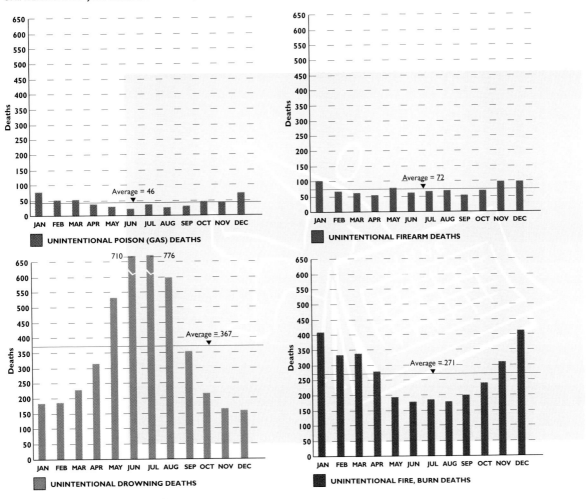

UNINTENTIONAL POISON (GAS) DEATHS

UNINTENTIONAL FIREARM DEATHS

UNINTENTIONAL DROWNING DEATHS

UNINTENTIONAL FIRE, BURN DEATHS

See page 94 for motor-vehicle deaths by month.

DEATH RATE TRENDS BY EVENT

The population death rate for all unintentional injuries decreased 4% from 1990 to 2000—from 36.9 down to 35.3.

The **motor-vehicle** death rate based on population decreased 17% from 1990 to 2000, but held steady at about 16 per 100,000 for most of the 1990s. Page 109 shows trends in motor-vehicle death rates based on registered vehicles and miles traveled. These rates show trends similar to the population death rate.

The death rate due to **falls** rose 20% from 1999 to 2000. It rose slowly during the early and mid 1990s but held steady for the past 3 years.

Death rates for **fires and burns, drowning, gas and vapor poisonings,** and **firearms,** which are low to begin with, have all decreased slowly over the past decade.

The death rate due to **solid and liquid poisonings** increased 110% from 1990 to 2000. Much of this increase may be attributed to the rise in unintentional overdoses of illegal drugs.

In addition to the graph below, the historical tables and graphs on pages 33–43 show the detailed numbers, rates, and trends for the four classes, principal types, and age groups from 1903 to the present.

UNINTENTIONAL-INJURY DEATH RATE TRENDS BY EVENT, UNITED STATES, 1990–2000

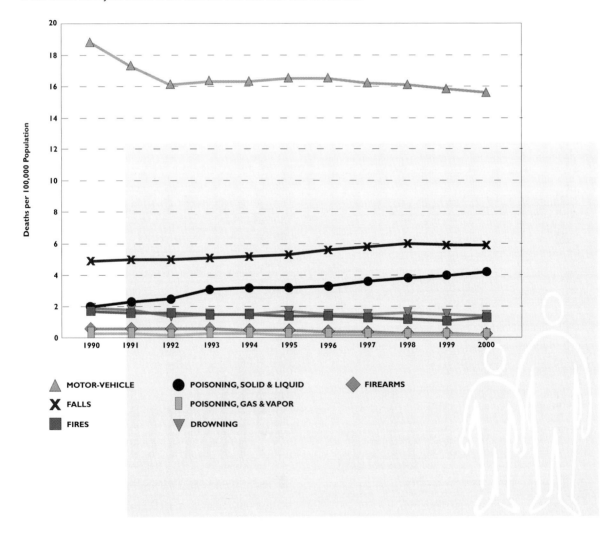

THE NATIONAL HEALTH INTERVIEW SURVEY

The National Health Interview Survey, conducted by the National Center for Health Statistics, is a continuous, personal-interview sampling of households to obtain information about the health status of household members, including injuries experienced during the 3 months prior to the interview. Responsible family members residing in the household supplied the information found in the survey. Of the nation's 101,018,000 households in 1997, 39,832 households containing 103,477 persons were interviewed. See below for definitions and comparability with other injury figures published in *Injury Facts®*.

ANNUAL RATE[a] OF LEADING EXTERNAL CAUSES OF INJURY AND POISONING EPISODES BY SEX AND AGE, UNITED STATES, 1997[b]

Sex and Age	External Cause of Injury and Poisoning					
	Fall	Struck By or Against Person or Object	Transportation[c]	Overexertion	Cutting/Piercing Instruments	Poisoning
Both sexes	**42.4**	**19.6**	**16.7**	**13.9**	**10.0**	**7.3**
Under 12 years	45.7	17.3	8.6	([d])	8.0	13.0
12–21 years	45.5	49.1	23.8	12.3	15.4	5.6
22–44 years	30.6	18.9	22.9	20.3	13.4	6.7
45–64 years	32.1	11.5	11.2	17.6	5.5	5.5
65 years and over	86.2	4.0	11.5	7.8	4.4	5.4
Male	**36.9**	**27.6**	**19.3**	**15.1**	**13.3**	**6.9**
Under 12 years	47.7	21.9	13.8	([d])	10.7	11.3
12–21 years	49.1	75.3	28.2	17.1	25.7	([d])
22–44 years	29.9	27.0	26.1	22.5	15.7	7.6
45–64 years	25.0	11.3	9.8	17.5	6.6	([d])
65 years and over	47.2	([d])	12.3	([d])	([d])	([d])
Female	**47.7**	**11.9**	**14.1**	**12.7**	**6.9**	**7.7**
Under 12 years	43.7	12.5	([d])	([d])	([d])	14.7
12–21 years	41.7	21.7	19.2	([d])	([d])	([d])
22–44 years	31.3	11.0	19.7	18.1	11.2	5.9
45–64 years	38.7	11.6	12.6	17.8	([d])	5.8
65 years and over	114.5	([d])	11.0	10.2	([d])	([d])

NUMBER AND PERCENT OF INJURY EPISODES BY PLACE OF OCCURRENCE AND SEX, UNITED STATES, 1997[b]

Place	Both Sexes		Male		Female	
	Number of Episodes (000)	%	Number of Episodes (000)	%	Number of Episodes (000)	%
All injury episodes	**32,438**	**100.0**	**17,646**	**100.0**	**14,792**	**100.0**
All places mentioned[e]	**32,900**	**101.4**	**17,911**	**101.5**	**14,989**	**101.3**
Home (inside)	7,832	24.1	3,098	17.6	4,734	32.0
Home (outside)	5,760	17.8	3,074	17.4	2,686	18.2
Street/highway	4,220	13.0	2,293	13.0	1,927	13.0
Sport facility	2,369	7.3	1,716	9.7	653	4.4
Industrial/construction	2,191	6.8	1,866	10.6	325	2.2
School	1,991	6.1	1,315	7.5	676	4.6
Trade/service	1,986	6.1	1,095	6.2	892	6.0
Park/recreation area	1,289	4.0	866	4.9	423	2.9
Other public building	920	2.8	447	2.5	473	3.2
Other (specified)f	2,414	7.4	999	5.7	1,415	9.6
Other	1,603	4.9	981	5.6	622	4.2
Refused/don't know	324	1.0	161	0.9	163	1.1

Source: Warner, M., Barnes, P.M., & Fingerhut, L.A. (2000, July). Injury and poisoning episodes and conditions: National Health Interview Survey, 1997. Vital and Health Statistics, Series 10 (No. 202). Hyattsville, MD: National Center for Health Statistics.
[a] *Per 1000 population.*
[b] *Latest official figures.*
[c] *Transportation includes the categories "Motor vehicle traffic;" "Pedalcycle, other;" "Pedestrian, other;" and "Transport, other."*
[d] *Figure does not meet standard of reliability or precision.*
[e] *"All Places Mentioned" is greater than the total number of injury episodes because respondents could indicate up to two places.*
f *"Other (specified)" place includes child care center or preschool, residential institution, health care facility, parking lot, farm, river, lake, stream, ocean, swimming pool, and mine or quarry.*

Injury Definitions

National Health Interview Survey Definitions. The National Health Interview Survey (NHIS) figures include injuries due to intentional violence as well as unintentional injuries. An injury or poisoning is included in the NHIS totals if it is *medically attended*. A *medically attended* injury or poisoning is one for which a physician has been consulted (in person or by telephone) for advice or treatment. Calls to poison control centers are considered contact with a health care professional and are included in this definition of medical attendance.

National Safety Council definition of injury. A disabling injury is defined as one that results in death, some degree of permanent impairment, or renders the injured person unable to effectively perform their regular duties or activities for a full day beyond the day of the injury. This definition applies to all unintentional injuries. All injury totals labeled "disabling injuries" in *Injury Facts®* are based on this definition. Some *rates* in the Work section are based on OSHA definitions of recordable cases (see Glossary).

Numerical differences between NHIS and National Safety Council injury totals are due mainly to the duration of disability. The Council's injury estimating procedure was revised for the 1993 edition of *Accident Facts®*. See the Technical Appendix for more information.

FALLS

About 11 million fall-related episodes of injury were estimated to have occurred annually in 1997–1998 according to special tabulations of data from the National Health Interview Survey (NHIS) provided by the National Center for Health Statistics. The NHIS is a personal-interview household survey that collects health-related data from a member of the household.

The table on the opposite page shows where the falls occurred and what the injured person was doing at the time. More than half of all the fall episodes (54.8%) occurred in the home or on home premises and 30.0% involved leisure activities. However, the place and activity percentages varied somewhat by sex and age. (Percentages are based on the number of fall episodes rather than the total number of places or activities mentioned. See footnote "b" below the table.)

Slightly less than half (48.4%) of falls to males occurred at home while 60.1% of falls to females happened at home. Home was the place for more than two thirds (67.2%) of falls to children under 12, more than three fourths (78.3%) of falls to those 65 and older, but less

than half (41.8%) of falls to persons 12–64 years old. About 10.0% of falls to children under 12 occurred at school and about 11.1% of falls to persons 12–64 occurred at a sports facility.

Leisure was the activity for about the same proportion of falls for both males (29.8%) and females (30.1%). Sports were the second most common activity for males (19.1%). For females, the second most common specified activity was working in the house or yard (14.7%). For children under 12, leisure (51.2%) and sports (10.3%) were the two most common specified activities. For persons 12–64 years old, leisure (26.3%) and working at a paid job (19.2%) were the two most common activities, but these were followed closely by sports (18.8%). For adults 65 and older, working in the house or yard (22.3%) and leisure (21.1%) were the most frequent specified activities.

See also page 21 for general injury information from the NHIS and page 138 for information on the type of fall.

FALL-RELATED INJURY EPISODES BY PLACE AND ACTIVITY, UNITED STATES, 1997–1998

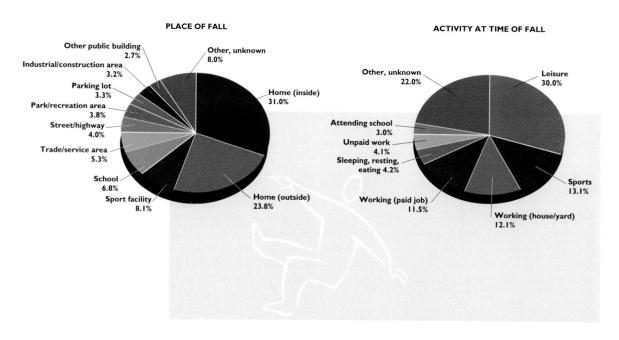

PLACE OF FALL

- Other public building 2.7%
- Industrial/construction area 3.2%
- Parking lot 3.3%
- Park/recreation area 3.8%
- Street/highway 4.0%
- Trade/service area 5.3%
- School 6.8%
- Sport facility 8.1%
- Other, unknown 8.0%
- Home (inside) 31.0%
- Home (outside) 23.8%

ACTIVITY AT TIME OF FALL

- Other, unknown 22.0%
- Attending school 3.0%
- Unpaid work 4.1%
- Sleeping, resting, eating 4.2%
- Working (paid job) 11.5%
- Working (house/yard) 12.1%
- Leisure 30.0%
- Sports 13.1%

AVERAGE ANNUAL NUMBER OF FALL-RELATED EPISODES BY PLACE OF FALL, ACTIVITY, SEX, AND AGE GROUP, UNITED STATES, 1997-1998

	Number of Episodes (in Thousands)					
	Both Sexes	Male	Female	0–11 Years	12–64 Years	65 Years or Over
All fall episodes	*11,081*	*5,003*	*6,078*	*2,173*	*6,449*	*2,459*
Place of fall						
All places mentioned[b]	11,160	5,026	6,134	2,176	6,502	2,482
Home (inside)	3,436	1,177	2,259	951	1,145	1,341
Home (outside)	2,639	1,245	1,394	509	1,545	586
Sport facility	893	547	346	161	715	(a)
School	749	440	308	217	532	—
Trade/service	584	226	358	(a)	438	100a
Street/highway	446	178	268	(a)	304	107a
Park/recreation area	421	283	139a	(a)	327	(a)
Parking lot	370	111a	259	(a)	251	98a
Industrial/construction	357	309	(a)	(a)	340	(a)
Other public building	294	86a	208	(a)	182	69a
Other (specified)[c]	438	170	268a	(a)	317	(a)
Other	463	212	251	(a)	352	(a)
Refused, Don't know	(a)	(a)	(a)	5	55	(a)
Activity at time of fall						
All activities mentioned[b]	11,137	5,035	6,102	2,194	6,470	2,473
Leisure	3,324	1,493	1,831	1,113	1,693	518
Sports	1,456	955	501	225	1,215	(a)
Working (house/yard)	1,335	444	891	(a)	764	548
Working paid job	1,276	739	537	(a)	1,239	(a)
Sleeping, resting, eating	461	154a	307	(a)	(a)	265
Unpaid work	452	155a	297	(a)	235	171a
Attending school	332	192a	140a	141a	191	—
Other (specified)[d]	217	98a	118a	87a	(a)	73a
Other	2,205	775	1,430	480	921	803
Refused, Don't know	79a	(a)	(a)	(a)	(a)	(a)

Source: National Center for Health Statistics, Office of Analysis, Epidemiology, and Health Promotion.
[a] These data have a relative standard error of 20%–30%. Data not shown have a relative standard error greater than 30%. Dashes indicates zero.
[b] "All places mentioned" and "All activities mentioned" are greater than the total number of fall episodes because respondents could indicate up to two places or activities.
[c] Other (specified) place includes child care center or preschool, residential institution, health care facility, farm, river, lake, stream, ocean, swimming pool and mine or quarry.
[d] Other (specified) activity includes driving, drinking, cooking, and being cared for.

PRINCIPAL CLASSES BY STATE

The states listed below participate in the Injury Mortality Tabulations reporting system. Reports from these states are used to make current year estimates. See the Technical Appendix for more information.

The estimated total number of unintentional-injury deaths for 2000 was unchanged from 1999. The number of unintentional-injury deaths in the Public Nonmotor-Vehicle class was down 6%, while the

Motor-Vehicle class was unchanged from 1999. The estimates for the Work and Home classes showed increases of 1% and 5%, respectively. The population death rate for the Public Nonmotor-Vehicle class decreased 7%, while the rates for the Total and the Motor-Vehicle class decreased 1% each. The rate for the Work class remained unchanged while the rate for the Home class increased 4%.

PRINCIPAL CLASSES OF UNINTENTIONAL-INJURY DEATHS BY STATE, 2000

State	Total[a]		Motor-Vehicle[b]		Work[c]		Home		Public Nonmotor-Vehicle	
	Deaths	Rate[d]	Deaths	Rate[d]	Deaths	Rate[d]	Deaths	Rate[d]	Deaths	Rate[d]
Total U.S.	97,300	35.3	43,000	15.6	5,200	1.9	29,500	10.7	22,000	8.0
Colorado	1,618	37.6	673	15.6	91	2.1	331	7.7	571	13.3
Delaware	227	29.0	136	17.4	5	0.6	73	9.3	13	1.7
Florida	6,137	38.4	2,393	15.0	223	1.4	1,350	8.4	2,253	14.1
Hawaii (8 mos.)	201	24.9	89	11.0	3	0.4	33	4.1	76	9.4
Idaho	522	40.3	287	22.2	13	1.0	123	9.5	94	7.3
Kansas	867	32.2	449	16.7	54	2.0	207	7.7	171	6.4
Missouri	2,505	44.8	1,238	22.1	72	1.3	585	10.5	583	10.4
New Jersey (10 mos.)	1,575	22.5	537	7.7	58	0.8	509	7.3	487	6.9
New Mexico	1,023	56.2	471	25.9	20	1.1	274	15.1	245	13.5
Oregon (7 mos.)	651	32.6	239	12.0	29	1.5	173	8.7	151	7.6
South Dakota	335	44.4	184	24.4	28	3.7	44	5.8	96	12.7

Source: Provisional reports of vital statistics registrars; deaths are by place of occurrence. U.S. totals are National Safety Council estimates.

[a] *The all-class total may not equal the sum of the separate class totals because Motor-Vehicle and other transportation deaths occurring to persons in the course of their employment are included in the Work death totals as well as the Motor-Vehicle and Public Nonmotor-Vehicle totals and also because unclassified deaths are included in the total.*

[b] *Differences between the figures given above and those on pages 102 and 103 are due in most cases to the inclusion of nontraffic deaths in this table.*

[c] *Work death totals may be too low where incomplete information on death certificates results in the deaths being included in the Public class. The Work totals may include some cases that are not compensable. For compensable cases only, see page 51.*

[d] *Deaths per 100,000 population, adjusted to annual basis where less than 12 months were reported.*

UNINTENTIONAL-INJURY DEATH RATES BY STATE

DEATH RATES PER 100,000 POPULATION BY STATE, 2000

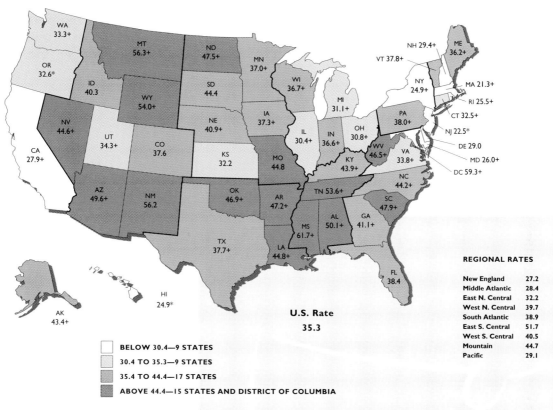

WA 33.3+
OR 32.6*
MT 56.3+
ND 47.5+
MN 37.0+
ID 40.3
SD 44.4
WI 36.7+
WY 54.0+
NV 44.6+
UT 34.3+
NE 40.9+
IA 37.3+
MI 31.1+
CA 27.9+
CO 37.6
KS 32.2
MO 44.8
IL 30.4+
IN 36.6+
OH 30.8+
NH 29.4+
ME 36.2+
VT 37.8+
NY 24.9+
MA 21.3+
RI 25.5+
CT 32.5+
NJ 22.5*
DE 29.0
MD 26.0+
DC 59.3+
PA 38.0+
WV 46.5+
VA 33.8+
AZ 49.6+
NM 56.2
OK 46.9+
AR 47.2+
TN 53.6+
KY 43.9+
NC 44.2+
SC 47.9+
MS 61.7+
AL 50.1+
GA 41.1+
TX 37.7+
LA 44.8+
FL 38.4
AK 43.4+
HI 24.9*

U.S. Rate 35.3

REGIONAL RATES

New England	27.2
Middle Atlantic	28.4
East N. Central	32.2
West N. Central	39.7
South Atlantic	38.9
East S. Central	51.7
West S. Central	40.5
Mountain	44.7
Pacific	29.1

BELOW 30.4—9 STATES
30.4 TO 35.3—9 STATES
35.4 TO 44.4—17 STATES
ABOVE 44.4—15 STATES AND DISTRICT OF COLUMBIA

Source: Rates estimated by the National Safety Council based on data from State Health Departments, National Center for Health Statistics, and U.S. Census Bureau.
+ 1998 National Center for Health Statistics.
*Partly estimated.

MAJOR DISASTERS, 2000

Disasters are front-page news even though the lives lost in the United States are relatively few when compared to the day-to-day life losses from ordinary injuries. The National Safety Council tracks major disasters resulting in unintentional-injury deaths. Listed below are the two major U.S. disasters taking 25 or more lives during 2000.

Type and Location	No. of Deaths	Date of Disaster
Crash of scheduled plane near Point Mugu, Calif.	88	January 31, 2000
Heat wave in the Southeast	46	July 8-20, 2000

Source: National Transportation Safety Board and National Weather Service.

LARGEST U.S. DISASTERS, 1981–2000

Year	Date	Type and Location	No. of Deaths
		Air Transportation	
1996	July 17	Crash of scheduled plane near East Moriches, N.Y.	230
1987	August 16	Crash of scheduled plane in Detroit, Mich.	156
1982	July 9	Crash of scheduled plane in Kenner, La.	154
1985	August 2	Crash of scheduled plane in Ft. Worth/Dallas, Texas Airport	135
1994	September 8	Crash of scheduled plane in Aliquippa, Pa.	132
1989	July 19	Crash of scheduled plane in Sioux City, Iowa	112
1996	May 11	Crash of scheduled plane near Miami, Fla.	110
2000	January 31	Crash of scheduled plane near Point Mugu, Calif.	88
1986	August 31	Two-plane collision over Los Angeles, Calif.	82
1982	January 13	Crash of scheduled plane in Washington, D.C.	78
1990	January 25	Crash of scheduled plane in Cove Neck, N.Y.	73
1994	October 31	Crash of scheduled plane in Indiana	68
1994	July 2	Crash of scheduled plane in Charlotte, N.C.	37
		Weather	
1995	July 11–27	Heat wave in Chicago, Ill.	465
1993	March 12–15	Severe snowstorm in Eastern States	270
1999	July 22–31	Heat wave in the Midwest	232
1998	May–July	Drought and heat wave in South and Southeast	200[a]
1996	January	Snowstorm and floods in Appalachians, Mid-Atlantic, and Northeast	187
1996	January–February	Cold wave in eastern two-thirds of the U.S.	100[a]
1993	June–July	Heat wave in Southeast	100[a]
1998	January 5	Winter storm and flooding in South and East	90[a]
1999	September 14–18	Hurricane Floyd, North Carolina and other states	78
1985	May 31	Storm and tornadoes in Pennsylvania and Ohio	74
1997	March	Tornadoes and flooding in South and Southeast	67
1985	November 4–5	Floods in W.Va., Va., Pa., and East Coast	65
1984	March 28–29	Storm and tornadoes in N.C., S.C., and East Coast	62
1999	May 3	Tornadoes in Oklahoma, Kansas, Texas, and Tennessee	54
1994	March 27	Tornado in Southeast	47
2000	July 8–20	Heat wave in the Southeast	46
1998	February 22	Tornadoes across central Florida	42
1996	September 5	Hurricane Fran in North Carolina and Virginia	36
1998	April 8	Tornado in central Alabama	34
1997	May 27	Tornadoes in Texas	29
1994	July 4–17	Floods in Georgia	28
		Work	
1987	April 24	Collapse of apartment building under construction in Bridgeport, Conn.	28
1982	March 19	Military plane exploded and crashed near Chicago, Ill.	27
1984	December 21	Mine fire in Orangeville, Utah	27
1991	September 3	Fire at food processing plant in Hamlet, N.C.	25
		Other Disasters	
1981	July 17	Collapse of aerial walkways in Kansas City, Mo., hotel	113
1994	January 17	Earthquake in San Andreas Fault, Calif.	61
1989	October 17	Earthquake in San Francisco, Calif., and surrounding area	61
1993	September 22	Bridge collapse under train, Mobile, Ala.	47
1981	October 26	Boat capsized near Hillsboro Beach, Fla.	33
1981	January 9	Fire in rest home for aged in Keansburg, N.J.	31

Source: National Safety Council, Accident Facts®, 1982-1998 editions, and Injury Facts®, 1999-2000 editions.
[a] Final death toll undetermined.

While you make a 10-minute safety speech, 2 persons will be killed and about 390 will suffer a disabling injury. Costs will amount to $9,750,000. On the average, there are 11 unintentional-injury deaths and about 2,340 disabling injuries every hour during the year.

Deaths and disabling injuries by class occurred in the nation at the following rates in 2000:

DEATHS AND DISABLING INJURIES BY CLASS, 2000

Class	Severity	One Every—	Number per ...			2000 Total
			Hour	Day	Week	
All	Deaths	5 minutes	11	267	1,870	97,300
	Injuries	2 seconds	2,340	56,200	394,200	20,500,000
Motor-Vehicle	Deaths	12 minutes	5	118	830	43,000
	Injuries	14 seconds	260	6,300	44,200	2,300,000
Work	Deaths	101 minutes	1	14	100	5,200
	Injuries	8 seconds	450	10,700	75,000	3,900,000
Workers Off-the-Job	Deaths	13 minutes	5	115	800	41,800
	Injuries	5 seconds	750	18,100	126,900	6,600,000
Home	Deaths	18 minutes	3	81	570	29,500
	Injuries	4 seconds	810	19,500	136,500	7,100,000
Public Nonmotor-Vehicle	Deaths	24 minutes	3	60	420	22,000
	Injuries	4 seconds	830	20,000	140,400	7,300,000

Source: National Safety Council estimates.

DEATHS EVERY HOUR . . .

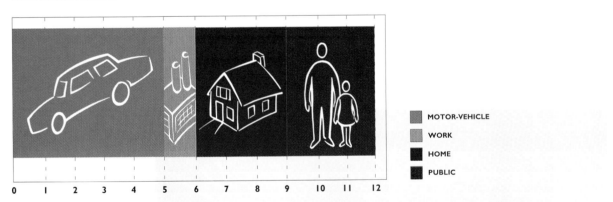

MOTOR-VEHICLE
WORK
HOME
PUBLIC

AN UNINTENTIONAL-INJURY DEATH EVERY FIVE MINUTES . . .

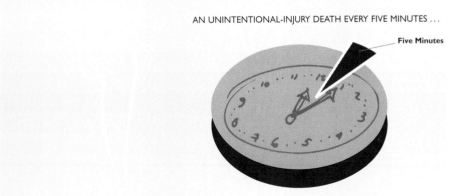

Five Minutes

INJURY-RELATED HOSPITAL EMERGENCY DEPARTMENT VISITS, 1998

About 37% of all hospital emergency department visits in the United States were injury related, according to information from the 1998 National Hospital Ambulatory Medical Care Survey conducted for the National Center for Health Statistics. There were approximately 100.4 million visits made to emergency departments, of which about 37.1 million were injury related. This resulted in an annual rate of about 37.3 emergency department visits per 100 persons, of which about 13.8 visits per 100 persons were injury related.

Males had a higher rate of injury-related visits than females. For males, about 16.2 visits per 100 males were recorded; for females the rate was 12.1 per 100 females. Those aged 15 to 24 had the highest rate of injury-related visits for males, and those aged 75 and over had the highest rate for females.

Falls and struck against or struck accidentally by objects or persons were the leading causes of injury-related emergency department visits, accounting for about 21% and 13% of the total, respectively. In total, about 7.7 million visits to emergency departments were made

in 1998 due to accidental falls, and about 4.7 million due to being struck against or struck accidentally by objects or persons. The next leading types were motor-vehicle accidents with 4.6 million visits (13% of the total), and accidents caused by cutting or piercing instruments, which accounted for about 3.1 million visits (8% of the total).

Nearly 29% of all injuries resulting in emergency department visits occurred at home, the most common place of injury. Street or highway was the place of injury for about 14% of the total, while recreation/sport area and industrial place each accounted for just over 6%. Other public building was the place of injury for 3% of the total, while school accounted for 2%. However, 40% of all injuries resulting in emergency department visits occurred in an "other or unknown place."

The table and charts on these pages show totals, rates, and percent distributions of injury-related visits to hospital emergency departments in 1998 by age, sex, cause of injury, and place of injury.

NUMBER AND PERCENT DISTRIBUTION OF EMERGENCY DEPARTMENT VISITS BY CAUSE OF INJURY, UNITED STATES, 1998

Cause of Injury and E-Code[a]	Number of Visits (000)	%
All Injury-Related Visits	**37,111**	**100.0%**
Unintentional Injuries, E800–E869, E880–E929	**28,636**	**77.2%**
Accidental Falls, E880–E886, E888	7,712	20.8%
Striking Against or Struck Accidentally by Objects or Persons, E916–E917	4,717	12.7%
Total Motor Vehicle Accidents, E810–E825	4,650	12.6%
Motor vehicle traffic, E810–E819	_4,259_	_11.5%_
Motor vehicle, nontraffic, E820–E825(.0, .5, .7, .9)	_391_	_1.1%_
Accidents Caused by Cutting or Piercing Instruments, E920	3,142	8.5%
Overexertion, E927	1,456	3.9%
Accidents Due to Natural and Environmental Factors, E900–E909, E928.0–E928.2	1,238	3.3%
Accidental Poisoning by Drugs, Medicinal Substances, Biologicals, Other Solid and Liquid Substances, Gases and Vapors, E850–E869	754	2.0%
Accidents Caused by Fire and Flames, Hot Substances or Object, Caustic or Corrosive Material, and Steam, E890–E899, E924	531	1.4%
Pedalcycle, Nontraffic and Other, E800–E807(.3), E820–E825(.6), E826.1, E826.9	496	1.3%
Machinery, E919	411	1.1%

Cause of Injury and E-Code[a]	Number of Visits (000)	%
Other Transportation, E800–E807(.0–.2, .8–.9), E826(.0, .2–.8), E827–E829, E831, E833–E845	174	0.5%
Other Mechanism[b], E830, E832, E846–E848, E910–E915, E918, E921–E923, E925–E926, E928.8, E929.0–E929.5	2,171	5.9%
Mechanism Unspecified, E887, E928.9, E929.8, E929.9	1,183	3.2%
Intentional Injuries, E950–E959, E960–E969, E970–E978, E990–E999	**2,168**	**5.8%**
Assault, E960–E969	1,618	4.4%
Unarmed Fight or Brawl and Striking by Blunt or Thrown Object, E960.0, E968.2	873	2.4%
Assault by Cutting and Piercing Instrument, E966	160	0.4%
Assault by Other and Unspecified Mechanism[c], E960.1, E962–E965, E967–E968.1, E968.3–E969.9	585	1.6%
Self-inflicted Injury, E950–E959	443	1.2%
Poisoning by Solid or Liquid Substances, Gases or Vapors, E950–E952	298	0.8%
Other and Unspecified Mechanism[d], E953–E959	145	0.4%
Other Causes of Violence, E970–E978, E990–E999	107	0.3%
Adverse Effects of Medical Treatment, E870–E879, E930–E949	**1,197**	**3.2%**
Other and Unknown[e]	**5,101**	**13.8%**

Source: McCaig, L.F. (2000). National Hospital Ambulatory Medical Care Survey: 1998 Emergency Department Summary (Advance Data, Number 313, May 10, 2000). Hyattsville, MD: National Center for Health Statistics.
Note: Sum of parts may not add to total due to rounding.
[a] Based on the International Classification of Diseases, 9th Revision, Clinical Modification (ICD-9-CM).
[b] Includes drowning, suffocation, firearm, and other mechanism.
[c] Includes assault by firearms and explosives, and other mechanism.
[d] Includes injury by cutting and piercing instrument, suffocation, and other and unspecified mechanism.
[e] Includes uncodable, illegible, and blank E-codes.

NUMBER AND PERCENT DISTRIBUTION OF EMERGENCY DEPARTMENT VISITS BY PLACE OF INJURY AND AGE, UNITED STATES, 1998

Place of Injury	All Ages		Under 18		18-64 Years		65 Years & Over	
	Number of Visits (000)	%	Number of Visits (000)	%	Number of Visits (000)	%	Number of Visits (000)	%
Total	37,111	100.0	10,458	100.0	22,560	100.0	4,093	100.0
Home	10,679	28.8	3,602	34.4	5,042	22.4	2,034	49.7
Street or Highway	5,195	14.0	1,063	10.2	3,814	16.9	317	7.7
Recreation/Sports Area	2,290	6.2	1,151	11.0	1,083	4.8	(a)	(a)
Industrial Places	2,263	6.1	(a)	(a)	2,166	9.6	(a)	(a)
Other Public Building	1,185	3.2	155	1.5	886	3.9	(a)	(a)
School	785	2.1	697	6.7	86	0.4	(a)	(a)
Other	1,266	3.3	211	2.0	806	3.6	208	5.1
Unknown	13,488	36.3	3,498	33.4	8,676	38.5	1,314	32.1

See source on page 28.
Note: Sum of parts may not add to total due to rounding.
aEstimate did not meet standard of reliability or precision.

RATE OF INJURY-RELATED VISITS TO EMERGENCY DEPARTMENTS BY PATIENT AGE AND SEX, 1998

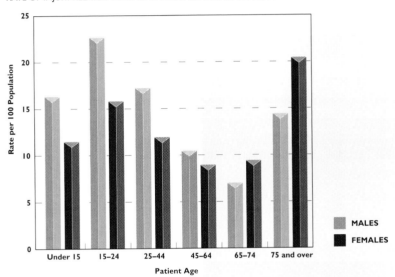

DISTRIBUTION OF EMERGENCY DEPARTMENT VISITS BY INTENTIONALITY AND AGE, UNITED STATES, 1998

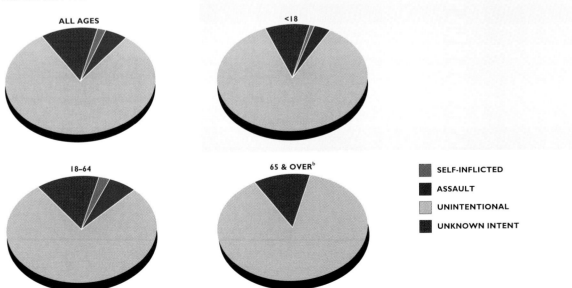

bEstimates for "self-inflicted" and "assault" did not meet standard of reliability or precision.

CHILDREN AND YOUTHS

For children and youths aged 1 to 24 years, unintentional injuries are the leading cause of death, accounting for more than 42% of the 43,669 total deaths of these persons in 1998. Overall, motor-vehicle crashes were the leading cause of unintentional-injury deaths for this age group, followed by drowning, solid and liquid poisonings, and fires and burns.

While unintentional-injury deaths decrease fairly steadily for those aged 1 to 10, they increase markedly for teenagers—from 310 for those age 12 to 1,744 for those age 18. Motor-vehicle crashes account for most of this increase.

For infants under 1 year of age, unintentional injuries are the fourth leading cause of death, following certain conditions originating in the perinatal period, congenital anomalies, and sudden infant death syndrome (see page 10). Although unintentional injuries only account for about 3% of deaths for those under age 1, the number of unintentional-injury deaths for this age is greater than that for those aged 15 and under.

UNINTENTIONAL-INJURY DEATHS BY EVENT, AGES 0–24, UNITED STATES, 1998

Age	Population (000)	Unintentional-Injury Deaths									
		All	Rates[a]	Motor-Vehicle	Drowning[b]	Poison (Solid, Liquid)	Firearms	Fires	Falls	Mechanical Suffocation	All Other
Under 1 year	3,791	754	19.9	162	63	8	0	41	20	312	148
1–24 years	91,590	18,538	20.2	12,653	1,761	817	381	752	337	254	1,583
1 year	3,750	614	16.4	205	188	7	3	60	16	32	103
2 years	3,752	511	13.6	178	161	4	1	67	10	19	71
3 years	3,800	435	11.4	181	82	5	14	74	13	10	56
4 years	3,897	375	9.6	195	65	2	1	57	7	13	35
5 years	3,950	354	9.0	181	50	2	7	53	8	9	44
6 years	4,022	300	7.5	159	49	0	5	43	5	5	34
7 years	4,060	321	7.9	180	57	2	4	37	6	8	27
8 years	3,885	279	7.2	150	45	1	9	31	4	5	34
9 years	4,012	290	7.2	164	42	1	9	32	3	10	28
10 years	3,941	278	7.1	153	40	0	6	25	2	12	40
11 years	3,837	276	7.2	165	27	0	7	29	4	16	28
12 years	3,832	310	8.1	178	37	2	8	18	5	14	48
13 years	3,858	375	9.7	222	42	3	24	20	7	7	50
14 years	3,774	471	12.5	316	55	8	23	12	11	5	41
15 years	3,893	635	16.3	462	65	7	25	9	16	6	45
16 years	3,920	1,215	31.0	967	81	20	32	10	9	11	85
17 years	3,931	1,411	35.9	1,111	107	33	29	22	19	8	82
18 years	3,880	1,744	44.9	1,400	101	68	29	26	28	6	86
19 years	3,918	1,585	40.5	1,221	85	92	26	19	22	9	111
20 years	3,781	1,469	38.9	1,086	103	97	28	21	18	12	104
21 years	3,670	1,550	42.2	1,139	92	103	34	29	37	8	108
22 years	3,415	1,286	37.7	927	67	114	20	25	34	8	91
23 years	3,412	1,255	36.8	891	55	129	21	17	25	7	110
24 years	3,400	1,199	35.3	822	65	116	16	16	28	14	122
0–4 years	18,990	2,689	14.2	921	559	26	19	299	66	386	413
5–9 years	19,929	1,544	7.7	834	243	7	34	196	26	37	167
10–14 years	19,242	1,710	8.9	1,034	201	13	68	104	29	54	207
15–19 years	19,542	6,590	33.7	5,161	439	220	141	86	94	40	409
20–24 years	17,678	6,759	38.2	4,865	382	559	119	108	142	49	535

Source: National Safety Council tabulations of National Center for Health Statistics mortality data.
Note: Data does not include "age unknown" cases, which totaled 110 in 1998.
[a]*Deaths per 100,000 population in each age group.*
[b]*Includes transport drownings.*

Falls account for half the unintentional-injury deaths for those aged 80 and older.

More than 78,000 adults aged 25 and older died as a result of unintentional injuries in 1998, with motor vehicles accounting for about 40% of these deaths. Data for five-year age groups indicate that motor-vehicle crashes are the most common type of unintentional-injury death through age 74. Poisoning by solids and liquids is the second most common type for age groups 25 through 54, and falls are the second most common type from age 55 through 74, at which point it becomes the primary cause of fatal injury for those aged 75 and older. Falls account for nearly one-half

of the unintentional-injury deaths of those in this age group.

Death rates per 100,000 population are relatively stable for those aged 25-49, averaging 32.7. Death rates increase with age for each group beginning with age 50. The average death rate for those aged 85 and older is 10 times higher than the average rate for those aged 25-49. All age groups older than 65 have death rates higher than the all-ages rate of 36.2.

UNINTENTIONAL-INJURY DEATHS BY EVENT, AGES 25 AND OLDER, UNITED STATES, 1998

| Age Group | Population (000) | Unintentional-Injury Deaths | | Motor-Vehicle | Falls | Poisoning by | | Suffocation by Ingestion | Fires, Burns | Surgical & Medical Mis-adventures[b] | Drowning[c] | All Other |
		Number	Rate[a]			Solids, Liquids	Gases, Vapors					
25–29	18,575	5,798	31.2	3,724	159	786	31	33	114	27	306	618
30–34	20,168	6,247	31.0	3,408	192	1,292	43	57	140	44	331	740
35–39	22,615	7,534	33.3	3,682	293	1,958	45	73	186	49	354	894
40–44	21,883	7,593	34.7	3,281	402	2,188	50	107	235	81	332	917
45–49	18,853	6,231	33.1	2,762	435	1,473	47	119	183	118	262	832
50–54	15,722	4,715	30.0	2,234	409	686	28	103	178	147	183	747
55–59	12,403	3,857	31.1	1,855	410	304	33	130	153	168	144	660
60–64	10,263	3,483	33.9	1,565	486	187	18	133	155	202	117	620
65–69	9,592	3,937	41.0	1,625	703	123	25	214	191	312	121	623
70–74	8,798	4,955	56.3	1,785	1,181	100	37	316	206	402	120	808
75–79	7,215	5,996	83.1	1,867	1,874	114	26	439	251	467	111	847
80–84	4,732	6,715	141.9	1,590	2,772	102	36	544	224	447	84	916
85–89	2,554	5,940	232.6	912	3,088	71	11	507	143	363	54	791
90–94	1,116	3,812	341.6	313	2,370	29	8	375	69	199	18	431
95–99	323	1,332	412.4	49	930	10	3	117	23	56	0	144
100 and over	57	288	505.3	4	208	2	0	27	9	12	2	24
25 and over	174,869	78,433	44.9	30,656	15,912	9,425	441	3,294	2,460	3,094	2,539	10,612
35 and over	136,126	66,388	48.8	23,524	15,561	7,347	367	3,204	2,206	3,023	1,902	9,254
45 and over	91,628	51,261	55.9	16,561	14,866	3,201	272	3,024	1,785	2,893	1,216	7,443
55 and over	57,053	40,315	70.7	11,565	14,022	1,042	197	2,802	1,424	2,628	771	5,864
65 and over	34,387	32,975	95.9	8,145	13,126	551	146	2,539	1,116	2,258	510	4,584
75 and over	15,997	24,083	150.5	4,735	11,242	328	84	2,009	719	1,544	269	3,153

Source: National Safety Council tabulations of National Center for Health Statistics mortality data.
Note: Data does not include "age unknown" cases, which totaled 110 in 1998.
[a] *Deaths per 100,000 population in each age group.*
[b] *Surgical and medical complications and misadventures.*
[c] *Includes transport drownings.*

TRENDS IN UNINTENTIONAL-INJURY DEATH RATES

Between 1912 and 2000, unintentional-injury deaths per 100,000 population were reduced 55% (after adjusting for the classification change in 1948) from 82.4 to 35.3. The reduction in the overall rate during a period when the nation's population nearly tripled has resulted in more than 4,400,000 fewer people being killed due to unintentional injuries than there would have been if the rate had not been reduced.

Age-adjusted rates, which eliminate the effect of shifts in the age distribution of the population, have decreased 67% from 1912 to 2000. The adjusted rates, which are shown in the graph on the opposite page, are standardized to the 1940 age distribution of the U.S. population. The break in the lines at 1948 shows the estimated effect of changes in the International Classification of Diseases. The break in the lines at 1992 resulted from the adoption of the Bureau of Labor Statistics Census of Fatal Occupational Injuries for work-related deaths.

The table below shows the change in the age distribution of the population since 1910. Note that the age groups shown are slightly different from the standard age groups used elsewhere in *Injury Facts*®.

The age-adjusted death rate for all unintentional-injuries increased and decreased significantly several times during the period from 1910 to 1940. Since 1940, there have been some setbacks, such as in the early 1960s, but the overall trend has been positive. The age-adjusted death rates for unintentional-injury deaths in the work and home classes have declined fairly steadily since they became available in the late 1920s. The rates in the public class declined for three decades, rose in the 1960s and then continued declining. The age-adjusted motor-vehicle death rate rose steadily from 1910 to the late 1930s as the automobile became more widely used. A sharp drop in use occurred during World War II and a sharp rise in rates occurred in the 1960s, with death rates reflecting economic cycles and a long-term downward trend since then.

UNITED STATES POPULATION, SELECTED YEARS

Year	All Ages	0–13	14–24	25–44	45–64	65 & Older
Number (in thousands)						
1910	92,407	27,806	20,024	27,037	13,555	3,985
1940	132,122	30,521	26,454	39,868	26,249	9,031
2000	275,306	54,640	42,330	82,335	61,167	34,837
Percent						
1910	100.0	30.1	21.7	29.3	14.7	4.3
1940	100.0	23.1	20.0	30.2	19.9	6.8
2000	100.0	19.8	15.4	29.9	22.2	12.7

Source: For 1910 and 1940: U. S. Bureau of the Census. (1960). Historical Statistics of the United States, Colonial Times to 1957. Washington, DC: U.S. Government Printing Office. For 2000: Population Projections Program, Population Division. (Internet Release Date: December 1999). Projections of the Total Resident Population by 5-year Age Groups, and Sex with Special Age Categories: Middle Series, 1999 to 2000. Washington, DC: U. S. Bureau of the Census. http://www.census.gov/population/www/projections/natsum-T3.html.

AGE-ADJUSTED DEATH RATES BY CLASS OF INJURY, UNITED STATES, 1910–2000

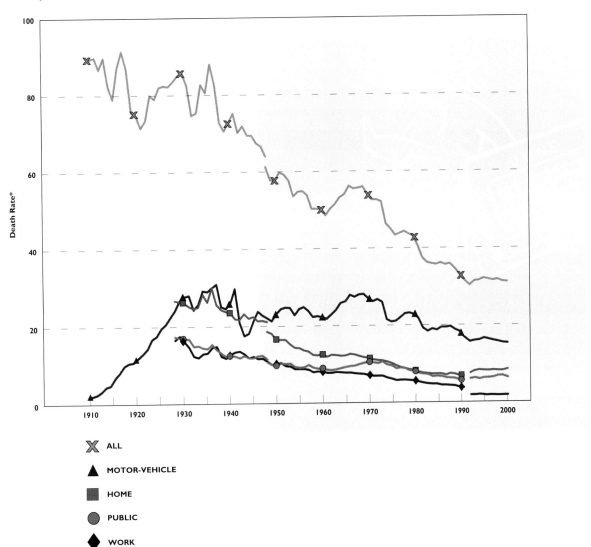

X   ALL

▲   MOTOR-VEHICLE

■   HOME

●   PUBLIC

◆   WORK

*Deaths per 100,000 population, adjusted to 1940 age distribution. The break at 1948 shows the estimated effect of classification changes. The break at 1992 is due to the adoption of the Bureau of Labor Statistics' Census of Fatal Occupational Injuries for work-related deaths.

PRINCIPAL CLASSES OF UNINTENTIONAL-INJURY DEATHS

PRINCIPAL CLASSES OF UNINTENTIONAL-INJURY DEATHS, UNITED STATES, 1903–2000

Year	Total[a] Deaths	Total[a] Rate[b]	Motor-Vehicle Deaths	Motor-Vehicle Rate[b]	Work Deaths	Work Rate[b]	Home Deaths	Home Rate[b]	Public Nonmotor-Vehicle Deaths	Public Nonmotor-Vehicle Rate[b]
1903	70,600	87.2	(c)	–	(c)	–	(c)	–	(c)	–
1904	71,500	86.6	(c)	–	(c)	–	(c)	–	(c)	–
1905	70,900	84.2	(c)	–	(c)	–	(c)	–	(c)	–
1906	80,000	93.2	400	0.5	(c)	–	(c)	–	(c)	–
1907	81,900	93.6	700	0.8	(c)	–	(c)	–	(c)	–
1908	72,300	81.2	800	0.9	(c)	–	(c)	–	(c)	–
1909	72,700	80.1	1,300	1.4	(c)	–	(c)	–	(c)	–
1910	77,900	84.4	1,900	2.0	(c)	–	(c)	–	(c)	–
1911	79,300	84.7	2,300	2.5	(c)	–	(c)	–	(c)	–
1912	78,400	82.5	3,100	3.3	(c)	–	(c)	–	(c)	–
1913	82,500	85.5	4,200	4.4	(c)	–	(c)	–	(c)	–
1914	77,000	78.6	4,700	4.8	(c)	–	(c)	–	(c)	–
1915	76,200	76.7	6,600	6.6	(c)	–	(c)	–	(c)	–
1916	84,800	84.1	8,200	8.1	(c)	–	(c)	–	(c)	–
1917	90,100	88.2	10,200	10.0	(c)	–	(c)	–	(c)	–
1918	85,100	82.1	10,700	10.3	(c)	–	(c)	–	(c)	–
1919	75,500	71.9	11,200	10.7	(c)	–	(c)	–	(c)	–
1920	75,900	71.2	12,500	11.7	(c)	–	(c)	–	(c)	–
1921	74,000	68.4	13,900	12.9	(c)	–	(c)	–	(c)	–
1922	76,300	69.4	15,300	13.9	(c)	–	(c)	–	(c)	–
1923	84,400	75.7	18,400	16.5	(c)	–	(c)	–	(c)	–
1924	85,600	75.6	19,400	17.1	(c)	–	(c)	–	(c)	–
1925	90,000	78.4	21,900	19.1	(c)	–	(c)	–	(c)	–
1926	91,700	78.7	23,400	20.1	(c)	–	(c)	–	(c)	–
1927	92,700	78.4	25,800	21.8	(c)	–	(c)	–	(c)	–
1928	95,000	79.3	28,000	23.4	19,000	15.8	30,000	24.9	21,000	17.4
1929	98,200	80.8	31,200	25.7	20,000	16.4	30,000	24.6	20,000	16.4
1930	99,100	80.5	32,900	26.7	19,000	15.4	30,000	24.4	20,000	16.3
1931	97,300	78.5	33,700	27.2	17,500	14.1	29,000	23.4	20,000	16.1
1932	89,000	71.3	29,500	23.6	15,000	12.0	29,000	23.2	18,000	14.4
1933	90,932	72.4	31,363	25.0	14,500	11.6	29,500	23.6	18,500	14.7
1934	100,977	79.9	36,101	28.6	16,000	12.7	34,000	26.9	18,000	14.2
1935	99,773	78.4	36,369	28.6	16,500	13.0	32,000	25.2	18,000	14.2
1936	110,052	85.9	38,089	29.7	18,500	14.5	37,000	28.9	19,500	15.2
1937	105,205	81.7	39,643	30.8	19,000	14.8	32,000	24.8	18,000	14.0
1938	93,805	72.3	32,582	25.1	16,000	12.3	31,000	23.9	17,000	13.1
1939	92,623	70.8	32,386	24.7	15,500	11.8	31,000	23.7	16,000	12.2
1940	96,885	73.4	34,501	26.1	17,000	12.9	31,500	23.9	16,500	12.5
1941	101,513	76.3	39,969	30.0	18,000	13.5	30,000	22.5	16,500	12.4
1942	95,889	71.6	28,309	21.1	18,000	13.4	30,500	22.8	16,000	12.0
1943	99,038	73.8	23,823	17.8	17,500	13.0	33,500	25.0	17,000	12.7
1944	95,237	71.7	24,282	18.3	16,000	12.0	32,500	24.5	16,000	12.0
1945	95,918	72.4	28,076	21.2	16,500	12.5	33,500	25.3	16,000	12.1
1946	98,033	70.0	33,411	23.9	16,500	11.8	33,000	23.6	17,500	12.5
1947	99,579	69.4	32,697	22.8	17,000	11.9	34,500	24.1	18,000	12.6
1948 (5th Rev.)[d]	98,001	67.1	32,259	22.1	16,000	11.0	35,000	24.0	17,000	11.6
1948 (6th Rev.)[d]	93,000	63.7	32,259	22.1	16,000	11.0	31,000	21.2	16,000	11.0
1949	90,106	60.6	31,701	21.3	15,000	10.1	31,000	20.9	15,000	10.1
1950	91,249	60.3	34,763	23.0	15,500	10.2	29,000	19.2	15,000	9.9
1951	95,871	62.5	36,996	24.1	16,000	10.4	30,000	19.6	16,000	10.4
1952	96,172	61.8	37,794	24.3	15,000	9.6	30,500	19.6	16,000	10.3
1953	95,032	60.1	37,955	24.0	15,000	9.5	29,000	18.3	16,500	10.4
1954	90,032	55.9	35,586	22.1	14,000	8.7	28,000	17.4	15,500	9.6
1955	93,443	56.9	38,426	23.4	14,200	8.6	28,500	17.3	15,500	9.4
1956	94,780	56.6	39,628	23.7	14,300	8.5	28,000	16.7	16,000	9.6
1957	95,307	55.9	38,702	22.7	14,200	8.3	28,000	16.4	17,500	10.3
1958	90,604	52.3	36,981	21.3	13,300	7.7	26,500	15.3	16,500	9.5
1959	92,080	52.2	37,910	21.5	13,800	7.8	27,000	15.3	16,500	9.3
1960	93,806	52.1	38,137	21.2	13,800	7.7	28,000	15.6	17,000	9.4
1961	92,249	50.4	38,091	20.8	13,500	7.4	27,000	14.8	16,500	9.0
1962	97,139	52.3	40,804	22.0	13,700	7.4	28,500	15.3	17,000	9.2
1963	100,669	53.4	43,564	23.1	14,200	7.5	28,500	15.1	17,500	9.3
1964	105,000	54.9	47,700	25.0	14,200	7.4	28,000	14.6	18,500	9.7
1965	108,004	55.8	49,163	25.4	14,100	7.3	28,500	14.7	19,500	10.1
1966	113,563	58.1	53,041	27.1	14,500	7.4	29,500	15.1	20,000	10.2
1967	113,169	57.3	52,924	26.8	14,200	7.2	29,000	14.7	20,500	10.4
1968	114,864	57.6	54,862	27.5	14,300	7.2	28,000	14.0	21,500	10.8
1969	116,385	57.8	55,791	27.7	14,300	7.1	27,500	13.7	22,500	11.2
1970	114,638	56.2	54,633	26.8	13,800	6.8	27,000	13.2	23,500	11.5
1971	113,439	54.8	54,381	26.3	13,700	6.6	26,500	12.8	23,500	11.4
1972	115,448	55.2	56,278	26.9	14,000	6.7	26,500	12.7	23,500	11.2
1973	115,821	54.8	55,511	26.3	14,300	6.8	26,500	12.5	24,500	11.6

See source and footnotes on page 35.

PRINCIPAL CLASSES OF UNINTENTIONAL-INJURY DEATHS, UNITED STATES, 1903–2000, Cont.

Year	Total[a] Deaths	Total[a] Rate[b]	Motor-Vehicle Deaths	Motor-Vehicle Rate[b]	Work Deaths	Work Rate[b]	Home Deaths	Home Rate[b]	Public Nonmotor-Vehicle Deaths	Public Nonmotor-Vehicle Rate[b]
1974	104,622	49.0	46,402	21.8	13,500	6.3	26,000	12.2	23,000	10.8
1975	103,030	47.8	45,853	21.3	13,000	6.0	25,000	11.6	23,000	10.6
1976	100,761	46.3	47,038	21.6	12,500	5.7	24,000	11.0	21,500	10.0
1977	103,202	47.0	49,510	22.5	12,900	5.9	23,200	10.6	22,200	10.1
1978	105,561	47.5	52,411	23.6	13,100	5.9	22,800	10.3	22,000	9.9
1979	105,312	46.9	53,524	23.8	13,000	5.8	22,500	10.0	21,000	9.4
1980	105,718	46.5	53,172	23.4	13,200	5.8	22,800	10.0	21,300	9.4
1981	100,704	43.9	51,385	22.4	12,500	5.4	21,700	9.5	19,800	8.6
1982	94,082	40.6	45,779	19.8	11,900	5.1	21,200	9.2	19,500	8.4
1983	92,488	39.6	44,452	19.0	11,700	5.0	21,200	9.1	19,400	8.3
1984	92,911	39.4	46,263	19.6	11,500	4.9	21,200	9.0	18,300	7.8
1985	93,457	39.3	45,901	19.3	11,500	4.8	21,600	9.1	18,800	7.9
1986	95,277	39.7	47,865	19.9	11,100	4.6	21,700	9.0	18,700	7.8
1987	95,020	39.2	48,290	19.9	11,300	4.7	21,400	8.8	18,400	7.6
1988	97,100	39.7	49,078	20.1	11,000	4.5	22,700	9.3	18,400	7.5
1989	95,028	38.5	47,575	19.3	10,900	4.4	22,500	9.1	18,200	7.4
1990	91,983	36.9	46,814	18.8	10,100	4.0	21,500	8.6	17,400	7.0
1991	89,347	35.4	43,536	17.3	9,800	3.9	22,100	8.8	17,600	7.0
1992	86,777	34.0	40,982	16.1	4,968[e]	1.9[e]	24,000[e]	9.4[e]	19,000[e]	7.4[e]
1993	90,523	35.1	41,893	16.3	5,035	2.0	26,100	10.1	19,700	7.6
1994	91,437	35.1	42,524	16.3	5,338	2.1	26,300	10.1	19,600	7.5
1995	93,320	35.5	43,363	16.5	5,018	1.9	27,200	10.3	20,100	7.6
1996	94,948	35.8	43,649	16.5	5,058	1.9	27,500	10.4	21,000	7.9
1997	95,644	35.7	43,458	16.2	5,162	1.9	27,700	10.3	21,700	8.1
1998[f]	97,835	36.2	43,501	16.1	5,120	1.9	29,000	10.7	22,600	8.4
1999[f]	97,300	35.7	43,000	15.8	5,170	1.9	28,200	10.3	23,400	8.6
2000[g]	97,300	35.3	43,000	15.6	5,200	1.9	29,500	10.7	22,000	8.0
Changes										
1990 to 2000	+6%	–4%	–8%	–17%	[h]	[h]	[h]	[h]	[h]	[h]
1999 to 2000	0%	–1%	0%	–1%	+1%	0%	+5%	+4%	–6%	–7%

Source: Total and motor-vehicle deaths, 1903–1932 based on National Center for Health Statistics death registration states; 1933–1948 (5th Rev.), 1949–1963, 1965–1998 are NCHS totals for the U.S. Work deaths for 1992–1999 are from the Bureau of Labor Statistics, Census of Fatal Occupational Injuries. All other figures are National Safety Council estimates.
[a] Duplications between Motor-Vehicle, Work, and Home are eliminated in the Total column.
[b] Rates are deaths per 100,000 population.
[c] Data insufficient to estimate yearly totals.
[d] In 1948 a revision was made in the International Classification of Diseases. The first figures for 1948 are comparable with those for earlier years, the second with those for later years.
[e] Adoption of the Census of Fatal Occupational Injuries figure for the Work class necessitated adjustments to the Home and Public classes. See the Technical Appendix for details.
[f] Revised.
[g] Preliminary.
[h] Comparison not valid for 1990-2000 because of change in estimating procedure (see footnote "e").

UNINTENTIONAL-INJURY DEATHS BY CLASS, UNITED STATES, 2000

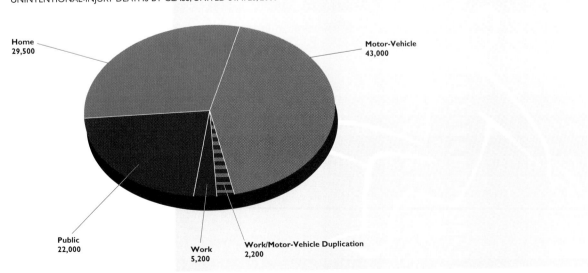

Home
29,500

Motor-Vehicle
43,000

Public
22,000

Work
5,200

Work/Motor-Vehicle Duplication
2,200

UNINTENTIONAL-INJURY DEATHS BY AGE

UNINTENTIONAL-INJURY DEATHS BY AGE, UNITED STATES, 1903–2000

Year	All Ages	Under 5 Years	5–14 Years	15–24 Years	25–44 Years	45–64 Years	65–74 Years	75 Years & Over[a]
1903	70,600	9,400	8,200	10,300	20,100	12,600	10,000	
1904	71,500	9,700	9,000	10,500	19,900	12,500	9,900	
1905	70,900	9,800	8,400	10,600	19,600	12,600	9,900	
1906	80,000	10,000	8,400	13,000	24,000	13,600	11,000	
1907	81,900	10,500	8,300	13,400	24,900	14,700	10,100	
1908	72,300	10,100	7,600	11,300	20,500	13,100	9,700	
1909	72,700	9,900	7,400	10,700	21,000	13,300	10,400	
1910	77,900	9,900	7,400	11,900	23,600	14,100	11,000	
1911	79,300	11,000	7,500	11,400	22,400	15,100	11,900	
1912	78,400	10,600	7,900	11,500	22,200	14,700	11,500	
1913	82,500	9,800	7,400	12,200	24,500	16,500	12,100	
1914	77,000	10,600	7,900	11,000	21,400	14,300	11,800	
1915	76,200	10,300	8,200	10,800	20,500	14,300	12,100	
1916	84,800	11,600	9,100	7,700	24,900	17,800	13,700	
1917	90,100	11,600	9,700	11,700	24,400	18,500	14,200	
1918	85,100	10,600	10,100	10,600	21,900	17,700	14,200	
1919	75,500	10,100	10,000	10,200	18,600	13,800	12,800	
1920	75,900	10,200	9,900	10,400	18,100	13,900	13,400	
1921	74,000	9,600	9,500	9,800	18,000	13,900	13,200	
1922	76,300	9,700	9,500	10,000	18,700	14,500	13,900	
1923	84,400	9,900	9,800	11,000	21,500	16,900	15,300	
1924	85,600	10,200	9,900	11,900	20,900	16,800	15,900	
1925	90,000	9,700	10,000	12,400	22,200	18,700	17,000	
1926	91,700	9,500	9,900	12,600	22,700	19,200	17,800	
1927	92,700	9,200	9,900	12,900	22,900	19,700	18,100	
1928	95,000	8,900	9,800	13,100	23,300	20,600	19,300	
1929	98,200	8,600	9,800	14,000	24,300	21,500	20,000	
1930	99,100	8,200	9,100	14,000	24,300	22,200	21,300	
1931	97,300	7,800	8,700	13,500	23,100	22,500	21,700	
1932	89,000	7,100	8,100	12,000	20,500	20,100	21,200	
1933	90,932	6,948	8,195	12,225	21,005	20,819	21,740	
1934	100,977	7,034	8,272	13,274	23,288	24,197	24,912	
1935	99,773	6,971	7,808	13,168	23,411	23,457	24,958	
1936	110,052	7,471	7,866	13,701	24,990	26,535	29,489	
1937	105,205	6,969	7,704	14,302	23,955	24,743	27,532	
1938	93,805	6,646	6,593	12,129	20,464	21,689	26,284	
1939	92,628	6,668	6,378	12,066	20,164	20,842	26,505	
1940	96,885	6,851	6,466	12,763	21,166	21,840	27,799	
1941	101,513	7,052	6,702	14,346	22,983	22,509	27,921	
1942	95,889	7,220	6,340	13,732	21,141	20,764	26,692	
1943	99,038	8,039	6,636	15,278	20,212	20,109	28,764	
1944	95,237	7,912	6,704	14,750	19,115	19,097	27,659	
1945	95,918	7,741	6,836	12,446	19,393	20,097	29,405	
1946	98,033	7,949	6,545	13,366	20,705	20,249	29,219	
1947	99,579	8,219	6,069	13,166	21,155	20,513	30,457	
1948 (5th Rev.)[b]	98,001	8,387	5,859	12,595	20,274	19,809	31,077	
1948 (6th Rev.)[b]	93,000	8,350	5,850	12,600	20,300	19,300	9,800	16,800
1949	90,106	8,469	5,539	11,522	19,432	18,302	9,924	16,918
1950	91,249	8,389	5,519	12,119	20,663	18,665	9,750	16,144
1951	95,871	8,769	5,892	12,366	22,363	19,610	10,218	16,653
1952	96,172	8,871	5,980	12,787	21,950	19,892	10,026	16,667
1953	95,032	8,678	6,136	12,837	21,422	19,479	9,927	16,553
1954	90,032	8,380	5,939	11,801	20,023	18,299	9,652	15,938
1955	93,443	8,099	6,099	12,742	29,911	19,199	9,929	16,464
1956	94,780	8,173	6,319	13,545	20,986	19,207	10,160	16,393
1957	95,307	8,423	6,454	12,973	20,949	19,495	10,076	16,937
1958	90,604	8,789	6,514	12,744	19,658	18,095	9,431	15,373
1959	92,080	8,748	6,511	13,269	19,666	18,937	9,475	15,474
1960	93,806	8,950	6,836	13,457	19,600	19,385	9,689	15,829
1961	92,249	8,622	6,717	13,431	19,273	19,134	9,452	15,620
1962	97,139	8,705	6,751	14,557	19,955	20,335	10,149	16,687
1963	100,669	8,688	6,962	15,889	20,529	21,262	10,194	17,145
1964	100,500	8,670	7,400	17,420	22,080	22,100	10,400	16,930
1965	108,004	8,586	7,391	18,688	22,228	22,900	10,430	17,781
1966	113,563	8,507	7,958	21,030	23,134	24,022	10,706	18,206
1967	113,169	7,825	7,874	21,645	23,255	23,826	10,645	18,099
1968	114,864	7,263	8,369	23,012	23,684	23,896	10,961	17,679
1969	116,385	6,973	8,186	24,668	24,410	24,192	10,643	17,313
1970	114,638	6,594	8,203	24,336	23,979	24,164	10,644	16,718
1971	113,439	6,496	8,143	24,733	23,535	23,240	10,494	16,798
1972	115,448	6,142	8,242	25,762	23,852	23,658	10,446	17,346
1973	115,821	6,037	8,102	26,550	24,750	23,059	10,243	17,080

See source and footnotes on page 37.

UNINTENTIONAL-INJURY DEATHS BY AGE, UNITED STATES, 1903–2000, Cont.

Year	All Ages	Under 5 Years	5–14 Years	15–24 Years	25–44 Years	45–64 Years	65–74 Years	75 Years & Over[a]
1974	104,622	5,335	7,037	24,200	22,547	20,334	9,323	15,846
1975	103,030	4,948	6,818	24,121	22,877	19,643	9,220	15,403
1976	100,761	4,692	6,308	24,316	22,399	19,000	8,823	15,223
1977	103,202	4,470	6,305	25,619	23,460	19,167	9,006	15,175
1978	105,561	4,766	6,118	26,622	25,024	18,774	9,072	15,185
1979	105,312	4,429	5,689	26,574	26,097	18,346	9,013	15,164
1980	105,718	4,479	5,224	26,206	26,722	18,140	8,997	15,950
1981	100,704	4,130	4,866	23,582	26,928	17,339	8,639	15,220
1982	94,082	4,108	4,504	21,306	25,135	15,907	8,224	14,898
1983	92,488	3,999	4,321	19,756	24,996	15,444	8,336	15,636
1984	92,911	3,652	4,198	19,801	25,498	15,273	8,424	16,065
1985	93,457	3,746	4,252	19,161	25,940	15,251	8,583	16,524
1986	95,277	3,843	4,226	19,975	27,201	14,733	8,499	16,800
1987	95,020	3,871	4,198	18,695	27,484	14,807	8,686	17,279
1988	97,100	3,794	4,215	18,507	28,279	15,177	8,971	18,157
1989	95,028	3,770	4,090	16,738	28,429	15,046	8,812	18,143
1990	91,983	3,496	3,650	16,241	27,663	14,607	8,405	17,921
1991	89,347	3,626	3,660	15,278	26,526	13,693	8,137	18,427
1992	86,777	3,286	3,388	13,662	25,808	13,882	8,165	18,586
1993	90,523	3,488	3,466	13,966	27,277	14,434	8,125	19,767
1994	91,437	3,406	3,508	13,898	27,012	15,200	8,279	20,134
1995	93,320	3,067	3,544	13,842	27,660	16,004	8,400	20,803
1996	94,948	2,951	3,433	13,809	27,092	16,717	8,780	22,166
1997	94,644	2,770	3,371	13,367	27,129	17,521	8,578	22,908
1998[c]	97,835	2,689	3,254	13,349	27,172	18,286	8,892	24,193
1999[c]	97,300	2,600	3,000	13,400	26,200	19,300	8,000	24,800
2000[d]	97,300	2,700	2,700	13,800	26,600	19,500	7,600	24,400
Changes								
1990 to 2000	+6%	−23%	−26%	−15%	−4%	+33%	−10%	+36%
1999 to 2000	0%	+4%	−10%	+3%	+2%	+1%	−5%	−2%

Source: 1903 to 1932 based on National Center for Health Statistics data for registration states; 1933–1948 (5th Rev.), 1949–1963, 1965–1998 are NCHS totals. All other figures are National Safety Council estimates. See Technical Appendix for comparability.
[a] Includes "age unknown." In 1998, these deaths numbered 110.
[b] In 1948, a revision was made in the International Classification of Diseases. The first figures for 1948 are comparable with those for earlier years, the second with those for later years.
[c] Revised.
[d] Preliminary.

UNINTENTIONAL-INJURY DEATHS AND POPULATION BY AGE, UNITED STATES, 2000

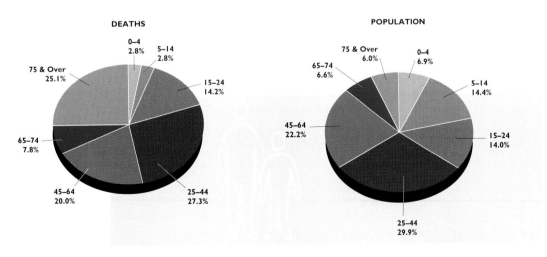

UNINTENTIONAL-INJURY DEATH RATES BY AGE

UNINTENTIONAL-INJURY DEATH RATES[a] BY AGE, UNITED STATES, 1903–2000

Year	Index	All Ages	Under 5 Years	5–14 Years	15–24 Years	25–44 Years	45–64 Years	65–74 Years	75 Years & Over[b]
1903	98.7	87.2	98.7	46.8	65.0	87.4	111.7		299.8
1904	103.2	86.6	99.1	50.9	64.9	84.6	108.1		290.0
1905	98.2	84.2	98.6	47.0	64.1	81.4	106.2		282.5
1906	114.5	93.2	99.1	46.5	77.1	97.3	111.7		306.0
1907	114.4	93.6	102.7	45.5	78.0	98.8	117.8		274.2
1908	100.0	81.2	97.5	41.2	64.4	79.5	102.2		256.7
1909	97.0	80.1	94.2	39.6	59.9	79.6	101.0		268.2
1910	103.1	84.4	92.8	39.1	65.3	87.3	104.0		276.0
1911	103.6	84.7	101.9	39.3	62.1	81.4	108.7		292.1
1912	100.0	82.5	97.1	40.5	62.3	79.2	103.2		275.8
1913	103.4	85.5	88.4	37.4	65.2	85.6	112.5		281.7
1914	95.1	78.6	94.3	38.9	58.5	73.2	94.6		268.1
1915	91.1	76.7	90.8	39.7	57.3	69.0	92.4		268.8
1916	100.6	84.1	101.4	43.3	40.8	82.5	112.1		297.6
1917	105.4	88.2	108.4	45.3	62.1	79.8	113.8		301.2
1918	100.1	82.1	91.0	46.5	58.7	72.2	106.3		294.2
1919	87.2	71.9	87.2	45.9	55.3	60.1	81.8		262.0
1920	86.3	71.2	87.4	44.9	55.5	56.9	85.6		289.5
1921	82.5	68.4	80.8	42.4	51.4	55.5	79.4		259.8
1922	84.7	69.4	80.6	41.5	51.4	57.1	81.4		265.1
1923	92.2	75.7	82.0	42.4	55.6	64.5	92.6		282.8
1924	91.1	75.6	82.9	42.4	58.6	61.7	90.2		283.5
1925	94.6	78.4	78.6	42.3	59.7	64.7	97.8		293.9
1926	95.1	78.7	77.9	41.4	59.9	65.4	98.2		298.7
1927	94.8	78.4	75.9	41.0	60.2	65.2	98.0		295.4
1928	91.4	79.3	74.4	40.4	59.9	65.6	99.9		306.2
1929	98.1	80.8	73.3	40.0	63.1	67.7	102.1		308.9
1930	97.9	80.5	71.8	36.9	62.3	67.0	102.9		317.9
1931	95.1	78.5	69.9	35.2	59.7	63.0	102.1		313.3
1932	86.1	71.3	65.1	32.8	52.7	55.6	89.3		296.9
1933	86.9	72.4	65.5	33.4	53.6	56.3	90.8		295.3
1934	95.4	79.9	68.1	33.9	57.8	61.8	103.3		328.5
1935	93.0	78.4	68.5	32.2	56.9	61.6	98.0		319.8
1936	101.5	85.9	74.4	32.9	58.8	65.3	108.6		367.4
1937	95.5	81.7	69.6	32.7	60.9	62.1	99.3		333.4
1938	84.0	72.3	65.3	28.5	51.3	52.5	85.4		308.9
1939	81.4	70.8	62.9	28.2	50.7	51.2	81.0		300.0
1940	84.1	73.4	64.8	28.8	53.5	53.2	83.4		305.7
1941	86.7	76.3	65.0	29.7	60.9	57.2	84.8		297.4
1942	81.0	71.6	63.9	27.9	59.8	52.4	77.1		275.5
1943	82.9	73.8	66.9	29.0	69.7	50.3	73.6		287.8
1944	80.2	71.7	63.2	29.1	72.9	48.9	68.9		268.6
1945	80.0	72.4	59.8	29.5	64.5	50.5	71.6		277.6
1946	77.8	70.0	60.2	28.1	61.7	48.8	70.9		267.9
1947	76.9	69.4	57.4	25.8	59.6	49.0	70.6		270.7
1948 (5th Rev.)[c]	73.9	67.1	56.3	24.6	56.8	46.2	66.8		267.4
1948 (6th Rev.)[c]	70.4	63.7	56.0	24.5	56.8	46.2	65.1	122.4	464.3
1949	66.7	60.6	54.4	23.0	52.2	43.5	60.6	120.4	450.7
1950	66.6	60.3	51.4	22.6	55.0	45.6	60.5	115.8	414.7
1951	69.0	62.5	50.8	23.6	57.7	49.0	62.7	117.1	413.6
1952	68.4	61.8	51.5	22.5	60.9	47.7	62.7	111.1	399.8
1953	66.6	60.1	49.5	22.1	61.4	46.4	60.5	106.7	383.6
1954	61.9	55.9	46.7	20.5	56.4	43.0	55.9	100.7	354.4
1955	63.2	56.9	43.9	20.7	60.1	44.7	57.7	100.8	350.2
1956	63.3	56.6	43.3	20.2	63.3	44.7	56.7	100.6	335.6
1957	62.2	55.9	43.5	19.9	59.5	44.6	56.6	97.5	333.3
1958	58.1	52.3	44.5	19.6	56.2	42.0	51.7	89.3	292.6
1959	58.1	52.2	43.6	18.9	56.5	42.1	53.2	87.7	284.7
1960	58.0	52.1	44.0	19.1	55.6	42.0	53.6	87.6	281.4
1961	56.1	50.4	42.0	18.1	54.0	41.2	52.1	83.8	267.9
1962	58.1	52.3	42.6	18.0	55.0	42.7	54.6	88.5	277.7
1963	59.5	53.4	42.8	18.2	57.2	44.0	56.3	87.9	277.0
1964	61.4	54.9	43.1	19.1	59.9	47.3	57.6	88.9	263.9
1965	62.3	55.8	43.4	18.7	61.6	47.7	58.8	88.5	268.7
1966	64.8	58.1	44.4	19.9	66.9	49.6	60.7	89.8	267.4
1967	64.0	57.3	42.2	19.4	66.9	49.7	59.2	88.5	257.4
1968	64.3	57.6	40.6	20.5	69.2	50.1	58.5	90.2	244.0
1969	64.6	57.8	40.2	20.0	71.8	51.2	58.4	86.6	232.0
1970	62.5	56.2	38.4	20.1	68.0	49.8	57.6	85.2	219.6
1971	60.7	54.8	37.7	20.1	66.1	48.4	54.7	82.7	213.2
1972	60.7	55.2	35.9	20.6	67.6	47.5	55.2	80.8	214.2
1973	60.1	54.8	35.8	20.6	68.2	48.0	53.3	77.3	206.3

See source and footnotes on page 39.

UNINTENTIONAL-INJURY DEATH RATES[a] BY AGE, UNITED STATES, 1903–2000, Cont.

Year	Index	All Ages	Under 5 Years	5–14 Years	15–24 Years	25–44 Years	45–64 Years	65–74 Years	75 Years & Over[b]
1974	53.5	49.0	32.4	18.2	60.9	42.7	46.7	68.7	186.7
1975	52.0	47.8	30.7	17.8	59.5	42.3	44.9	66.2	175.5
1976	50.1	46.3	30.0	16.7	58.9	40.3	43.2	62.0	168.4
1977	50.6	47.0	28.7	17.0	61.3	40.9	43.4	61.5	164.0
1978	51.2	47.5	30.3	16.9	63.1	42.3	42.4	60.5	159.7
1979	50.4	46.9	27.6	16.1	62.6	42.7	41.3	58.8	154.8
1980	49.7	46.5	27.2	15.0	61.7	42.3	40.8	57.5	158.6
1981	46.8	43.9	24.4	14.2	55.9	41.2	39.0	54.4	147.4
1982	43.2	40.6	23.8	13.2	51.2	37.3	35.8	50.9	140.0
1983	41.8	39.6	22.8	12.7	48.2	36.0	34.7	50.8	142.8
1984	41.5	39.4	20.6	12.4	48.9	35.7	34.3	50.7	142.8
1985	41.3	39.3	21.0	12.6	47.9	35.3	34.2	50.9	143.0
1986	41.7	39.7	21.4	12.6	50.5	36.1	33.0	49.6	141.5
1987	41.1	39.2	21.4	12.4	48.1	35.7	33.0	49.8	141.6
1988	41.5	39.7	20.9	12.3	48.5	36.1	33.4	50.9	145.3
1989	40.1	38.5	20.4	11.8	44.8	35.7	32.8	49.3	141.5
1990	38.5	36.9	18.5	10.4	44.0	34.2	31.6	46.4	136.5
1991	36.8	35.4	18.9	10.2	42.0	32.3	29.3	44.5	136.7
1992	35.1	34.0	16.8	9.3	37.8	31.3	28.7	44.2	134.5
1993	36.2	35.1	17.7	9.4	38.8	33.0	29.1	43.6	139.9
1994	36.1	35.1	17.3	9.4	38.4	32.5	29.9	44.3	139.2
1995	36.4	35.5	15.7	9.3	38.2	33.2	30.6	44.8	140.6
1996	36.5	35.8	15.3	8.9	38.1	32.3	31.1	47.0	145.9
1997	36.2	35.7	14.5	8.7	36.5	32.5	31.6	46.3	146.2
1998[d]	36.4	36.2	14.2	8.3	35.9	32.6	31.9	48.3	151.1
1999[d]	35.9	35.7	13.8	7.6	35.4	31.6	32.6	43.5	151.8
2000[e]	35.7	35.3	14.3	6.8	35.9	32.3	31.9	41.8	146.6

Changes									
1990 to 2000		–4%	–23%	–35%	–18%	–6%	+1%	–10%	+7%
1999 to 2000		–1%	+4%	–11%	+1%	+2%	–2%	–4%	–3%

2000 Population (Millions)									
Total		275.306[f]	18.865	39.689	38.415	82.335	61.167	18.189	16.648
Male		134.554[f]	9.639	20.318	19.660	40.847	29.617	8.210	6.264
Female		140.752[f]	9.227	19.371	18.755	41.487	31.550	9.979	10.384

Source: All figures are National Safety Council estimates. See Technical Appendix for comparability.
[a] *Rates are deaths per 100,000 resident population in each age group. The All Ages crude rates are based on U.S. Census Bureau figures. The index numbers (1912=100.0) are based on rates standardized for age (base 1940) to remove the influence of changes in age distribution between 1903 and 2000.*
[b] *Includes age unknown.*
[c] *In 1948, a revision was made in the International Classification of Diseases. The first figures for 1948 are comparable with those for earlier years, the second with those for later years.*
[d] *Revised.*
[e] *Preliminary.*
[f] *Sum of parts may not equal total due to rounding.*

PRINCIPAL TYPES OF UNINTENTIONAL-INJURY DEATHS

PRINCIPAL TYPES OF UNINTENTIONAL-INJURY DEATHS, UNITED STATES, 1903–2000

Year	Total	Motor-Vehicle	Falls	Drowning[a]	Fires, Burns[b]	Ingest. of Food, Object	Firearms	Poison (Solid, Liquid)	Poison (Gas, Vapor)	All Other
1903	70,600	(c)	(c)	9,200	(c)	(c)	2,500	(c)	(c)	58,900
1904	71,500	(c)	(c)	9,300	(c)	(c)	2,800	(c)	(c)	59,400
1905	70,900	(c)	(c)	9,300	(c)	(c)	2,000	(c)	(c)	59,600
1906	80,000	400	(c)	9,400	(c)	(c)	2,100	(c)	(c)	68,100
1907	81,900	700	(c)	9,000	(c)	(c)	1,700	(c)	(c)	70,500
1908	72,300	800	(c)	9,300	(c)	(c)	1,900	(c)	(c)	60,300
1909	72,700	1,300	(c)	8,500	(c)	(c)	1,600	(c)	(c)	61,300
1910	77,900	1,900	(c)	8,700	(c)	(c)	1,900	(c)	(c)	65,400
1911	79,300	2,300	(c)	9,000	(c)	(c)	2,100	(c)	(c)	65,900
1912	78,400	3,100	(c)	8,600	(c)	(c)	2,100	(c)	(c)	64,600
1913	82,500	4,200	15,100	10,300	8,900	(c)	2,400	3,200	(c)	38,400
1914	77,000	4,700	15,000	8,700	9,100	(c)	2,300	3,300	(c)	33,900
1915	76,200	6,600	15,000	8,600	8,400	(c)	2,100	2,800	(c)	32,700
1916	84,800	8,200	15,200	8,900	9,500	(c)	2,200	2,900	(c)	37,900
1917	90,100	10,200	15,200	7,600	10,800	(c)	2,300	2,800	(c)	41,200
1918	85,100	10,700	13,200	7,000	10,200	(c)	2,500	2,700	(c)	38,800
1919	75,500	11,200	11,900	9,100	9,100	(c)	2,800	3,100	(c)	28,300
1920	75,900	12,500	12,600	6,100	9,300	(c)	2,700	3,300	(c)	29,400
1921	74,000	13,900	12,300	7,800	7,500	(c)	2,800	2,900	(c)	26,800
1922	76,300	15,300	13,200	7,000	8,300	(c)	2,900	2,800	(c)	26,800
1923	84,400	18,400	14,100	6,800	9,100	(c)	2,900	2,800	2,700	27,600
1924	85,600	19,400	14,700	7,400	7,400	(c)	2,900	2,700	2,900	28,200
1925	90,000	21,900	15,500	7,300	8,600	(c)	2,800	2,700	2,800	28,400
1926	91,700	23,400	16,300	7,500	8,800	(c)	2,800	2,600	3,200	27,100
1927	92,700	25,800	16,500	8,100	8,200	(c)	3,000	2,600	2,700	25,800
1928	95,000	28,000	17,000	8,600	8,400	(c)	2,900	2,800	2,800	24,500
1929	98,200	31,200	17,700	7,600	8,200	(c)	3,200	2,600	2,800	24,900
1930	99,100	32,900	18,100	7,500	8,100	(c)	3,200	2,600	2,500	24,200
1931	97,300	33,700	18,100	7,600	7,100	(c)	3,100	2,600	2,100	23,000
1932	89,000	29,500	18,600	7,500	7,100	(c)	3,000	2,200	2,100	19,000
1933	90,932	31,363	18,962	7,158	6,781	(c)	3,014	2,135	1,633	19,886
1934	100,977	36,101	20,725	7,077	7,456	(c)	3,033	2,148	1,643	22,794
1935	99,773	36,369	21,378	6,744	7,253	(c)	2,799	2,163	1,654	21,413
1936	110,052	38,089	23,562	6,659	7,939	(c)	2,817	2,177	1,665	27,144
1937	105,205	39,643	22,544	7,085	7,214	(c)	2,576	2,190	1,675	22,278
1938	93,805	32,582	23,239	6,881	6,491	(c)	2,726	2,077	1,428	18,381
1939	92,623	32,386	23,427	6,413	6,675	(c)	2,618	1,963	1,440	17,701
1940	96,885	34,501	23,356	6,202	7,521	(c)	2,375	1,847	1,583	19,500
1941	101,513	39,969	22,764	6,389	6,922	(c)	2,396	1,731	1,464	19,878
1942	95,889	28,309	22,632	6,696	7,901	(c)	2,678	1,607	1,741	24,325
1943	99,038	23,823	24,701	7,115	8,726	921	2,282	1,745	2,014	27,711
1944	95,237	24,282	22,989	6,511	8,372	896	2,392	1,993	1,860	25,942
1945	95,918	28,076	23,847	6,624	7,949	897	2,385	1,987	2,120	22,033
1946	98,033	33,411	23,109	6,442	7,843	1,076	2,801	1,961	1,821	19,569
1947	99,579	32,697	24,529	6,885	8,033	1,206	2,439	1,865	1,865	14,060
1948 (5th Rev.)[d]	98,001	32,259	24,836	6,428	7,743	1,315	2,191	1,753	2,045	19,611
1948 (6th Rev.)[d]	93,000	32,259	22,000	6,500	6,800	1,299	2,330	1,600	2,020	17,192
1949	90,106	31,701	22,308	6,684	5,982	1,341	2,326	1,634	1,617	16,513
1950	91,249	34,763	20,783	6,131	6,405	1,350	2,174	1,584	1,769	16,290
1951	95,871	36,996	21,376	6,489	6,788	1,456	2,247	1,497	1,627	17,395
1952	96,172	37,794	20,945	6,601	6,922	1,434	2,210	1,440	1,397	17,429
1953	95,032	37,955	20,631	6,770	6,579	1,603	2,277	1,391	1,223	16,603
1954	90,032	35,586	19,771	6,334	6,083	1,627	2,271	1,339	1,223	15,798
1955	93,443	38,426	20,192	6,344	6,352	1,608	2,120	1,431	1,163	15,807
1956	94,780	39,628	20,282	6,263	6,405	1,760	2,202	1,422	1,213	15,605
1957	95,307	38,702	20,545	6,613	6,269	2,043	2,369	1,390	1,143	16,233
1958	90,604	36,981	18,248	6,582[e]	7,291[e]	2,191[e]	2,172	1,429	1,187	14,523
1959	92,080	37,910	18,774	6,434	6,898	2,189	2,258	1,661	1,141	14,815
1960	93,806	38,137	19,023	6,529	7,645	2,397	2,334	1,679	1,253	14,809
1961	92,249	38,091	18,691	6,525	7,102	2,499	2,204	1,804	1,192	14,141
1962	97,139	40,804	19,589	6,439	7,534	1,813	2,092	1,833	1,376	15,659
1963	100,669	43,564	19,335	6,347	8,172	1,949	2,263	2,061	1,489	15,489
1964	105,000	47,700	18,941	6,709	7,379	1,865	2,275	2,100	1,360	16,571
1965	108,004	49,163	19,984	6,799	7,347	1,836	2,344	2,110	1,526	16,895
1966	113,563	53,041	20,066	7,084	8,084	1,831	2,558	2,283	1,648	16,968
1967	113,169	52,924	20,120	7,076	7,423	1,980	2,896	2,506	1,574	16,670
1968	114,864	54,862	18,651	7,372[e]	7,335	3,100[e]	2,394[e]	2,583	1,526	17,041
1969	116,385	55,791	17,827	7,699	7,163	3,712	2,309	2,967	1,549	16,368
1970	114,638	54,633	16,926	7,860	6,718	2,753	2,406	3,679	1,620	18,043
1971	113,439	54,381	16,755	7,396	6,776	2,877	2,360	3,710	1,646	17,538
1972	115,448	56,278	16,744	7,586	6,714	2,830	2,442	3,728	1,690	17,436
1973	115,821	55,511	16,506	8,725	6,503	3,013	2,618	3,683	1,652	17,610

See source and footnotes on page 41.

PRINCIPAL TYPES OF UNINTENTIONAL-INJURY DEATHS, UNITED STATES, 1903–2000, Cont.

Year	Total	Motor-Vehicle	Falls	Drowning[a]	Fires, Burns[b]	Ingest. of Food, Object	Firearms	Poison (Solid, Liquid)	Poison (Gas, Vapor)	All Other
1974	104,622	46,402	16,339	7,876	6,236	2,991	2,513	4,016	1,518	16,731
1975	103,030	45,853	14,896	8,000	6,071	3,106	2,380	4,694	1,577	16,453
1976	100,761	47,038	14,136	6,827	6,338	3,033	2,059	4,161	1,569	15,600
1977	103,202	49,510	13,773	7,126	6,357	3,037	1,982	3,374	1,596	16,447
1978	105,561	52,411	13,690	7,026	6,163	3,063	1,806	3,035	1,737	16,630
1979	105,312	53,524	13,216	6,872	5,991	3,243	2,004	3,165	1,472	15,825
1980	105,718	53,172	13,294	7,257	5,822	3,249	1,955	3,089	1,242	16,638
1981	100,704	51,385	12,628	6,277	5,697	3,331	1,871	3,243	1,280	14,992
1982	94,082	45,779	12,077	6,351	5,210	3,254	1,756	3,474	1,259	14,922
1983	92,488	44,452	12,024	6,353	5,028	3,387	1,695	3,382	1,251	14,916
1984	92,911	46,263	11,937	5,388	5,010	3,541	1,668	3,808	1,103	14,193
1985	93,457	45,901	12,001	5,316	4,938	3,551	1,649	4,091	1,079	14,931
1986	95,277	47,865	11,444	5,700	4,835	3,692	1,452	4,731	1,009	14,549
1987	95,020	48,290	11,733	5,100	4,710	3,688	1,440	4,415	900	14,744
1988	97,100	49,078	12,096	4,966	4,965	3,805	1,501	5,353	873	14,463
1989	95,028	47,575	12,151	4,015	4,716	3,578	1,489	5,603	921	14,980
1990	91,983	46,814	12,313	4,685	4,175	3,303	1,416	5,055	748	13,474
1991	89,347	43,536	12,662	4,818	4,120	3,240	1,441	5,698	736	13,096
1992	86,777	40,982	12,646	3,542	3,958	3,182	1,409	6,449	633	13,976
1993	90,523	41,893	13,141	3,807	3,900	3,160	1,521	7,877	660	14,564
1994	91,437	42,524	13,450	3,942	3,986	3,065	1,356	8,309	685	14,120
1995	93,320	43,363	13,986	4,350	3,761	3,185	1,225	8,461	611	14,378
1996	94,948	43,649	14,986	3,959	3,741	3,206	1,134	8,872	638	14,763
1997	95,644	43,458	15,447	4,051	3,490	3,275	981	9,587	576	14,779
1998[f]	97,835	43,501	16,274	4,406	3,255	3,515	866	10,255	546	15,217
1999[f]	97,300	43,000	16,000	4,000	3,100	3,100	800	11,000	400	15,900
2000[g]	97,300	43,000	16,200	3,900	3,600	3,400	600	11,700	400	14,500
Changes										
1990 to 2000	+6%	–8%	+32%	–17%	–14%	+3%	–58%	+131%	–47%	+8%
1999 to 2000	0%	0%	+1%	–3%	+16%	+10%	–25%	+6%	0%	–9%

Source: National Center for Health Statistics and National Safety Council. See Technical Appendix for comparability.
[a] *Includes drowning in water transport accidents.*
[b] *Includes burns by fire, and deaths resulting from conflagration regardless of nature of injury.*
[c] *Comparable data not available.*
[d] *In 1948, a revision was made in the International Classification of Diseases. The first figures for 1948 are comparable with those for earlier years, the second with those for later years.*
[e] *Data are not comparable to previous years shown due to classification changes in 1958 and 1968.*
[f] *Revised.*
[g] *Preliminary.*

UNINTENTIONAL-INJURY DEATH RATES FOR PRINCIPAL TYPES

UNINTENTIONAL-INJURY DEATH RATES[a] FOR PRINCIPAL TYPES, UNITED STATES, 1903–2000

Year	Total	Motor-Vehicle	Falls	Drowning[b]	Fires, Burns[c]	Ingest. of Food, Object	Firearms	Poison (Solid, Liquid)	Poison (Gas, Vapor)	All Other
1903	87.2	(d)	(d)	11.4	(d)	(d)	3.1	(d)	(d)	72.7
1904	86.6	(d)	(d)	11.3	(d)	(d)	3.4	(d)	(d)	71.9
1905	84.2	(d)	(d)	11.1	(d)	(d)	2.4	(d)	(d)	70.7
1906	93.2	0.5	(d)	11.0	(d)	(d)	2.4	(d)	(d)	79.3
1907	93.6	0.8	(d)	10.4	(d)	(d)	2.0	(d)	(d)	80.4
1908	81.2	0.9	(d)	10.5	(d)	(d)	2.1	(d)	(d)	67.7
1909	80.1	1.4	(d)	9.4	(d)	(d)	1.8	(d)	(d)	67.5
1910	84.4	2.0	(d)	9.4	(d)	(d)	2.1	(d)	(d)	70.9
1911	84.7	2.5	(d)	9.6	(d)	(d)	2.2	(d)	(d)	70.4
1912	82.5	3.3	(d)	9.0	(d)	(d)	2.2	(d)	(d)	68.0
1913	85.5	4.4	15.5	10.6	9.1	(d)	2.5	3.3	(d)	40.1
1914	78.6	4.8	15.1	8.8	9.1	(d)	2.3	3.3	(d)	35.2
1915	76.7	6.6	14.9	8.6	8.4	(d)	2.1	2.8	(d)	33.3
1916	84.1	8.1	14.9	8.7	9.3	(d)	2.2	2.8	(d)	38.1
1917	88.2	10.0	14.7	7.4	10.5	(d)	2.2	2.7	(d)	40.7
1918	82.1	10.3	12.8	6.8	9.9	(d)	2.4	2.6	(d)	37.3
1919	71.9	10.7	11.4	6.9	8.7	(d)	2.7	3.0	(d)	28.5
1920	71.2	11.7	11.8	5.7	8.7	(d)	2.5	3.1	(d)	27.7
1921	68.4	12.9	11.3	7.2	6.9	(d)	2.6	2.7	(d)	24.8
1922	69.4	13.9	12.0	6.4	7.5	(d)	2.6	2.5	(d)	24.5
1923	75.7	16.5	12.6	6.1	8.1	(d)	2.6	2.5	2.4	24.9
1924	75.6	17.1	12.9	6.5	8.4	(d)	2.5	2.4	2.5	23.3
1925	78.4	19.1	13.4	6.3	7.4	(d)	2.4	2.3	2.4	25.1
1926	78.7	20.1	13.9	6.4	7.5	(d)	2.4	2.2	2.7	23.5
1927	78.4	21.8	13.9	6.8	6.9	(d)	2.5	2.2	2.3	22.0
1928	79.3	23.4	14.1	7.1	7.0	(d)	2.4	2.3	2.3	20.7
1929	80.8	25.7	14.5	6.2	6.7	(d)	2.6	2.1	2.3	20.7
1930	80.5	26.7	14.7	6.1	6.6	(d)	2.6	2.1	2.0	19.7
1931	78.5	27.2	14.6	6.1	5.7	(d)	2.5	2.1	1.7	18.6
1932	71.3	23.6	14.9	6.0	5.7	(d)	2.4	1.8	1.7	15.2
1933	72.4	25.0	15.1	5.7	5.4	(d)	2.4	1.7	1.3	15.8
1934	79.9	28.6	16.4	5.6	5.9	(d)	2.4	1.7	1.3	18.0
1935	78.4	28.6	16.8	5.3	5.7	(d)	2.2	1.7	1.3	16.8
1936	85.9	29.7	18.4	5.2	6.2	(d)	2.2	1.7	1.3	21.2
1937	81.7	30.8	17.5	5.5	5.6	(d)	2.0	1.7	1.3	17.3
1938	72.3	25.1	17.9	5.3	5.0	(d)	2.1	1.6	1.1	14.2
1939	70.8	24.7	17.9	4.9	5.1	(d)	2.0	1.5	1.1	13.6
1940	73.4	26.1	17.7	4.7	5.7	(d)	1.8	1.4	1.2	14.8
1941	76.3	30.0	17.1	4.8	5.2	(d)	1.8	1.3	1.1	15.0
1942	71.6	21.1	16.9	5.0	5.9	(d)	2.0	1.2	1.3	18.2
1943	73.8	17.8	18.4	5.3	6.5	0.7	1.7	1.3	1.5	20.6
1944	71.7	18.3	17.3	4.9	6.3	0.7	1.8	1.5	1.4	19.5
1945	72.4	21.2	18.0	5.0	6.0	0.7	1.8	1.5	1.6	16.6
1946	70.0	23.9	16.5	4.6	5.6	0.8	2.0	1.4	1.3	13.9
1947	69.4	22.8	17.1	4.8	5.6	0.8	1.7	1.3	1.3	14.0
1948 (5th Rev.)[e]	67.1	22.1	17.0	4.4	5.3	0.9	1.5	1.2	1.4	13.3
1948 (6th Rev.)[e]	63.7	22.1	15.1	4.5	4.7	0.9	1.6	1.1	1.4	12.3
1949	60.6	21.3	15.0	4.5	4.0	0.9	1.6	1.1	1.1	11.1
1950	60.3	23.0	13.7	4.1	4.2	0.9	1.4	1.1	1.2	10.7
1951	62.5	24.1	13.9	4.2	4.4	1.0	1.5	1.0	1.1	11.3
1952	61.8	24.3	13.5	4.2	4.5	0.9	1.4	0.9	0.9	11.2
1953	60.1	24.0	13.0	4.3	4.2	1.0	1.4	0.9	0.8	10.2
1954	55.9	22.1	12.3	3.9	3.8	1.0	1.4	0.8	0.8	9.8
1955	56.9	23.4	12.3	3.9	3.9	1.0	1.3	0.9	0.7	9.5
1956	56.6	23.7	12.1	3.7	3.8	1.1	1.3	0.8	0.7	9.4
1957	55.9	22.7	12.1	3.9	3.7	1.2	1.4	0.8	0.7	9.4
1958	52.3	21.3	10.5	3.8[f]	4.2[f]	1.3[f]	1.3	0.8	0.7	8.4
1959	52.2	21.5	10.6	3.7	3.9	1.2	1.3	0.9	0.7	8.4
1960	52.1	21.2	10.6	3.6	4.3	1.3	1.3	0.9	0.7	8.2
1961	50.4	20.8	10.2	3.6	3.9	1.4	1.2	1.0	0.7	7.6
1962	52.3	22.0	10.5	3.5	4.1	1.0	1.1	1.0	0.7	8.4
1963	53.4	23.1	10.3	3.4	4.3	1.0	1.2	1.1	0.8	8.2
1964	54.9	25.0	9.9	3.5	3.9	1.0	1.2	1.1	0.7	8.4
1965	55.8	25.4	10.3	3.5	3.8	1.0	1.2	1.1	0.8	8.7
1966	58.1	27.1	10.3	3.6	4.8	0.9	1.3	1.2	0.8	8.1
1967	57.3	26.8	10.2	3.6	3.8	1.0	1.5	1.3	0.8	8.3
1968	57.6	27.5	9.4	3.7[f]	3.7[f]	1.6[f]	1.2[f]	1.3	0.8	8.4
1969	57.8	27.7	8.9	3.8	3.6	1.8	1.2	1.5	0.8	8.5
1970	56.2	26.8	8.3	3.9	3.3	1.4	1.2	1.8	0.8	8.7
1971	54.8	26.3	8.1	3.6	3.3	1.4	1.1	1.8	0.8	8.4
1972	55.2	26.9	8.0	3.6	3.2	1.4	1.2	1.8	0.8	8.3
1973	54.8	26.3	7.8	4.1	3.1	1.4	1.2	1.7	0.8	8.4

See source and footnotes on page 43.

NATIONAL SAFETY COUNCIL® INJURY FACTS® 2001 EDITION

UNINTENTIONAL-INJURY DEATH RATES[a] FOR PRINCIPAL TYPES, UNITED STATES, 1903–2000, Cont.

Year	Total	Motor-Vehicle	Falls	Drowning[b]	Fires, Burns[c]	Ingest. of Food, Object	Firearms	Poison (Solid, Liquid)	Poison (Gas, Vapor)	All Other
1974	49.0	21.8	7.7	3.7	2.9	1.4	1.2	1.8	0.7	7.8
1975	47.8	21.3	6.9	3.7	2.8	1.4	1.1	2.2	0.7	7.7
1976	46.3	21.6	6.5	3.1	2.9	1.4	0.9	1.9	0.7	7.3
1977	47.0	22.5	6.3	3.2	2.9	1.4	0.9	1.5	0.7	7.6
1978	47.5	23.6	6.2	3.2	2.8	1.4	0.8	1.4	0.8	7.3
1979	46.9	23.8	5.9	3.1	2.7	1.4	0.9	1.4	0.7	7.0
1980	46.5	23.4	5.9	3.2	2.6	1.4	0.9	1.4	0.5	7.2
1981	43.9	22.4	5.5	2.7	2.5	1.5	0.8	1.4	0.6	6.5
1982	40.6	19.8	5.2	2.7	2.2	1.4	0.8	1.5	0.5	6.5
1983	39.6	19.0	5.1	2.7	2.2	1.4	0.7	1.4	0.5	6.6
1984	39.4	19.6	5.1	2.3	2.1	1.5	0.7	1.6	0.5	6.0
1985	39.3	19.3	5.0	2.2	2.1	1.5	0.7	1.7	0.5	6.3
1986	39.7	19.9	4.8	2.4	2.0	1.5	0.6	2.0	0.4	6.1
1987	39.2	19.9	4.8	2.1	1.9	1.5	0.6	1.8	0.4	6.2
1988	39.7	20.1	4.9	2.0	2.0	1.6	0.6	2.2	0.4	5.9
1989	38.5	19.3	4.9	1.9	1.9	1.4	0.6	2.3	0.4	5.8
1990	36.9	18.8	4.9	1.9	1.7	1.3	0.6	2.0	0.3	5.4
1991	35.4	17.3	5.0	1.8	1.6	1.3	0.6	2.3	0.3	5.2
1992	34.0	16.1	5.0	1.4	1.6	1.2	0.6	2.5	0.2	5.4
1993	35.1	16.3	5.1	1.5	1.5	1.2	0.6	3.1	0.3	5.5
1994	35.1	16.3	5.2	1.5	1.5	1.2	0.5	3.2	0.3	5.4
1995	35.5	16.5	5.3	1.7	1.4	1.2	0.5	3.2	0.2	5.5
1996	35.8	16.5	5.6	1.5	1.4	1.2	0.4	3.3	0.2	5.7
1997	35.7	16.2	5.8	1.5	1.3	1.2	0.4	3.6	0.2	5.5
1998[g]	36.2	16.1	6.0	1.6	1.2	1.3	0.3	3.8	0.2	5.7
1999[g]	35.7	15.8	5.9	1.5	1.1	1.1	0.3	4.0	0.1	5.9
2000[h]	35.3	15.6	5.9	1.4	1.3	1.2	0.2	4.2	0.1	5.3
Changes										
1990 to 2000	−4%	−17%	+20%	−26%	−24%	−8%	−67%	+110%	−67%	−2%
1999 to 2000	−1%	−1%	0%	−7%	+18%	+9%	−33%	+5%	0%	−10%

Source: National Safety Council estimates. See Technical Appendix for comparability.
[a] *Deaths per 100,000 population.*
[b] *Includes drowning in water transport accidents.*
[c] *Includes burns by fire, and deaths resulting from conflagration regardless of nature of injury.*
[d] *Comparable data not available.*
[e] *In 1948, a revision was made in the International Classification of Diseases. The first figures for 1948 are comparable with those for earlier years, the second with those for later years.*
[f] *Data are not comparable to previous years shown due to classification changes in 1958 and 1968.*
[g] *Revised.*
[h] *Preliminary.*

WORK

Between 1912 and 2000, unintentional work deaths per 100,000 population were reduced 90%, from 21 to 2. In 1912, an estimated 18,000 to 21,000 workers' lives were lost. In 2000, in a workforce nearly quadrupled in size and producing nine times the goods and services, there were only 5,200 work deaths.

The National Safety Council adopted the Bureau of Labor Statistics' Census of Fatal Occupational Injuries (CFOI) figure, beginning with the 1992 data year, as

the authoritative count of work-related deaths. The Technical Appendix discusses the change in the Council's estimating procedures.

The CFOI system counts intentional as well as unintentional work injuries. Each year between 850 and 1,300 homicides and suicides are identified and counted. These fatal injuries are not included in the unintentional-injury estimates below.

Unintentional-Injury Deaths 5,200
Unintentional-Injury Deaths per 100,000 workers 3.8
Disabling Injuries 3,900,000
Workers 136,402,000
Costs . . . .$131.2 billion

UNINTENTIONAL INJURIES AT WORK BY INDUSTRY, UNITED STATES, 2000

Industry Division	Workers[a] (000)	Deaths[a]		Deaths per 100,000 Workers[a]		Disabling Injuries
		2000	Change from 1999	2000	Change from 1999	
All industries	136,402	5,200	+1%	3.8	0%	3,900,000
Agriculture[b]	3,380	780	+1%	22.5	−([c])%	130,000
Mining, quarrying[b]	520	110	−9%	21.2	−1%	20,000
Construction	8,949	1,220	+5%	13.6	−1%	470,000
Manufacturing	19,868	660	−1%	3.3	−3%	630,000
Transportation and public utilities	8,084	930	+1%	11.5	0%	380,000
Trade[b]	27,723	420	−1%	1.5	0%	750,000
Services[b]	47,611	630	+2%	1.3	0%	940,000
Government	20,267	450	+([c])%	2.2	0%	580,000

Source: National Safety Council estimates based on data from the Bureau of Labor Statistics, National Center for Health Statistics, state vital statistics departments, and state industrial commissions.
[a] *Deaths include persons of all ages. Workers and death rates include persons 16 years and older.*
[b] *Agriculture includes forestry, fishing, and agricultural services. Mining includes oil and gas extraction. Trade includes wholesale and retail trade. Services includes finance, insurance, and real estate.*
[c] *Less than 0.5%.*

UNINTENTIONAL WORK-INJURY DEATHS AND DEATH RATES, UNITED STATES, 1992–2000

Year	Deaths	Workersa	Death Rateb
1992	4,968	119,168	4.2
1993	5,035	120,778	4.2
1994	5,338	124,470	4.3
1995	5,018	126,248	4.0
1996	5,069	127,997	4.0
1997	5,160	130,810	3.9
1998d	5,120	132,772	3.9
1999d	5,170	134,688	3.8
2000e	5,200	136,402	3.8

Source: Deaths through 1999 are from the Bureau of Labor Statistics, Census of Fatal Occupational Injuries. Employment is from the Bureau of Labor Statistics and is based on the Current Population Survey. All other data are National Safety Council estimates.
[a] *In thousands. Workers are persons ages 16 and older gainfully employed, including owners, managers, other paid employees, the self-employed, unpaid family workers, and active duty resident military personnel. Due to changes in procedures, estimates of workers from 1992 to the present are not comparable to prior years.*
[b] *Deaths per 100,000 workers.*
[c] *Deaths include persons of all ages. Workers and death rates include persons 16 years and older. Because of adoption of the Census of Fatal Occupational Injuries, deaths and rates from 1992 to the present are not comparable to prior years. See Technical Appendix for change in estimating procedure.*
[d] *Revised.*
[e] *Preliminary.*

WORKERS' UNINTENTIONAL-INJURY DEATHS, AND DEATH RATES, UNITED STATES, 1992–2000

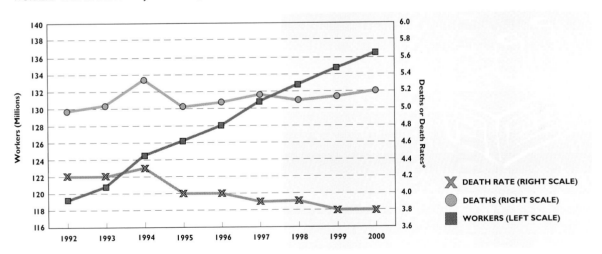

DEATH RATE (RIGHT SCALE)
DEATHS (RIGHT SCALE)
WORKERS (LEFT SCALE)

Deaths in thousands; rate per 100,000 workers.

OCCUPATIONAL-INJURY DEATHS AND DEATH RATES, UNITED STATES, 1992–2000

Year	Total	Homicide & Suicide	Unintentional								
			All Industriesa	Agri-cultureb	Mining, Quarryingc	Construc-tion	Manufac-turing	Transpor-tation & Public Utilities	Traded	Servicese	Govern-ment
Deaths											
1992	6,217	1,249	4,968	779	175	889	707	769	415	601	585
1993	6,331	1,296	5,035	842	169	895	698	754	450	633	524
1994	6,632	1,294	5,338	814	177	1,000	734	820	492	676	531
1995	6,275	1,257	5,018	770	155	1,021	640	785	462	608	527
1996	6,202	1,133	5,069	768	152	1,073	663	923	454	671	321
1997	6,238	1,078	5,160	799	156	1,075	678	882	451	593	504
1998f	6,055	935	5,120	808	143	1,134	631	830	443	634	465
1999f	6,023	853	5,170	774	121	1,166	669	917	423	619	448
2000g	—	—	5,200	780	110	1,220	660	930	420	630	450
Deaths per 100,000 Workers											
1992	5.2	1.0	4.2	23.2	26.4	13.7	3.6	11.5	1.7	1.6	3.0
1993	5.2	1.0	4.2	26.0	25.3	13.3	3.6	11.0	1.8	1.6	2.6
1994	5.3	1.0	4.3	22.8	26.5	14.4	3.7	11.6	1.9	1.7	2.7
1995	4.9	0.9	4.0	21.5	24.8	14.3	3.1	11.0	1.8	1.5	2.7
1996	4.8	0.9	4.0	21.3	26.8	14.4	3.2	12.7	1.7	1.6	1.6
1997	4.8	0.8	3.9	22.5	24.7	13.7	3.3	11.6	1.7	1.3	2.6
1998f	4.5	0.7	3.9	22.7	23.1	14.1	3.1	10.8	1.6	1.4	2.4
1999f	4.5	0.6	3.8	22.6	21.5	13.8	3.4	11.5	1.5	1.3	2.2
2000g	—	—	3.8	22.5	21.2	13.6	3.3	11.5	1.5	1.3	2.2

Source: Deaths are from Bureau of Labor Statistics, Census of Fatal Occupational Injuries, except 2000 which are National Safety Council estimates. Rates are National Safety Council estimates based on Bureau of Labor Statistics employment data. Deaths include persons of all ages. Death rates include persons 16 years and older. Dashes indicate data not available.
a Includes deaths with industry unknown.
b Agriculture includes forestry, fishing, and agricultural services.
c Mining includes oil and gas extraction.
d Trade includes wholesale and retail trade.
e Services includes finance, insurance, and real estate.
f Revised.
g Preliminary.

OCCUPATIONAL UNINTENTIONAL-INJURY DEATH RATES, UNITED STATES, 2000

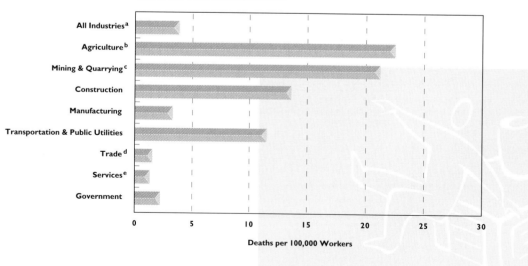

See footnotes in table above.

The true cost to the nation, to employers, and to individuals of work-related deaths and injuries is much greater than the cost of workers' compensation insurance alone. The figures presented below show the National Safety Council's estimates of the total costs of occupational deaths and injuries. Cost estimating procedures were revised for the 1993 edition of *Accident Facts®*. In general, cost estimates are not comparable from year to year. As additional or more precise data become available, they are used from that year forward. Previously estimated figures are not revised.

Total Cost in 2000 . . . .$131.2 billion
Includes wage and productivity losses of $67.6 billion, medical costs of $24.2 billion, and administrative expenses of $22.3 billion. Includes employer costs of $11.5 billion such as the money value of time lost by

workers other than those with disabling injuries, who are directly or indirectly involved in injuries, and the cost of time required to investigate injuries, write up injury reports, etc. Also includes damage to motor vehicles in work injuries of $2.2 billion and fire losses of $3.4 billion.

Cost per Worker $960
This figure indicates the value of goods or services each worker must produce to offset the cost of work injuries. It is *not* the average cost of a work injury.

Cost per Death $980,000

Cost per Disabling Injury $28,000
These figures include estimates of wage losses, medical expenses, administrative expenses, and employer costs, and exclude property damage costs except to motor vehicles.

TIME LOST BECAUSE OF WORK INJURIES

DAYS LOST

TOTAL TIME LOST IN 2000 125,000,000

Due to Injuries in 2000 80,000,000
Includes primarily the actual time lost during the year from disabling injuries, except that it does not include time lost on the day of the injury or time required for further medical treatment or check-up following the injured person's return to work.

Fatalities are included at an average loss of 150 days per case, and permanent impairments are included at actual days lost plus an allowance for lost efficiency resulting from the impairment.

Not included is time lost by persons with nondisabling injuries or other persons directly or indirectly involved in the incidents.

DAYS LOST

Due to Injuries in Prior Years 45,000,000
This is an indicator of the productive time lost in 2000 due to permanently disabling injuries that occurred in prior years.

DAYS LOST

**TIME LOSS IN FUTURE YEARS FROM
2000 INJURIES** 60,000,000
Includes time lost in future years due to on-the-job deaths and permanently disabling injuries that occurred in 2000.

WORKER DEATHS AND INJURIES ON AND OFF THE JOB

Nearly 9 out of 10 deaths and about three fifths of the disabling injuries suffered by workers in 2000 occurred off the job. The ratios of off-the-job deaths and injuries to on-the-job were 8.0 to 1 and 1.7 to 1, respectively. Production time lost due to off-the-job injuries totaled about 160,000,000 days in 2000, compared with 80,000,000 days lost by workers injured on the job. Production time lost in future years due to off-the-job injuries in 2000 will total an estimated 400,000,000 days, more than six times the 60,000,000 days lost in

future years from 2000's on-the-job injuries. Off-the-job injuries to workers cost the nation at least $178.6 billion in 2000.

The basis of the rates shown in the table below was changed from 1,000,000 hours to 200,000 hours beginning with the 1998 edition. This change was made so that the rates would be on the same basis as the occupational injury and illness incidence rates shown elsewhere in *Injury Facts*.

ON- AND OFF-THE-JOB INJURIES, UNITED STATES, 2000

| Place | Deaths | | Disabling Injuries | |
	Number	Rate[a]	Number	Rate[a]
On- and off-the-job	**47,000**	**0.012**	**10,500,000**	**2.6**
On-the-job	5,200	0.004	3,900,000	2.7
Off-the-job	41,800	0.016	6,600,000	2.5
Motor-vehicle	22,800	0.084	1,200,000	4.4
Public nonmotor-vehicle	8,300	0.020	2,800,000	6.6
Home	10,700	0.006	2,600,000	1.4

Source: National Safety Council estimates. Procedures for allocating time spent on and off the job were revised for the 1990 edition. Rate basis changed to 200,000 hours for the 1998 edition. Death and injury rates are not comparable to rate estimates prior to the 1998 edition.
[a] *Per 200,000 hours exposure by place.*

WORKERS' ON- AND OFF-THE JOB INJURIES, 2000

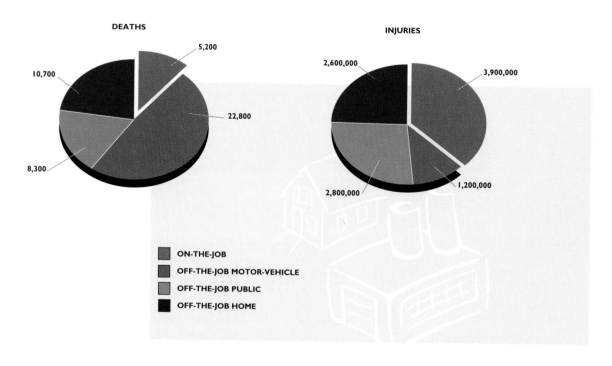

WORKERS' COMPENSATION CASES

According to the National Academy of Social Insurance, an estimated $43.4 billion, including benefits under deductible provisions, was paid out under workers' compensation in 1999 (the latest year for which data were available), an increase of about 2.5% from 1998. Of this total, $25.3 billion was for income benefits and $18.1 billion was for medical and hospitalization costs. Private carriers paid about $23.8 billion of the total workers' compensation benefits in 1999. In 1999,

approximately 123.9 million workers were covered by workers' compensation—an increase of 2.5% over the 120.9 million in 1998.

The table below shows the trend in the number of compensated or reported cases in each reporting state. Due to the differences in population, industries, and coverage of compensation laws, comparison among states should not be made.

WORKERS' COMPENSATION CASES, UNITED STATES, 1998–2000

State	Deaths[a]			Cases[a]			1999 Compensation Paid ($000)
	2000	1999	1998	2000	1999	1998	
Alabama	97	101	98	24,345	27,170	27,820	596,233
Alaska	34	33	32	28,086	28,551	28,814	137,630
Arizona	113	75	89	—	—	—	427,841
Arkansas	81	96	96	14,452	13,351	13,979	165,854
Colorado[b]	—	108	110	—	32,706	33,441	702,458
Connecticut	41	60	43	82,514	75,175	61,659	722,156
Delaware	15	14	11	22,661	20,564	18,421	105,436
Florida[b]	—	221	294	—	81,474	81,363	2,079,830
Georgia[c]	—	262	233	—	44,472	45,796	816,249
Hawaii	—	26	17	—	30,309	30,727	211,138
Iowa	62	66	72	30,938	33,494	35,228	283,983
Kentucky	72	86	74	43,590	49,214	49,460	430,953
Louisiana[c]	—	87	107	—	19,146	18,975	428,808
Maine	34[d]	32	26	16,962[d]	16,631	12,716	249,674
Maryland	—	66	42	—	18,982	17,860	1,169,386
Michigan[c, e]	92	134	123	54,201	51,459	52,481	1,392,806
Minnesota[c]	—	45	65	—	34,300	32,900	744,600
Mississippi[c]	—	99	100	—	15,991	16,335	253,532
Missouri	98	161	156	159,088	168,704	170,245	592,993
Nebraska	54	53	53	68,057	66,339	68,206	173,149
New Jersey[c, f]	—	—	—	54,513	53,883	61,468	987,378
New Mexico[g]	13	23	12	18,744	15,842	15,624	117,168
North Carolina	227	161	143	66,871	68,469	74,939	710,100
North Dakota	20	13	21	20,045	20,034	20,683	77,236
Ohio	175	194	123	280,873	288,242	296,158	2,018,923
Oregon[c]	45[d]	47	52	25,047[d]	25,802	27,049	398,965
South Dakota[c]	29	24	19	29,711	30,081	28,656	80,331
Utah	50	51	62	76,795	74,956	73,883	219,338
Washington	79	78	76	247,113	248,086	248,552	1,418,255
Wisconsin[c, h]	77	67	63	52,860	58,620	48,047	652,281

Source: Deaths and Cases—State workers' compensation authorities for calendar or fiscal year. 1999 Compensation Paid—Mont, D., Burton, J. F., Jr., Reno, V., & Thompson, C. (May, 2001). Workers' compensation: benefits, coverage, and costs, 1999 new estimates and 1996–1998 revisions. Washington, DC: National Academy of Social Insurance. States not listed did not respond to the survey. Dash (—) indicates data not available.

Definitions:
Reported case—a reported case may or may not be work-related and may not receive compensation.
Compensated case—a case determined to be work-related and for which compensation was paid.

[a] Reported cases involving medical and indemnity benefits, unless otherwise noted.
[b] Lost time claims.
[c] Closed or compensated cases.
[d] Preliminary.
[e] Loss time claims over 7 days.
[f] Closed or compensated cases, not specified whether they were medical benefits only or medical and indemnity benefits.
[g] Compensated and compensable claims and indemnity cases only.
[h] Indemnity benefits only.

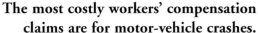

WORKERS' COMPENSATION
CLAIMS COSTS, 1998–1999

The data in the graphs below and on page 53 are from the National Council on Compensation Insurance's (NCCI) Detailed Claim Information (DCI) file, a stratified random sample of lost-time claims in 41 states. Total incurred costs consist of medical and indemnity payments plus case reserves on open claims, and are calculated as of the second report (18 months after the initial report of injury). Injuries that result in medical payments only, without lost time, are not included. For open claims, costs include all payments as of the second report plus case reserves for future payments.

Cause of Injury. The most costly lost-time workers' compensation claims, according to the NCCI data, are for those resulting from motor-vehicle crashes. These injuries averaged nearly $22,200 per workers' compensation claim filed in 1998 and 1999. The other types with above average costs were those involving a fall or slip ($12,486), cumulative trauma ($11,420), or a burn ($10,989). The average cost for all claims combined was $10,610.

Nature of Injury. The most costly lost-time workers' compensation claims by the nature of the injury are for those resulting from amputation. These injuries averaged $27,714 per workers' compensation claim filed in 1998 and 1999. The next highest costs were for injuries resulting in fracture ($14,544), "other trauma" ($13,995), and carpal tunnel syndrome ($12,501). The average cost for all natures of injury combined was $10,610.

Part of Body. When viewed by part of body, the most costly lost-time workers' compensation claims are for those involving the head or central nervous system. These injuries averaged $22,958 per workers' compensation claim filed in 1998 and 1999. The next highest costs were for injuries involving multiple body parts ($19,284); neck ($16,095); leg ($14,612); knee ($11,366); arm or shoulder ($10,861); hip, thigh, or pelvis ($10,778); and lower back ($10,698). The average cost for all parts of body combined was $10,610.

AVERAGE TOTAL INCURRED COSTS PER CLAIM BY CAUSE OF INJURY, 1998–1999

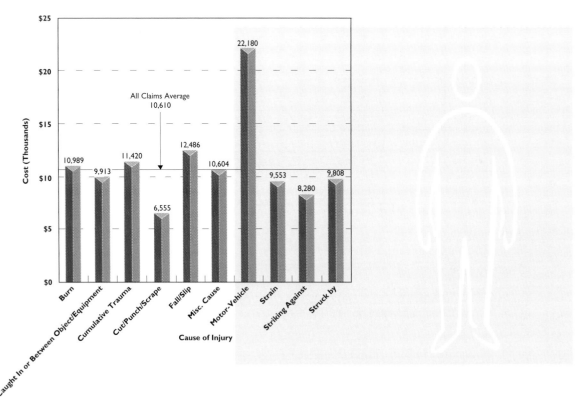

AVERAGE TOTAL INCURRED COSTS PER CLAIM BY NATURE OF INJURY, 1998–1999

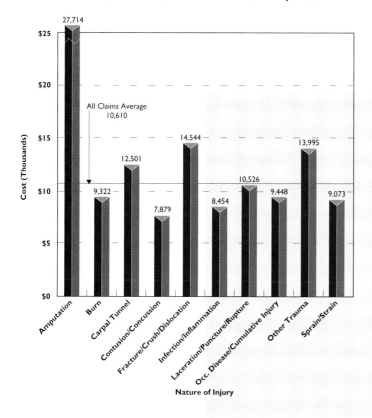

All Claims Average
10,610

Cost (Thousands)

Amputation	27,714
Burn	9,322
Carpal Tunnel	12,501
Contusion/Concussion	7,879
Fracture/Crush/Dislocation	14,544
Infection/Inflammation	8,454
Laceration/Puncture/Rupture	10,526
Occ. Disease/Cumulative Injury	9,448
Other Trauma	13,995
Sprain/Strain	9,073

Nature of Injury

AVERAGE TOTAL INCURRED COSTS PER CLAIM BY PART OF BODY, 1998–1999

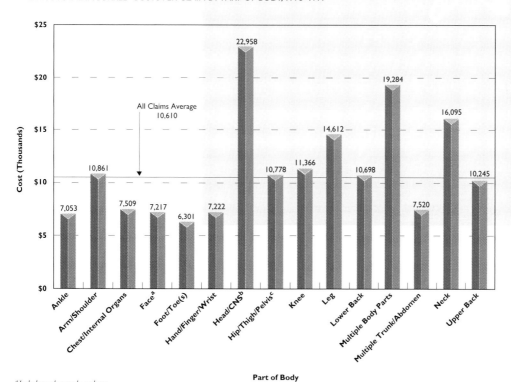

All Claims Average
10,610

Cost (Thousands)

Ankle	7,053
Arm/Shoulder	10,861
Chest/Internal Organs	7,509
Face[a]	7,217
Foot/Toe(s)	6,301
Hand/Finger/Wrist	7,222
Head/CNS[b]	22,958
Hip/Thigh/Pelvis[c]	10,778
Knee	11,366
Leg	14,612
Lower Back	10,698
Multiple Body Parts	19,284
Multiple Trunk/Abdomen	7,520
Neck	16,095
Upper Back	10,245

Part of Body

[a] Includes teeth, mouth, and eyes.
[b] Central nervous system.
[c] Includes sacrum and coccyx.

CONFINED SPACES

Confined spaces are those that, by design, have limited openings for entry and exit, unfavorable ventilation, and are not intended for continuous occupancy by employees. Confined spaces may include storage tanks and compartments, process vessels, pits, silos, vats, boilers, ventilation and exhaust ducts, sewers, tunnels, underground utility vaults, pipelines, and other similar structures.

Occupational injuries and illnesses associated with confined spaces are those that arise from inhalation of harmful substances or oxygen depletion. Sometimes engulfment in loose materials such as grain, sand, or earth (as in a trench cave-in) are also included. The data presented here are the results of a National Safety Council analysis of Bureau of Labor Statistics data.

Inhalation of harmful substances in enclosed, restricted, or confined spaces resulted in an estimated 548 nonfatal cases involving days away from work in 1999 in all private industry. There has been a steady decrease in the estimated annual number of cases from 1994 when there were nearly 3,000. Over the 8-year period from 1992 through 1999, there were 304 deaths, an average of 38 per year. The most common occupations of fatally injured workers were farm occupations (about 13%),

engine mechanics (about 10%), nonconstruction laborers (about 7%), and construction laborers (about 6%). Carbon monoxide accounted for 33% of the deaths and hydrogen sulfide for 10%. Methane and oxides of nitrogen each accounted for about 7% of the deaths.

Oxygen depletion in enclosed, restricted, or confined spaces resulted in 55 deaths from 1992 through 1999, or about 7 annually. Workers in manufacturing accounted for 31% of the deaths, service industries for 18%, and construction for 16%. Estimates of nonfatal injuries in this category did not meet publication criteria.

Engulfment in materials is a general category that includes excavation or trenching cave-in, other cave-in, and landslide. There were about 170–310 nonfatal injuries and 58 fatal injuries annually due to cave-in or landslide in recent years. Thirty-two percent of the deaths involved construction laborers and another 18% involved other construction trades occupations. About 15% involved mining occupations. About half of the fatalities (49%) were due to asphyxiation; 19% each due to internal injuries and multiple injuries; and about 9% to intracranial injuries.

LOCATION OF CONFINED SPACE-RELATED FATALITIES, UNITED STATES, 1992–1999

Location	Inhalation of Substance	Oxygen Depletion	Engulfment
Total	**304**	**55**	**468**
Home	21	—	36
Farm	53	—	28
Mine	7	—	101
Industrial place	144	30	226
Place for recreation or sport	—	—	—
Street and highway	—	—	26
Public building	15	—	—
Resident institution	—	—	—
Other specified places	46	14	40
Place unspecified	11	—	7

Source: National Safety Council tabulation of Bureau of Labor Statistics, Census of Fatal Occupational Injuries data.
Note: Dashes indicate fewer than 5 deaths.

According to the Bureau of Labor Statistics, the back was the body part most frequently affected in injuries involving days away from work in 1999, accounting for about a quarter of the total 1,702,470 injuries in private industry. The fingers were the second most injured parts of body, followed by multiple-part, knee, and head injuries. Overall, the manufacturing and service industries had the highest number of injuries, combining to make up nearly 47% of the total.

NUMBER OF NONFATAL OCCUPATIONAL INJURIES INVOLVING DAYS AWAY FROM WORK[a] BY PART OF BODY AFFECTED AND INDUSTRY DIVISION, PRIVATE INDUSTRY, UNITED STATES, 1999

| Part of Body Affected | Private Industry[b] | Goods Producing | | | | Service Producing | | | | |
		Agri-culture[b, c]	Mining[c]	Construc-tion	Manufac-turing	Trans. & Public Utilities	Wholesale Trade	Retail Trade	Finance, Insurance, & Real Estate	Services
Total[d]	1,702,470	34,941	11,138	193,765	403,568	196,725	136,110	291,648	39,472	394,922
Head	107,696	2,889	642	15,892	29,520	12,011	7,698	15,528	1,939	21,577
Eye	53,096	1,710	268	9,936	18,674	3,669	3,576	6,533	599	8,130
Neck	30,889	497	246	2,456	5,691	4,594	2,901	4,580	605	9,230
Trunk	631,173	10,583	3,990	62,562	140,973	79,593	57,262	104,033	12,010	160,166
Shoulder	93,787	1,621	479	8,416	23,219	14,372	8,166	15,082	1,344	21,089
Back	424,251	6,600	2,584	40,998	89,297	51,692	37,784	71,414	8,333	115,549
Upper extremities	397,118	9,820	2,436	45,858	125,123	32,286	24,245	76,296	8,868	72,186
Wrist	84,410	1,208	399	6,948	27,456	7,176	4,618	13,827	3,301	19,476
Hand, except finger	70,809	2,306	478	8,240	20,621	4,983	4,380	15,871	1,170	12,761
Finger	149,475	3,802	1,042	20,372	51,671	9,501	9,247	30,388	2,552	20,901
Lower extremities	350,202	7,956	2,705	47,058	70,751	44,939	29,717	60,041	8,059	78,975
Knee	127,953	2,056	1,022	16,796	25,644	16,714	9,815	22,414	2,386	31,105
Foot, except toe	59,782	1,392	474	8,748	13,455	7,374	5,663	10,720	1,275	10,682
Toe	17,867	353	92	2,223	4,112	2,291	1,379	3,947	263	3,207
Body systems	21,910	382	174	1,629	4,677	2,943	1,335	2,776	1,211	6,783
Multiple parts	148,188	2,053	1,112	16,160	23,509	19,379	12,013	25,162	5,840	42,960

Source: Bureau of Labor Statistics (2001). Occupational Injuries and Illnesses in the United States—Profiles Data 1992–1999, CD-ROM Disk 1 (National and Boston, Philadelphia, and Chicago Regions), Version 7.6.
[a] Days-away-from-work cases include those that result in days away from work with or without restricted work activity.
[b] Excludes farms with less than 11 employees.
[c] Agriculture includes forestry and fishing; mining includes quarrying and oil and gas extraction.
[d] Data may not sum to column totals because of rounding and exclusion of nonclassifiable responses.

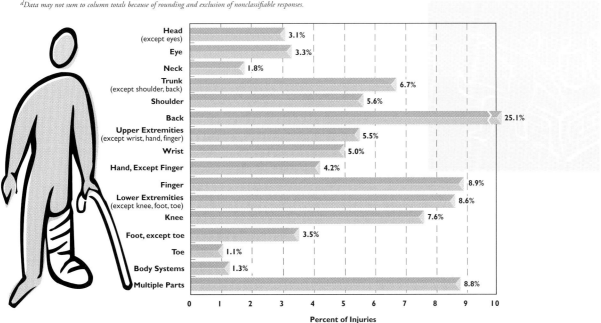

FATAL OCCUPATIONAL INJURIES BY STATE

In general, the states with the largest number of persons employed have the largest number of work-related fatalities. Four of the largest states—California, Texas, Florida, and New York—accounted for over one-fourth of the total fatalities in the United States. Each state's industry mix, geographical features, age of population, and other characteristics of the workforce must be considered when evaluating state fatality profiles.

FATAL OCCUPATIONAL INJURIES BY STATE AND EVENT OR EXPOSURE, UNITED STATES, 1999

State	Deaths per 100,000 workers[a]	Deaths[b]	Percent of Deaths					
			Transportation[c]	Assaults & Violent Acts[d]	Contact with Objects & Equipment	Falls	Exposure to Harmful Substances or Environments	Fires & Explosions
Total[e]	4.5	6,023	43	15	17	12	9	4
Alabama	6.0	123	38	10	22	11	10	8
Alaska	14.2	42	74	7	12	—	—	—
Arizona	3.1	70	39	23	24	4	9	—
Arkansas	6.5	76	49	8	12	5	17	8
California	3.8	591	44	19	14	12	7	3
Colorado	4.5	98	47	18	15	10	5	4
Connecticut	2.3	38	34	34	13	11	—	—
Delaware	3.7	14	36	29	—	—	—	—
District of Columbia	5.3	14	21	21	—	36	—	—
Florida	4.9	345	39	17	15	16	10	2
Georgia	5.8	229	44	17	16	10	9	3
Hawaii	5.7	32	28	56	—	—	—	—
Idaho	6.9	43	44	9	23	12	7	—
Illinois	3.4	208	34	17	19	14	11	4
Indiana	5.7	171	46	15	16	12	7	3
Iowa	5.2	80	52	—	26	4	10	8
Kansas	5.8	81	49	5	23	12	6	—
Kentucky	6.4	120	49	14	18	8	7	3
Louisiana	7.2	141	39	9	26	8	16	4
Maine	5.9	38	50	9	22	9	—	—
Maryland	3.1	82	40	29	12	11	6	—
Massachussetts	2.6	83	32	10	13	24	6	15
Michigan	3.7	182	34	15	18	13	10	10
Minnesota	2.7	72	65	7	17	7	4	—
Mississippi	10.6	128	52	6	20	14	6	—
Missouri	6.0	164	48	11	19	10	10	3
Montana	10.9	49	45	10	29	6	—	6
Nebraska	7.3	65	51	9	26	6	—	5
Nevada	6.3	57	37	18	19	18	7	—
New Hampshire	2.2	14	36	21	—	—	—	—
New Jersey	2.6	103	34	17	17	21	9	—
New Mexico	5.1	39	54	13	10	13	—	—
New York	2.9	241	30	25	12	18	11	2
North Carolina	5.9	222	43	19	14	11	10	2
North Dakota	6.8	22	36	—	41	—	—	—
Ohio	4.0	222	43	12	20	15	9	2
Oklahoma	6.2	99	44	14	13	11	12	5
Oregon	4.2	69	52	7	26	7	7	—
Pennsylvania	3.9	221	41	12	18	15	5	7
Rhode Island	2.3	11	36	—	—	—	27	—
South Carolina	7.4	139	53	16	9	9	8	6
South Dakota	11.6	45	58	7	16	—	13	—
Tennessee	5.7	154	49	12	18	8	8	4
Texas	4.8	468	44	15	15	12	12	3
Utah	5.2	54	56	6	24	11	—	—
Vermont	4.3	14	43	29	—	—	—	—
Virginia	4.5	154	42	17	12	12	13	3
Washington	3.0	88	49	9	19	15	7	—
West Virginia	7.5	57	35	12	33	9	9	—
Wisconsin	3.7	105	45	11	22	10	10	3
Wyoming	12.9	32	56	—	28	9	—	—

[a]Death rates are National Safety Council estimates.
[b]Includes other events and exposures such as bodily reaction in addition to those shown separately.
[c]Includes highway, nonhighway, air, water, rail, and fatalities to workers struck by vehicles.
[d]Includes homicides, self-inflicted injuries, and animal attacks.
[e]Includes 21 fatalities that occurred outside the territorial boundaries of the United States in 1999.
Note: Percentages may not add to 100 due to rounding. Dashes indicate less than 0.5% or data that are not available.
Source: United States Department of Labor, Bureau of Labor Statistics. (2000, August). National Census of Fatal Occupational Injuries, 1999. (Release USDL00-236) Washington, DC: Author.
United States Department of Labor, Bureau of Labor Statistics. (2001, June). Geographic Profile of Employment and Unemployment, 1999. (Bulletin 2537). Table 12. Washington, DC: Author.

Safety professionals in business and industry often want to compare, or benchmark, the occupational injury and illness incidence rates of their establishments with a national average. The only national averages available are the incidence rates compiled by the U.S. Bureau of Labor Statistics (BLS) through its annual Survey of Occupational Injuries and Illnesses.[a] The National Safety Council substantially changed the nature of the award program through which rates were compiled in previous years. Such rates are no longer available from the Council.

The first step in benchmarking is to calculate the incidence rates for the establishment. The basic formula for computing incidence rates is *(N x 200,000)/EH,* where *N* is the number of cases, *EH* is the number of hours worked by all employees during the time period, and *200,000* is the base for 100 full-time workers (working 40 hours per week, 50 weeks per year). Because the BLS rates are based on reports from entire establishments, both the OSHA 200 Log and the number of employee hours *(EH)* should cover the whole establishment being benchmarked. In addition, both the hours worked and the log should cover the same time period (e.g., a month, quarter, or full year).

There are four rates that are most often benchmarked.

Total Cases—defined as the incidence rate of total OSHA-recordable cases per 200,000 hours worked. For this rate, *N* is the count of the number of cases with check marks in columns 2, 6, 9, and 13 of the OSHA 200 Log.

Total Lost Workday Cases—defined as the incidence rate of cases with either days away from work, days of restricted work activity, or both. For this rate, *N* is the count of cases with entries in columns 2 and 9 of the Log.

Cases With Days Away From Work—defined as the incidence rate of cases with days away from work (with

or without days of restricted activity). For this rate, *N* is the count of cases with entries in columns 3 and 10 of the Log.

Cases Without Lost Workdays—defined as the incidence rate of cases with neither days away from work nor days of restricted work activity. For this rate, *N* is the count of cases with entries in columns 6 and 13 of the Log.

After computing one or more of the rates, the next step is to determine the Standard Industrial Classification (SIC) code for the establishment.[b] This code is used to find the appropriate BLS rate for comparison. A convenient way to find an SIC code is to use the search feature on the OSHA Internet site (http://www.osha.gov/oshstats/sicser.html). Otherwise, call a regional BLS office for assistance.

Once the SIC code is known, the comparable BLS rates may be found by (a) consulting the table of rates on pages 60–62, (b) visiting the BLS Internet site (http://stats.bls.gov/oshhome.htm), or (c) by calling a regional BLS office. Note that some tables on the Internet site provide incidence rates by size of establishment and rate quartiles within each SIC code. Quartiles divide the reporting establishments into four equal parts. One fourth of the establishments had rates lower than the first quartile rate; one fourth had rates between the first quartile and the median; one fourth had rates between the median and the third quartile; and one fourth had rates greater than the third quartile.

An alternative way of benchmarking is to compare the current incidence rates for an establishment to its own prior historical rates to determine if the rates are improving and if progress is satisfactory (using criteria set by the organization).

[a] *Bureau of Labor Statistics. (1997).* BLS Handbook of Methods. *Washington, DC: U.S. Government Printing Office. (Or on the Internet at http://stats.bls.gov/opub/hom/ homch9_a1htm.)*
[b] *Executive Office of the President, Office of Management and Budget. (1987).* Standard Industrial Classification Manual. *Springfield, VA: National Technical Information Service.*

TRENDS IN OCCUPATIONAL INCIDENCE RATES

All four occupational injury and illness incidence rates published by the Bureau of Labor Statistics for 1999 decreased from 1998. The incidence rate for total nonfatal cases was 6.3 per 100 full-time workers in 1999, down 6% from the 1998 rate of 6.7. The 1999 incidence rate for total lost workday cases was 3.0, down 3% from 3.1 in 1998. The incidence rate for lost workday cases with days away from work was 1.9 in

1999, down 5% from 2.0 in 1998. The incidence rate in 1999 for nonfatal cases without lost workdays was 3.3, a decrease of 6% from the 1998 rate of 3.5.

Beginning with 1992 data, the Bureau of Labor Statistics revised its annual survey to include only nonfatal cases and stopped publishing the incidence rate of lost workdays.

OCCUPATIONAL INJURY AND ILLNESS INCIDENCE RATES, BUREAU OF LABOR STATISTICS, UNITED STATES, 1973–1999

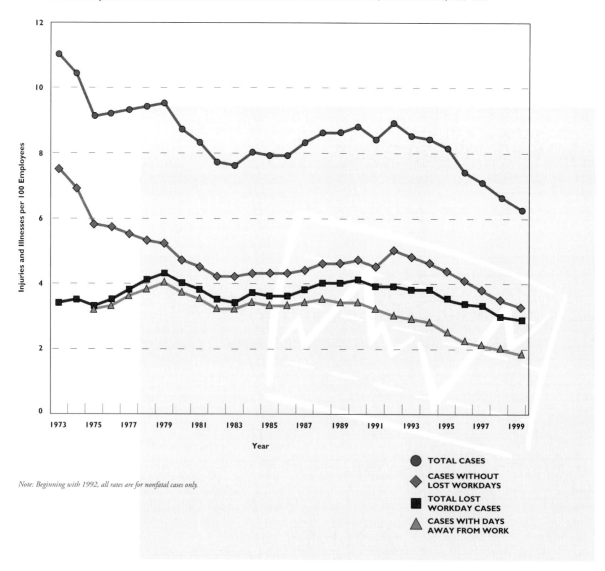

Note: Beginning with 1992, all rates are for nonfatal cases only.

OCCUPATIONAL INJURIES AND ILLNESSES

The tables below and on pages 60–62 present the results of the 1999 Survey of Occupational Injuries and Illnesses conducted by the Bureau of Labor Statistics (BLS), U.S. Department of Labor. The survey collects data on injuries and illnesses (from the OSHA 200 Log) and employee-hours worked from a nationwide sample of about 174,000 establishments representing the private sector of the economy. The survey excludes public employees, private households, the self-employed, and farms with fewer than 11 employees. The incidence rates give the number of cases per 100 full-time workers per year using 200,000 employee-hours as the equivalent. Definitions of the terms are given in the Glossary on page 167.

Beginning with 1992 data, the BLS revised its annual survey to include only nonfatal cases and stopped publishing incidence rates of lost workdays.

BLS ESTIMATES OF NONFATAL OCCUPATIONAL INJURY AND ILLNESS INCIDENCE RATES BY INDUSTRY DIVISION, 1998-1999

	Incidence Rates[c]							
		Lost Workday Cases					
	Total Cases		Total		With Days Away from Work		Cases Without Lost Workdays	
Industry Division	1999	1998	1999	1998	1999	1998	1999	1998
Private Sector[d]	6.3	6.7	3.0	3.1	1.9	2.0	3.3	3.5
Agriculture, forestry, and fishing[d]	7.3	7.9	3.4	3.9	2.4	3.0	3.9	4.0
Mining	4.4	4.9	2.7	2.9	2.0	2.2	1.7	2.0
Construction	8.6	8.8	4.2	4.0	3.3	3.3	4.4	4.8
Manufacturing	9.2	9.7	4.6	4.7	2.2	2.3	4.6	5.0
Transportation and public utilities	7.3	7.3	4.4	4.3	3.1	3.2	2.8	3.0
Wholesale and retail trade	6.1	6.5	2.7	2.8	1.8	1.8	3.4	3.6
Finance, insurance, and real estate	1.8	1.9	0.8	0.7	0.6	0.5	1.1	1.2
Services	4.9	5.2	2.2	2.4	1.5	1.5	2.6	2.9

Source: Bureau of Labor Statistics.
[a] Industry Division and 2 and 3 digit SIC code totals on pages 60-62 include data for industries not shown separately.
[b] Standard Industrial Classification Manual, 1987 Edition, for industries shown on pages 60-62.
[c] Incidence Rate = $\dfrac{\text{Number of injuries \& illnesses x 200,000}}{\text{Total hours worked by all employees during period covered}}$
where 200,000 is the base for 100 full-time workers (working 40 hours per week, 50 weeks per year). The "Total Cases" rate is based on the number of cases with check marks in columns 2, 6, 9, and 13 of the OSHA 200 Log. The "Total Lost Workday Cases" rate is based on columns 2 and 9. The "Lost Workday Cases With Days Away From Work" rate is based on columns 3 and 10. The "Cases Without Lost Workdays" rate is based on columns 6 and 13.
[d] Excludes farms with less than 11 employees.

BLS ESTIMATES OF NONFATAL OCCUPATIONAL INJURY AND ILLNESS INCIDENCE RATES FOR SELECTED INDUSTRIES, 1999

Industry[a]	SIC Code[b]	Total Cases	Lost Workday Cases Total	With Days Away from Work	Cases Without Lost Workdays
			Incidence Rates[c]		
PRIVATE SECTOR[d]	—	**6.3**	**3.0**	**1.9**	**3.3**
Agriculture, Forestry, and Fishing[d]	—	**7.3**	**3.4**	**2.4**	**3.9**
Agricultural production	01-02	7.7	3.6	2.5	4.1
Agricultural services	07	7.1	3.3	2.4	3.8
Forestry	08	6.1	2.9	2.2	3.2
Mining	—	**4.4**	**2.7**	**2.0**	**1.7**
Metal mining	10	5.0	2.9	1.7	2.1
Coal mining	12	7.4	5.5	5.2	1.9
Oil and gas extraction	13	3.5	1.8	1.2	1.7
Crude petroleum and natural gas	131	1.7	0.9	0.8	0.8
Oil and gas field services	138	4.8	2.4	1.5	2.4
Nonmetallic minerals, except fuels	14	4.3	2.8	2.0	1.4
Construction	—	**8.6**	**4.2**	**3.3**	**4.4**
General building contractors	15	8.0	3.7	2.9	4.3
Residential building construction	152	7.4	3.6	3.0	3.8
Nonresidential building construction	154	8.9	3.9	3.0	5.0
Heavy construction, except building	16	7.8	3.8	2.8	4.0
Highway and street construction	161	8.9	4.0	2.8	4.8
Heavy construction, except highway	162	7.3	3.7	2.7	3.7
Special trade contractors	17	8.9	4.4	3.6	4.5
Plumbing, heating, air-conditioning	171	10.2	4.5	3.5	5.7
Painting and paper hanging	172	4.6	2.8	2.4	1.8
Electrical work	173	7.7	3.4	2.8	4.3
Masonry, stonework and plastering	174	9.7	5.1	4.4	4.5
Carpentry and floor work	175	10.8	5.2	4.2	5.6
Roofing, siding, and sheet metal work	176	11.2	6.5	5.4	4.7
Miscellaneous special trade contractors	179	8.1	4.3	3.3	3.8
Manufacturing	—	**9.2**	**4.6**	**2.2**	**4.6**
Durable goods	—	10.1	4.8	2.4	5.3
Lumber and wood products	24	13.0	6.7	3.9	6.3
Logging	241	8.4	5.0	4.9	3.3
Sawmills and planing mills	242	12.9	6.9	4.4	6.0
Millwork, plywood and structural members	243	13.0	6.6	3.5	6.4
Wood containers	244	15.1	9.0	6.1	6.2
Wood buildings and mobile homes	245	17.7	8.4	3.9	9.3
Furniture and fixtures	25	11.5	5.9	2.5	5.7
Household furniture	251	11.0	5.5	2.3	5.5
Office furniture	252	10.3	5.3	2.2	5.0
Public building and related furniture	253	14.9	8.2	3.1	6.7
Stone, clay, and glass products	32	10.7	5.4	3.0	5.3
Flat glass	321	12.2	4.8	1.4	7.4
Glass and glassware, pressed or blown	322	10.9	5.9	2.7	5.0
Products of purchased glass	323	10.6	4.9	1.8	5.7
Structural clay products	325	11.9	5.2	2.3	6.7
Concrete, gypsum, and plaster products	327	11.2	6.1	4.0	5.1
Miscellaneous nonmetallic mineral products	329	8.7	4.1	2.1	4.5
Primary metal industries	33	12.9	6.3	3.1	6.7
Blast furnace and basic steel products	331	9.6	4.4	2.6	5.2
Iron and steel foundries	332	20.1	8.8	3.9	11.4
Primary nonferrous metals	333	13.9	6.7	2.1	7.2
Nonferrous rolling and drawing	335	9.7	5.1	2.3	4.5
Nonferrous foundries (castings)	336	15.8	8.8	4.4	7.0
Fabricated metal products	34	12.6	6.0	3.1	6.6
Metal cans and shipping containers	341	9.2	4.4	2.3	4.8
Cutlery, hand tools, and hardware	342	9.9	5.2	2.4	4.7
Plumbing and heating, except electric	343	13.5	6.1	2.6	7.4
Fabricated structural metal products	344	13.3	6.5	4.0	6.7
Screw machine products, bolts, etc.	345	12.3	5.1	2.1	7.2
Metal forgings and stampings	346	16.9	7.2	3.2	9.7
Metal services, n.e.c.	347	9.6	4.7	2.4	4.8
Ordnance and accessories, n.e.c.	348	6.1	3.3	1.4	2.8
Miscellaneous fabricated metal products	349	11.4	6.0	3.0	5.4
Industrial machinery and equipment	35	8.5	3.7	2.0	4.8
Engines and turbines	351	8.2	3.5	2.1	4.6
Farm and garden machinery	352	9.8	4.6	2.6	5.2
Construction and related machinery	353	11.6	5.3	3.0	6.3
Metalworking machinery	354	8.3	3.3	1.9	5.0
Special industry machinery	355	9.3	3.8	2.4	5.5
General industrial machinery	356	9.7	4.3	2.3	5.3
Computer and office equipment	357	2.7	1.2	0.6	1.5
Refrigeration and service machinery	358	11.7	5.2	2.1	6.5

See source and footnotes on page 59.
n.e.c. = not elsewhere classified.

BLS ESTIMATES OF NONFATAL OCCUPATIONAL INJURY AND ILLNESS INCIDENCE RATES FOR SELECTED INDUSTRIES, 1999, Cont.

Industry[a]	SIC Code[b]	Incidence Rates[c]			
		Total Cases	Lost Workday Cases		Cases Without Lost Workdays
			Total	With Days Away from Work	
Industrial machinery, n.e.c.	359	9.3	3.9	2.3	5.4
Electronic and other electric equipment	36	5.7	2.8	1.2	2.9
Electric distribution equipment	361	7.6	3.4	1.7	4.3
Electrical industrial apparatus	362	7.3	3.2	1.5	4.1
Household appliances	363	11.0	5.2	2.1	5.8
Electric lighting and wiring equipment	364	7.1	3.9	1.8	3.2
Household audio and video equipment	365	5.7	2.9	1.5	2.7
Communications equipment	366	3.1	1.4	0.7	1.7
Electronic components and accessories	367	4.1	2.1	0.9	2.1
Misc. electrical equipment and supplies	369	8.7	4.2	1.6	4.5
Transportation equipment	37	13.7	6.4	2.7	7.3
Motor vehicles and equipment	371	16.8	7.7	3.1	9.2
Aircraft and parts	372	8.2	4.1	1.7	4.1
Ship and boat building and repairing	373	18.0	9.1	3.9	8.9
Railroad equipment	374	7.9	4.0	2.0	3.9
Guided missiles, space vehicles, parts	376	2.8	1.3	0.6	1.5
Instruments and related products	38	4.0	1.8	0.9	2.2
Search and navigation equipment	381	2.3	0.9	0.6	1.3
Measuring and controlling devices	382	3.9	1.7	0.9	2.2
Medical instruments and supplies	384	4.9	2.2	1.0	2.8
Ophthalmic goods	385	5.0	2.4	1.4	2.6
Miscellaneous manufacturing industries	39	8.4	4.0	1.9	4.4
Musical instruments	393	9.4	2.7	1.6	6.8
Toys and sporting goods	394	10.6	5.8	2.2	4.8
Pens, pencils, office, and art supplies	395	6.7	3.8	1.8	2.9
Costume jewelry and notions	396	5.6	2.2	1.4	3.4
Nondurable goods	—	7.8	4.2	1.9	3.6
Food and kindred products	20	12.7	7.3	2.8	5.3
Meat products	201	17.9	10.6	2.3	7.3
Dairy products	202	11.8	7.3	4.3	4.5
Preserved fruits and vegetables	203	10.2	5.4	2.4	4.7
Grain mill products	204	8.0	4.1	2.4	3.9
Bakery products	205	10.4	6.2	3.1	4.2
Sugar and confectionery products	206	9.9	4.3	1.7	5.6
Fats and oils	207	8.7	5.3	2.5	3.4
Beverages	208	11.5	6.9	3.3	4.5
Miscellaneous foods and kindred products	209	10.1	5.9	3.1	4.2
Tobacco products	21	5.5	2.2	1.7	3.3
Textile mill products	22	6.4	3.2	1.2	3.2
Broadwoven fabric mills, cotton	221	5.1	2.5	0.4	2.6
Broadwoven fabric mills, manmade	222	5.6	2.9	1.2	2.8
Broadwoven fabric mills, wool	223	4.9	2.2	0.8	2.8
Knitting mills	225	5.9	2.8	0.8	3.0
Textile finishing, except wool	226	7.3	3.4	2.0	3.8
Carpets and rugs	227	6.7	3.6	0.9	3.1
Yarn and thread mills	228	6.0	2.8	0.7	3.2
Miscellaneous textile goods	229	9.1	4.9	2.6	4.3
Apparel and other textile products	23	5.8	2.8	1.4	3.0
Men's and boys' suits and coats	231	6.7	3.3	2.4	3.4
Men's and boys' furnishings	232	7.4	3.6	1.6	3.8
Women's and misses' outerwear	233	2.3	1.2	0.7	1.2
Women's and children's undergarments	234	7.0	2.7	1.7	4.3
Girls' and children's outerwear	236	4.2	2.0	1.8	2.2
Miscellaneous apparel and accessories	238	5.3	2.0	1.6	3.2
Miscellaneous fabricated textile products	239	7.6	3.8	1.6	3.8
Paper and allied products	26	7.0	3.7	1.8	3.3
Paper mills	262	5.9	2.6	1.3	3.3
Paperboard mills	263	6.2	3.4	1.9	2.8
Paperboard containers and boxes	265	7.8	4.4	1.9	3.4
Printing and publishing	27	5.0	2.6	1.6	2.4
Newspapers	271	5.3	2.6	1.9	2.7
Periodicals	272	1.8	0.8	0.5	0.9
Books	273	5.1	3.0	1.5	2.1
Commercial printing	275	5.8	3.1	1.7	2.7
Manifold business forms	276	5.9	2.3	1.4	3.6
Blankbooks and bookbinding	278	6.3	3.5	2.2	2.7
Chemicals and allied products	28	4.4	2.3	1.1	2.2
Industrial inorganic chemicals	281	4.1	2.1	1.2	2.0
Plastics materials and synthetics	282	4.2	2.1	0.9	2.1
Drugs	283	3.8	1.9	0.8	1.8
Soap, cleaners, and toilet goods	284	5.0	2.6	1.3	2.4
Paints and allied products	285	6.7	3.2	1.8	3.5
Industrial organic chemicals	286	3.3	1.7	0.9	1.5
Agricultural chemicals	287	5.4	2.1	1.0	3.3

See source and footnotes on page 59.
n.e.c. = not elsewhere classified.

Industry[a]	SIC Code[b]	Total Cases	Lost Workday Cases Total	Lost Workday Cases With Days Away from Work	Cases Without Lost Workdays
Miscellaneous chemical products	289	6.2	3.7	2.1	2.5
Petroleum and coal products	29	4.1	1.8	1.0	2.3
Petroleum refining	291	2.5	1.1	0.7	1.4
Asphalt paving and roofing materials	295	5.2	2.4	1.5	2.8
Rubber and miscellaneous plastics products	30	10.1	5.5	2.8	4.7
Tires and inner tubes	301	10.4	6.2	2.4	4.2
Hose and belting and gaskets and packing	305	8.6	4.6	2.0	4.0
Fabricated rubber products, n.e.c.	306	9.8	5.6	2.8	4.3
Miscellaneous plastic products, n.e.c.	308	10.3	5.5	2.9	4.9
Leather and leather products	31	10.3	5.0	1.6	5.3
Leather tanning and finishing	311	15.7	10.4	2.7	5.3
Footwear, except rubber	314	10.7	3.8	1.6	6.9
Transportation and Public Utilities	—	**7.3**	**4.4**	**3.1**	**2.8**
Railroad transportation	40	3.6	2.8	2.4	0.8
Local and interurban passenger transit	41	9.1	4.7	3.5	4.4
Local and suburban transportation	411	11.7	6.1	4.3	5.6
School buses	415	6.9	3.2	2.6	3.6
Trucking and warehousing	42	8.7	5.1	3.6	3.6
Trucking & courier services, except air	421	8.7	5.2	3.7	3.5
Public warehousing and storage	422	8.7	4.5	2.7	4.2
Water transportation	44	8.0	4.4	3.8	3.6
Transportation by air	45	13.3	9.4	6.6	3.9
Air transportation, scheduled	451	14.4	10.4	7.3	4.0
Transportation services	47	3.8	2.2	1.3	1.6
Communications	48	3.1	1.7	1.2	1.4
Telephone communications	481	2.8	1.7	1.3	1.1
Cable and other pay television services	484	6.4	3.1	1.7	3.3
Electric, gas, and sanitary services	49	6.1	3.3	1.7	2.9
Electric services	491	4.9	2.2	1.0	2.7
Gas production and distribution	492	4.7	2.4	1.4	2.3
Combination utility services	493	5.8	3.0	1.5	2.9
Sanitary services	495	9.9	6.4	3.4	3.5
Wholesale and Retail Trade	—	**6.1**	**2.7**	**1.8**	**3.4**
Wholesale trade	—	6.3	3.3	2.0	3.0
Wholesale trade–durable goods	50	5.6	2.6	1.7	2.9
Lumber and construction materials	503	9.8	4.6	2.7	5.2
Electrical goods	506	2.6	1.4	0.9	1.2
Machinery, equipment, and supplies	508	5.7	2.5	1.8	3.1
Wholesale trade–nondurable goods	51	7.3	4.2	2.6	3.1
Groceries and related products	514	10.6	6.6	4.1	3.9
Petroleum and petroleum products	517	4.6	2.3	1.7	2.3
Retail trade	—	6.1	2.5	1.7	3.6
Building materials and garden supplies	52	8.3	3.8	2.4	4.5
General merchandise stores	53	8.5	4.6	2.4	3.9
Food stores	54	7.9	3.4	2.4	4.5
Automotive dealers and service stations	55	5.7	2.1	1.6	3.6
Apparel and accessory stores	56	3.2	1.4	0.9	1.8
Home furniture, furnishings, and equipment	57	4.7	2.4	1.6	2.4
Eating and drinking places	58	5.6	1.8	1.4	3.8
Miscellaneous retail	59	4.1	1.8	1.1	2.3
Finance, Insurance, and Real Estate	—	**1.8**	**0.8**	**0.6**	**1.1**
Depository institutions	60	1.5	0.6	0.4	1.0
Insurance agents, brokers, and service	64	0.9	0.3	0.2	0.6
Real estate	65	3.9	1.9	1.4	2.0
Services	—	**4.9**	**2.2**	**1.5**	**2.6**
Hotels and other lodging places	70	7.8	3.7	2.1	4.1
Personal services	72	3.0	1.6	1.0	1.4
Business services	73	3.0	1.4	0.9	1.6
Services to buildings	734	5.7	2.8	2.2	2.9
Auto repair, services, and parking	75	6.1	2.9	2.3	3.2
Miscellaneous repair services	76	5.2	2.6	1.8	2.6
Amusement and recreation services	79	6.7	3.0	1.7	3.8
Health services	80	7.5	3.4	2.2	4.0
Nursing and personal care facilities	805	13.5	7.6	4.5	5.9
Hospitals	806	9.2	4.0	2.5	5.2
Legal services	81	1.0	0.4	0.3	0.6
Educational services	82	2.9	1.1	0.8	1.8
Social services	83	5.6	2.7	1.9	2.9
Child day care services	835	2.6	1.0	0.8	1.5
Engineering and management services	87	1.7	0.7	0.5	1.0

See source and footnotes on page 59.
n.e.c. = not elsewhere classified.

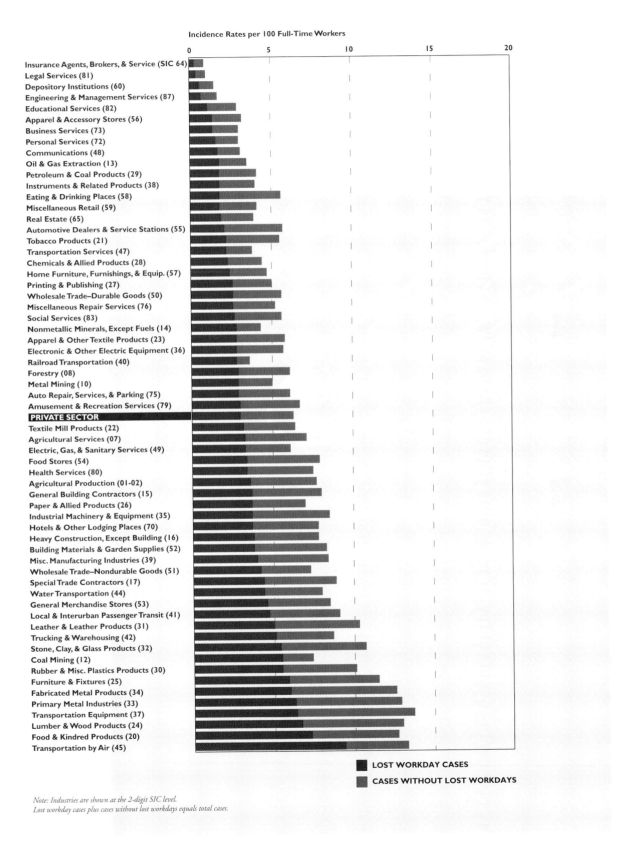

Incidence Rates per 100 Full-Time Workers

Insurance Agents, Brokers, & Service (SIC 64)
Legal Services (81)
Depository Institutions (60)
Engineering & Management Services (87)
Educational Services (82)
Apparel & Accessory Stores (56)
Business Services (73)
Personal Services (72)
Communications (48)
Oil & Gas Extraction (13)
Petroleum & Coal Products (29)
Instruments & Related Products (38)
Eating & Drinking Places (58)
Miscellaneous Retail (59)
Real Estate (65)
Automotive Dealers & Service Stations (55)
Tobacco Products (21)
Transportation Services (47)
Chemicals & Allied Products (28)
Home Furniture, Furnishings, & Equip. (57)
Printing & Publishing (27)
Wholesale Trade–Durable Goods (50)
Miscellaneous Repair Services (76)
Social Services (83)
Nonmetallic Minerals, Except Fuels (14)
Apparel & Other Textile Products (23)
Electronic & Other Electric Equipment (36)
Railroad Transportation (40)
Forestry (08)
Metal Mining (10)
Auto Repair, Services, & Parking (75)
Amusement & Recreation Services (79)
PRIVATE SECTOR
Textile Mill Products (22)
Agricultural Services (07)
Electric, Gas, & Sanitary Services (49)
Food Stores (54)
Health Services (80)
Agricultural Production (01-02)
General Building Contractors (15)
Paper & Allied Products (26)
Industrial Machinery & Equipment (35)
Hotels & Other Lodging Places (70)
Heavy Construction, Except Building (16)
Building Materials & Garden Supplies (52)
Misc. Manufacturing Industries (39)
Wholesale Trade–Nondurable Goods (51)
Special Trade Contractors (17)
Water Transportation (44)
General Merchandise Stores (53)
Local & Interurban Passenger Transit (41)
Leather & Leather Products (31)
Trucking & Warehousing (42)
Stone, Clay, & Glass Products (32)
Coal Mining (12)
Rubber & Misc. Plastics Products (30)
Furniture & Fixtures (25)
Fabricated Metal Products (34)
Primary Metal Industries (33)
Transportation Equipment (37)
Lumber & Wood Products (24)
Food & Kindred Products (20)
Transportation by Air (45)

■ **LOST WORKDAY CASES**
■ **CASES WITHOUT LOST WORKDAYS**

Note: Industries are shown at the 2-digit SIC level.
Lost workday cases plus cases without lost workdays equals total cases.

FATAL OCCUPATIONAL INJURIES AND NONFATAL INJURIES AND ILLNESSES BY INDUSTRY DIVISION

The tables on pages 65 through 73 present data on the characteristics of injured/ill workers and the injuries and illnesses that affected them. These data indicate how many workers are killed by on-the-job injuries and how many are affected by nonfatal injuries and illnesses. The data can be used to help set priorities for safety and health programs and for benchmarking.

The fatality information covers only deaths due to injuries and comes from the Bureau of Labor Statistics (BLS) Census of Fatal Occupational Injuries. The data are 8-year totals for the calendar years 1992–1999. The 8 years were combined because counts for many of the items would be too small to publish if data for a single year were used.

The data on nonfatal cases cover both injuries and illnesses and come from the BLS Survey of Occupational Injuries and Illnesses for the 1999 reference year. The Survey also is used to produce the incidence rates shown on the preceding pages. The estimates on the following pages are the number of

cases involving days away from work (with or without days of restricted work activity).

Data are presented for the sex, age, occupation, and race or ethnic origin of the worker and for the nature of injury/illness, the part of body affected, the source of injury/illness, and the event or exposure that produced the injury/illness.

The text at the top of each page describes the kind of establishments that are included in the industry division, the number of workers in the industry division for 1999, and the annual average number of workers for the 1992–1999 period.

Page 65 shows nonfatal injury/illness data for the private sector of the economy (excluding government entities) and fatal injury data for all industries. Pages 66 through 72 present the data for private sector industry divisions. Page 73 presents the fatal injury data for the Government industry division (the BLS Survey does not cover government entities at the national level).

The nonfatal occupational injury and illness data cover only the private sector of the economy and exclude employees in federal, state, and local government entities. The fatal injury data cover employees in both the private sector and government.

There were 134,688,000 people employed in 1999, of which 114,569,000 worked in the private sector and 20,118,000 in government. Over the 8 years from 1992 through 1999, total employment averaged 127,116,000 per year with 107,395,000 in the private sector.

NUMBER OF NONFATAL OCCUPATIONAL INJURIES AND ILLNESSES INVOLVING DAYS AWAY FROM WORK[a] AND FATAL OCCUPATIONAL INJURIES BY SELECTED WORKER AND CASE CHARACTERISTICS, UNITED STATES

Characteristic	Private Industry[b,c] Nonfatal Cases, 1999	All Industries Fatalities, 1992–1999
Total	**1,702,470**	**49,958**
Sex		
Men	1,129,243	46,039
Women	558,127	3,917
Age		
Under 14	—	—
14 to 15	866	231[d]
16 to 19	58,206	1,276
20 to 24	197,841	3,901
25 to 34	457,555	11,144
35 to 44	483,545	12,444
45 to 54	310,502	10,083
55 to 64	138,391	6,651
65 and over	22,538	4,152
Occupation		
Managerial and professional	94,671	5,530
Technical, sales, and administrative support	249,426	6,394
Service	289,479	4,146
Farming, forestry, and fishing	42,899	7,363
Precision production, craft, and repair	297,965	8,770
Operators, fabricators, and laborers	719,728	16,604
Military	N/A	728
Race or ethnic origin		
White, non-Hispanic	859,591	33,245
Black, non-Hispanic	155,149	4,509
Hispanic	182,896	5,137
Asian or Pacific Islander	25,328	1,425
American Indian or Alaskan Native	6,812	269
Not reported	472,693	5,377
Nature of injury, illness		
Sprains, strains	739,742	65
Fractures	113,734	278
Cuts, lacerations, punctures	153,762	8,136
Bruises, contusions	155,965	20
Heat burns	27,108	1,169
Chemical burns	11,614	54
Amputations	9,985	—
Carpal tunnel syndrome	27,922	—
Tendonitis	16,582	—
Multiple injuries	59,343	13,587
Soreness, pain	109,257	10
Back pain	43,198	8
All other	277,455	26,654

Characteristic	Private Industry[b,c] Nonfatal Cases, 1999	All Industries Fatalities, 1992–1999
Part of body affected		
Head	107,696	12,268
Eye	53,096	5
Neck	30,889	1,024
Trunk	631,173	10,152
Back	424,251	629
Shoulder	93,787	19
Upper extremities	397,118	125
Finger	149,475	13
Hand, except finger	70,809	10
Wrist	84,410	6
Lower extremities	350,202	444
Knee	127,953	60
Foot, toe	77,649	25
Body systems	21,910	8,191
Multiple	148,188	17,338
All other	15,294	431
Source of injury, illness		
Chemicals, chemical products	28,773	1,255
Containers	244,574	670
Furniture, fixtures	58,537	140
Machinery	114,183	4,067
Parts and materials	192,005	3,385
Worker motion or position	267,060	22
Floor, ground surfaces	272,026	5,050
Hand tools	77,942	878
Vehicles	137,660	21,111
Health care patient	72,363	13
All other	237,346	13,382
Event or exposure		
Contact with object, equipment	459,606	7,999
Struck by object	229,158	4,524
Struck against object	116,517	117
Caught in object, equipment, material	76,968	3,331
Fall to lower level	93,881	4,717
Fall on same level	190,701	440
Slips, trips	54,761	11
Overexertion	459,441	49
Overexertion in lifting	264,837	29
Repetitive motion	73,195	—
Exposed to harmful substance	76,223	4,638
Transportation accidents	73,246	20,793
Fires, explosions	3,486	1,583
Assault, violent act	23,225	9,340
by person	16,644	7,378
by other	6,581	1,962
All other	194,705	403

Source: National Safety Council tabulations of Bureau of Labor Statistics data.
Note: Because of rounding and data exclusion of nonclassifiable responses, data may not sum to the totals. Dashes indicate data that do not meet publication guidelines. "N/A" means not applicable.
[a] Days away from work include those that result in days away from work with or without restricted work activity.
[b] Excludes farms with fewer than 11 employees.

[c] Data conforming to OSHA definitions for mining operators in coal, metal, and nonmetal mining and for employees in railroad transportation are provided to BLS by the Mine Safety and Health Administration, U.S. Department of Labor; and the Federal Railroad Administration, U.S. Department of Transportation. Independent mining contractors are excluded from the coal, metal, and nonmetal mining industries.
[d] Includes ages 15 and younger.

AGRICULTURE, FORESTRY, AND FISHING

The Agriculture, Forestry, and Fishing industry division includes production of crops and livestock, animal specialties, agricultural services, forestry (but excluding logging, which is in the Manufacturing industry division), and commercial fishing, hunting, and trapping.

Employment in Agriculture, Forestry, and Fishing totaled 3,348,000 in 1999 and averaged 3,408,000 per year from 1992 through 1999. It is the second smallest industry division after Mining.

NUMBER OF NONFATAL OCCUPATIONAL INJURIES AND ILLNESSES INVOLVING DAYS AWAY FROM WORK[a] AND FATAL OCCUPATIONAL INJURIES BY SELECTED WORKER AND CASE CHARACTERISTICS, UNITED STATES, AGRICULTURE, FORESTRY, AND FISHING

Characteristic	Nonfatal Cases[b], 1999	Fatalities, 1992–1999
Total	**34,941**	**6,638**
Sex		
Men	28,638	6,432
Women	6,155	205
Age		
Under 14	—	—
14 to 15	—	149[c]
16 to 19	1,322	191
20 to 24	5,431	387
25 to 34	10,498	992
35 to 44	9,689	1,175
45 to 54	4,747	999
55 to 64	2,063	1,067
65 and over	439	1,667
Occupation		
Managerial and professional	541	90
Technical, sales, and administrative support	1,469	136
Service	532	24
Farming, forestry, and fishing	27,387	6,052
Precision production, craft, and repair	1,336	51
Operators, fabricators, and laborers	3,505	268
Race or ethnic origin		
White, non-Hispanic	14,019	4,807
Black, non-Hispanic	1,340	242
Hispanic	14,642	780
Asian or Pacific Islander	211	90
American Indian or Alaskan Native	108	49
Not reported	4,622	670
Nature of injury, illness		
Sprains, strains	11,563	—
Fractures	3,662	25
Cuts, lacerations, punctures	4,090	331
Bruises, contusions	3,236	—
Heat burns	285	80
Chemical burns	199	—
Amputations	264	—
Carpal tunnel syndrome	214	—
Tendonitis	232	—
Multiple injuries	1,154	1,466
Soreness, pain	1,606	—
Back pain	750	—
All other	8,437	4,729

Characteristic	Nonfatal Cases[b], 1999	Fatalities, 1992–1999
Part of body affected		
Head	2,889	1,277
Eye	1,710	—
Neck	497	152
Trunk	10,583	1,739
Back	6,600	68
Shoulder	1,621	—
Upper extremities	9,820	29
Finger	3,802	—
Hand, except finger	2,306	—
Wrist	1,208	—
Lower extremities	7,956	65
Knee	2,056	—
Foot, toe	1,744	—
Body systems	382	1,672
Multiple	2,053	1,671
All other	762	33
Source of injury, illness		
Chemicals, chemical products	421	105
Containers	2,717	93
Furniture, fixtures	305	—
Machinery	2,616	995
Parts and materials	2,458	264
Worker motion or position	4,974	—
Floor, ground surfaces	5,184	418
Hand tools	2,448	65
Vehicles	2,564	3,391
Health care patient	—	—
All other	11,253	1,305
Event or exposure		
Contact with object, equipment	11,465	1,539
Struck by object	5,108	806
Struck against object	2,769	14
Caught in object, equipment, material	2,218	714
Fall to lower level	2,649	425
Fall on same level	2,885	24
Slips, trips	1,009	—
Overexertion	5,627	—
Overexertion in lifting	3,388	—
Repetitive motion	799	—
Exposed to harmful substance	1,874	677
Transportation accidents	1,502	3,389
Fires, explosions	—	98
Assault, violent act	2,895	448
by person	43	131
by other	2,852	317
All other	4,201	38

Source: National Safety Council tabulations of Bureau of Labor Statistics data.

Note: Because of rounding and data exclusion of nonclassifiable responses, data may not sum to the totals. Dashes indicate data that do not meet publication guidelines.

[a] *Days away from work include those that result in days away from work with or without restricted work activity.*

[b] *Excludes farms with fewer than 11 employees.*

[c] *Includes ages 15 and younger.*

The Mining industry division includes metal mining, coal mining, oil and gas extraction, and mining and quarrying of nonmetallic minerals such as stone, sand, and gravel.

Mining is the smallest industry division. Mining employment in 1999 amounted to 562,000 workers. Over the 8 years from 1992 through 1999, employment in Mining averaged 626,000 per year.

NUMBER OF NONFATAL OCCUPATIONAL INJURIES AND ILLNESSES INVOLVING DAYS AWAY FROM WORKª AND FATAL OCCUPATIONAL INJURIES BY SELECTED WORKER AND CASE CHARACTERISTICS, UNITED STATES, MINING

Characteristic	Nonfatal Cases[b], 1999	Fatalities, 1992–1999
Total	11,318	1,273
Sex		
Men	10,999	1,257
Women	289	16
Age		
Under 14	—	—
14 to 15	—	—
16 to 19	178	21
20 to 24	780	119
25 to 34	2,532	337
35 to 44	3,425	364
45 to 54	3,300	274
55 to 64	836	107
65 and over	32	50
Occupation		
Managerial and professional	279	66
Technical, sales, and administrative support	123	29
Service	40	13
Farming, forestry, and fishing	—	—
Precision production, craft, and repair	5,346	688
Operators, fabricators, and laborers	5,226	473
Race or ethnic origin		
White, non-Hispanic	2,242	947
Black, non-Hispanic	133	42
Hispanic	1,088	145
Asian or Pacific Islander	19	—
American Indian or Alaskan Native	—	16
Not reported	7,832	120
Nature of injury, illness		
Sprains, strains	4,406	—
Fractures	1,771	5
Cuts, lacerations, punctures	789	35
Bruises, contusions	1,141	—
Heat burns	141	44
Chemical burns	56	—
Amputations	90	—
Carpal tunnel syndrome	73	—
Tendonitis	—	—
Multiple injuries	700	419
Soreness, pain	332	—
Back pain	119	—
All other	1,816	767

Characteristic	Nonfatal Cases[b], 1999	Fatalities, 1992–1999
Part of body affected		
Head	642	271
Eye	268	—
Neck	246	22
Trunk	3,990	254
Back	2,584	10
Shoulder	479	—
Upper extremities	2,436	—
Finger	1,042	—
Hand, except finger	478	—
Wrist	399	—
Lower extremities	2,705	10
Knee	1,022	—
Foot, toe	565	—
Body systems	174	231
Multiple	1,112	476
All other	14	5
Source of injury, illness		
Chemicals, chemical products	875	78
Containers	700	22
Furniture, fixtures	54	6
Machinery	1,471	236
Parts and materials	1,912	156
Worker motion or position	428	—
Floor, ground surfaces	2,085	76
Hand tools	486	8
Vehicles	649	361
Health care patient	—	—
All other	2,658	329
Event or exposure		
Contact with object, equipment	4,573	484
Struck by object	2,520	231
Struck against object	946	5
Caught in object, equipment, material	1,066	247
Fall to lower level	1,081	86
Fall on same level	897	7
Slips, trips	98	—
Overexertion	3,249	—
Overexertion in lifting	1,193	—
Repetitive motion	142	—
Exposed to harmful substance	485	138
Transportation accidents	169	385
Fires, explosions	33	137
Assault, violent act	—	25
by person	—	13
by other	—	12
All other	592	9

Source: National Safety Council tabulations of Bureau of Labor Statistics data.
Note: Because of rounding and data exclusion of nonclassifiable responses, data may not sum to the totals. Dashes indicate data that do not meet publication guidelines.
ª Days away from work include those that result in days away from work with or without restricted work activity.
[b] Data conforming to OSHA definitions for mining operators in coal, metal, and nonmetal mining are provided to BLS by the Mine Safety and Health Administration, U.S. Department of Labor. Independent mining contractors are excluded from the coal, metal, and nonmetal mining industries.

CONSTRUCTION

The Construction industry division includes establishments engaged in construction of buildings, heavy construction other than buildings, and special trade contractors such as plumbing, electrical, carpentry, etc.

In 1999, employment in the Construction industry division totaled 8,479,000 workers. Employment over the 1992–1999 period averaged 7,395,000 workers per year.

NUMBER OF NONFATAL OCCUPATIONAL INJURIES AND ILLNESSES INVOLVING DAYS AWAY FROM WORK[a] AND FATAL OCCUPATIONAL INJURIES BY SELECTED WORKER AND CASE CHARACTERISTICS, UNITED STATES, CONSTRUCTION

Characteristic	Nonfatal Cases, 1999	Fatalities, 1992–1999
Total	**193,765**	**8,768**
Sex		
Men	188,591	8,642
Women	4,601	126
Age		
Under 14	—	—
14 to 15	—	10[b]
16 to 19	4,989	262
20 to 24	26,959	805
25 to 34	58,207	2,236
35 to 44	59,233	2,447
45 to 54	28,266	1,677
55 to 64	10,552	992
65 and over	833	327
Occupation		
Managerial and professional	2,128	546
Technical, sales, and administrative support	2,533	105
Service	451	20
Farming, forestry, and fishing	364	28
Precision production, craft, and repair	114,614	4,429
Operators, fabricators, and laborers	72,607	3,618
Race or ethnic origin		
White, non-Hispanic	121,504	5,853
Black, non-Hispanic	9,563	624
Hispanic	28,757	1,221
Asian or Pacific Islander	1,255	82
American Indian or Alaskan Native	1,085	50
Not reported	31,602	938
Nature of injury, illness		
Sprains, strains	72,371	5
Fractures	19,085	36
Cuts, lacerations, punctures	26,017	257
Bruises, contusions	13,866	—
Heat burns	2,394	153
Chemical burns	1,886	—
Amputations	1,358	—
Carpal tunnel syndrome	1,173	—
Tendonitis	751	—
Multiple injuries	8,539	2,590
Soreness, pain	9,656	—
Back pain	3,813	—
All other	36,670	5,719

Characteristic	Nonfatal Cases, 1999	Fatalities, 1992–1999
Part of body affected		
Head	15,892	2,339
Eye	9,936	—
Neck	2,546	131
Trunk	62,562	1,379
Back	40,998	75
Shoulder	8,416	—
Upper extremities	45,858	12
Finger	20,372	—
Hand, except finger	8,240	—
Wrist	6,948	—
Lower extremities	47,058	53
Knee	16,796	5
Foot, toe	10,971	5
Body systems	1,629	1,929
Multiple	16,160	2,881
All other	2,060	44
Source of injury, illness		
Chemicals, chemical products	2,686	166
Containers	9,237	110
Furniture, fixtures	3,262	36
Machinery	10,971	1,037
Parts and materials	48,196	1,219
Worker motion or position	25,995	—
Floor, ground surfaces	34,869	2,602
Hand tools	15,979	100
Vehicles	9,871	2,175
Health care patient	—	—
All other	32,697	1,322
Event or exposure		
Contact with object, equipment	67,628	1,655
Struck by object	34,835	821
Struck against object	15,387	14
Caught in object, equipment, material	9,272	816
Fall to lower level	22,381	2,619
Fall on same level	13,774	41
Slips, trips	6,067	—
Overexertion	40,181	—
Overexertion in lifting	23,578	—
Repetitive motion	3,516	—
Exposed to harmful substance	7,226	1,493
Transportation accidents	6,499	2,399
Fires, explosions	829	244
Assault, violent act	486	254
by person	328	125
by other	158	129
All other	25,178	58

Source: National Safety Council tabulations of Bureau of Labor Statistics data.
Note: Because of rounding and data exclusion of nonclassifiable responses, data may not sum to the totals. Dashes indicate data that do not meet publication guidelines.
[a] Days away from work include those that result in days away from work with or without restricted work activity.
[b] Includes ages 15 and younger.

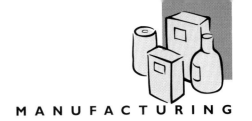

MANUFACTURING

The Manufacturing industry division includes establishments engaged in the mechanical or chemical transformation of materials or substances into new products. It includes durable and nondurable goods such as food, textiles, apparel, lumber, wood products, paper and paper products, printing, chemicals and pharmaceuticals, petroleum and coal products, rubber and plastics products, metals and metal products, machinery, electrical equipment, transportation equipment, and others.

Manufacturing employment in 1999 was 19,993,000 workers. Average annual employment from 1992 through 1999 was 20,197,000 workers.

NUMBER OF NONFATAL OCCUPATIONAL INJURIES AND ILLNESSES INVOLVING DAYS AWAY FROM WORKᵃ AND FATAL OCCUPATIONAL INJURIES BY SELECTED WORKER AND CASE CHARACTERISTICS, UNITED STATES, MANUFACTURING

Characteristic	Nonfatal Cases[b], 1999	Fatalities, 1992–1999	Characteristic	Nonfatal Cases[b], 1999	Fatalities, 1992–1999
Total	**403,568**	**5,937**	**Part of body affected**		
			Head	29,520	1,549
Sex			*Eye*	*18,674*	—
Men	301,640	5,601	Neck	5,691	107
Women	100,387	336	Trunk	140,973	1,266
			Back	*89,297*	*81*
Age			*Shoulder*	*23,219*	—
Under 14	—	—	Upper extremities	125,123	25
14 to 15	10	13[b]	*Finger*	*51,671*	—
16 to 19	7,996	130	*Hand, except finger*	*20,621*	—
20 to 24	42,018	431	*Wrist*	*27,456*	—
25 to 34	109,087	1,279	Lower extremities	70,751	73
35 to 44	118,438	1,606	*Knee*	*25,644*	*15*
45 to 54	81,895	1,297	*Foot, toe*	*17,568*	—
55 to 64	36,434	894	Body systems	4,677	888
65 and over	3,220	278	Multiple	23,509	1,988
			All other	3,324	41
Occupation					
Managerial and professional	5,606	599	**Source of injury, illness**		
Technical, sales, and administrative support	22,838	426	Chemicals, chemical products	9,537	234
Service	7,191	108	Containers	54,118	182
Farming, forestry, and fishing	2,776	922	Furniture, fixtures	10,636	22
Precision production, craft, and repair	72,332	1,125	Machinery	46,952	961
Operators, fabricators, and laborers	290,866	2,722	Parts and materials	71,735	600
			Worker motion or position	79,290	—
Race or ethnic origin			Floor, ground surfaces	42,127	440
White, non-Hispanic	219,286	4,024	Hand tools	22,623	73
Black, non-Hispanic	35,364	631	Vehicles	19,034	1,766
Hispanic	46,386	510	Health care patient	13	—
Asian or Pacific Islander	6,143	99	All other	47,505	1,655
American Indian or Alaskan Native	1,481	27			
Not reported	94,909	646	**Event or exposure**		
			Contact with object, equipment	134,923	2,219
Nature of injury, illness			*Struck by object*	*56,948*	*1,390*
Sprains, strains	157,359	15	*Struck against object*	*31,293*	*26*
Fractures	27,884	34	*Caught in object, equipment, material*	*34,767*	*801*
Cuts, lacerations, punctures	41,801	478	Fall to lower level	13,217	399
Bruises, contusions	34,773	3	Fall on same level	32,121	74
Heat burns	6,655	242	Slips, trips	10,295	5
Chemical burns	3,800	31	Overexertion	101,958	13
Amputations	5,289	—	*Overexertion in lifting*	*55,468*	*9*
Carpal tunnel syndrome	12,147	—	Repetitive motion	34,057	—
Tendonitis	7,093	—	Exposed to harmful substance	20,892	563
Multiple injuries	12,286	1,525	Transportation accidents	8,399	1,736
Soreness, pain	21,742	—	Fires, explosions	772	371
Back pain	*8,377*	—	Assault, violent act	755	503
All other	72,741	3,606	*by person*	*454*	*304*
			by other	*301*	*199*
			All other	46,181	54

Source: National Safety Council tabulations of Bureau of Labor Statistics data.
Note: Because of rounding and data exclusion of nonclassifiable responses, data may not sum to the totals. Dashes indicate data that do not meet publication guidelines.
ᵃ Days away from work include those that result in days away from work with or without restricted work activity.
ᵇ Includes ages 15 and younger.

TRANSPORTATION AND PUBLIC UTILITIES

This industry division includes transportation by rail, highway, air, water, or pipeline and associated transportation services; communications by telephone, radio, television, cable, or satellite; and electric, gas, and sanitary services.

Employment in the Transportation and Public Utilities industry division totaled 7,948,000 in 1999 and averaged 7,283,000 workers per year from 1992 through 1999.

NUMBER OF NONFATAL OCCUPATIONAL INJURIES AND ILLNESSES INVOLVING DAYS AWAY FROM WORK[a] AND FATAL OCCUPATIONAL INJURIES BY SELECTED WORKER AND CASE CHARACTERISTICS, UNITED STATES, TRANSPORTATION AND PUBLIC UTILITIES[b]

Characteristic	Nonfatal Cases, 1999	Fatalities, 1992–1999
Total	**196,725**	**8,010**
Sex		
Men	149,767	7,610
Women	39,605	400
Age		
Under 14	—	—
14 to 15	—	—
16 to 19	3,364	69
20 to 24	16,407	400
25 to 34	54,404	1,728
35 to 44	61,782	2,242
45 to 54	39,806	2,079
55 to 64	15,197	1,122
65 and over	1,859	357
Occupation		
Managerial and professional	3,178	317
Technical, sales, and administrative support	27,633	858
Service	12,301	124
Farming, forestry, and fishing	253	23
Precision production, craft, and repair	26,478	747
Operators, fabricators, and laborers	126,544	5,927
Race or ethnic origin		
White, non-Hispanic	68,828	5,288
Black, non-Hispanic	15,578	1,034
Hispanic	8,908	630
Asian or Pacific Islander	1,607	183
American Indian or Alaskan Native	447	28
Not reported	101,358	847
Nature of injury, illness		
Sprains, strains	95,657	8
Fractures	11,644	26
Cuts, lacerations, punctures	9,778	897
Bruises, contusions	20,407	—
Heat burns	864	272
Chemical burns	595	7
Amputations	550	—
Carpal tunnel syndrome	2,012	—
Tendonitis	1,019	—
Multiple injuries	6,849	2,866
Soreness, pain	16,916	—
Back pain	7,205	—
All other	30,435	3,932

Characteristic	Nonfatal Cases, 1999	Fatalities, 1992–1999
Part of body affected		
Head	12,011	1,714
Eye	3,669	—
Neck	4,594	142
Trunk	79,593	1,425
Back	51,692	88
Shoulder	14,372	—
Upper extremities	32,286	9
Finger	9,501	—
Hand, except finger	4,983	—
Wrist	7,176	—
Lower extremities	44,939	56
Knee	16,714	11
Foot, toe	9,665	—
Body systems	2,943	1,118
Multiple	19,379	3,463
All other	980	83
Source of injury, illness		
Chemicals, chemical products	2,535	141
Containers	40,509	83
Furniture, fixtures	3,561	6
Machinery	5,003	211
Parts and materials	16,052	408
Worker motion or position	30,677	—
Floor, ground surfaces	30,487	265
Hand tools	3,409	63
Vehicles	36,344	5,612
Health care patient	1,823	—
All other	26,325	1,217
Event or exposure		
Contact with object, equipment	42,143	652
Struck by object	21,467	413
Struck against object	11,766	9
Caught in object, equipment, material	5,931	227
Fall to lower level	13,458	233
Fall on same level	18,518	31
Slips, trips	7,243	—
Overexertion	55,937	—
Overexertion in lifting	29,824	—
Repetitive motion	5,553	—
Exposed to harmful substance	6,771	531
Transportation accidents	18,157	5,415
Fires, explosions	268	136
Assault, violent act	1,098	963
by person	674	821
by other	423	142
All other	27,580	47

Source: National Safety Council tabulations of Bureau of Labor Statistics data.
Note: Because of rounding and data exclusion of nonclassifiable responses, data may not sum to the totals. Dashes indicate data that do not meet publication guidelines.
[a] Days away from work include those that result in days away from work with or without restricted work activity.
[b] Data conforming to OSHA definitions for employees in railroad transportation are provided to BLS by the Federal Railroad Administration, U.S. Department of Transportation.

WHOLESALE AND RETAIL TRADE

Establishments in Wholesale Trade generally sell merchandise to retailers; to industrial, commercial, institutional, farm, construction contractors, or professional business users; to other wholesalers; or to agents or brokers. Retail Trade establishments generally sell merchandise for personal or household consumption.

Wholesale trade employed 5,172,000 people in 1999 and an average of 4,889,000 people annually from 1992 through 1999. Retail trade had 22,301,000 workers in 1999 and an 8-year average of 21,124,000 per year for 1992-1999.

NUMBER OF NONFATAL OCCUPATIONAL INJURIES AND ILLNESSES INVOLVING DAYS AWAY FROM WORK[a] AND FATAL OCCUPATIONAL INJURIES BY SELECTED WORKER AND CASE CHARACTERISTICS, UNITED STATES, WHOLESALE AND RETAIL TRADE

Characteristic	Nonfatal Cases, 1999	Fatalities, 1992–1999
Total	**427,757**	**7,483**
Sex		
Men	277,138	6,454
Women	148,109	1,027
Age		
Under 14	—	—
14 to 15	347	24[b]
16 to 19	28,933	309
20 to 24	62,906	721
25 to 34	113,233	1,670
35 to 44	109,129	1,719
45 to 54	65,107	1,447
55 to 64	30,818	982
65 and over	7,573	598
Occupation		
Managerial and professional	15,665	907
Technical, sales, and administrative support	112,166	3,297
Service	81,006	673
Farming, forestry, and fishing	2,683	51
Precision production, craft, and repair	47,037	487
Operators, fabricators, and laborers	167,070	2,015
Race or ethnic origin		
White, non-Hispanic	227,383	4,444
Black, non-Hispanic	33,786	745
Hispanic	43,324	857
Asian or Pacific Islander	7,839	658
American Indian or Alaskan Native	1,510	23
Not reported	113,915	756
Nature of injury, illness		
Sprains, strains	187,609	10
Fractures	26,739	41
Cuts, lacerations, punctures	46,730	3,512
Bruises, contusions	40,923	—
Heat burns	10,220	142
Chemical burns	2,515	—
Amputations	1,449	—
Carpal tunnel syndrome	4,647	—
Tendonitis	2,971	—
Multiple injuries	14,868	1,275
Soreness, pain	28,163	—
Back pain	*11,055*	—
All other	60,924	2,499

Characteristic	Nonfatal Cases, 1999	Fatalities, 1992–1999
Part of body affected		
Head	23,226	2,205
Eye	*10,109*	—
Neck	7,481	213
Trunk	161,295	1,946
Back	*109,198*	*139*
Shoulder	*23,248*	*7*
Upper extremities	100,541	14
Finger	*39,635*	—
Hand, except finger	*20,251*	—
Wrist	*18,445*	—
Lower extremities	89,758	66
Knee	*32,230*	*10*
Foot, toe	*21,709*	—
Body systems	4,111	610
Multiple	37,175	2,361
All other	4,170	68
Source of injury, illness		
Chemicals, chemical products	5,046	132
Containers	95,465	88
Furniture, fixtures	18,530	19
Machinery	30,374	216
Parts and materials	32,599	278
Worker motion or position	58,248	—
Floor, ground surfaces	76,771	334
Hand tools	21,215	335
Vehicles	36,612	2,343
Health care patient	—	—
All other	52,849	3,734
Event or exposure		
Contact with object, equipment	118,780	570
Struck by object	*65,180*	*320*
Struck against object	*31,063*	*12*
Caught in object, equipment, material	*15,186*	*234*
Fall to lower level	20,974	246
Fall on same level	59,503	80
Slips, trips	15,075	—
Overexertion	116,585	5
Overexertion in lifting	*76,773*	—
Repetitive motion	11,694	—
Exposed to harmful substance	18,195	280
Transportation accidents	18,083	2,184
Fires, explosions	1,020	172
Assault, violent act	4,072	3,895
by person	*2,924*	*3,554*
by other	*1,148*	*341*
All other	43,778	48

Source: National Safety Council tabulations of Bureau of Labor Statistics data.
Note: Because of rounding and data exclusion of nonclassifiable responses, data may not sum to the totals. Dashes indicate data that do not meet publication guidelines.
[a] Days away from work include those that result in days away from work with or without restricted work activity.
[b] Includes ages 15 and younger.

SERVICES

Establishments in the Services industry division provide services, rather than merchandise, for individuals, businesses, government agencies, and other organizations. Broad categories in this industry division include lodging places, personal and business services, automobile services, repair services, motion pictures, amusement and recreation services, health, legal, education, social services, and others.

Services is the largest industry division with 38,157,000 workers in 1999 and an annual average of 34,487,000 from 1992 through 1999.

NUMBER OF NONFATAL OCCUPATIONAL INJURIES AND ILLNESSES INVOLVING DAYS AWAY FROM WORK[a] AND FATAL OCCUPATIONAL INJURIES BY SELECTED WORKER AND CASE CHARACTERISTICS, UNITED STATES, SERVICES[b]

Characteristic	Nonfatal Cases, 1999	Fatalities, 1992–1999
Total	**434,394**	**7,666**
Sex		
Men	172,471	6,220
Women	258,982	1,443
Age		
Under 14	—	—
14 to 15	—	20[c]
16 to 19	11,424	168
20 to 24	43,339	581
25 to 34	109,596	1,681
35 to 44	121,849	1,872
45 to 54	87,382	1,585
55 to 64	42,492	1,071
65 and over	8,582	676
Occupation		
Managerial and professional	67,274	2,482
Technical, sales, and administrative support	82,663	1,152
Service	187,959	1,563
Farming, forestry, and fishing	9,433	207
Precision production, craft, and repair	30,822	1,004
Operators, fabricators, and laborers	53,911	1,192
Race or ethnic origin		
White, non-Hispanic	206,331	5,048
Black, non-Hispanic	59,385	769
Hispanic	39,792	738
Asian or Pacific Islander	8,254	246
American Indian or Alaskan Native	2,176	48
Not reported	118,457	817
Nature of injury, illness		
Sprains, strains	210,778	15
Fractures	22,949	76
Cuts, lacerations, punctures	24,558	1,755
Bruises, contusions	41,619	6
Heat burns	6,549	141
Chemical burns	2,563	—
Amputations	985	—
Carpal tunnel syndrome	7,656	—
Tendonitis	4,513	—
Multiple injuries	14,947	2,084
Soreness, pain	30,843	5
Back pain	11,880	—
All other	66,433	3,581

Characteristic	Nonfatal Cases, 1999	Fatalities, 1992–1999
Part of body affected		
Head	23,516	1,900
Eye	8,729	—
Neck	9,835	167
Trunk	172,176	1,461
Back	123,882	103
Shoulder	22,433	—
Upper extremities	81,054	24
Finger	23,453	—
Hand, except finger	13,931	—
Wrist	22,777	—
Lower extremities	87,034	82
Knee	33,491	10
Foot, toe	15,428	6
Body systems	7,994	1,204
Multiple	48,800	2,742
All other	3,985	86
Source of injury, illness		
Chemicals, chemical products	7,674	333
Containers	41,829	67
Furniture, fixtures	22,189	41
Machinery	16,797	303
Parts and materials	19,054	362
Worker motion or position	67,449	6
Floor, ground surfaces	80,504	718
Hand tools	11,781	201
Vehicles	32,586	3,221
Health care patient	70,473	12
All other	64,058	2,402
Event or exposure		
Contact with object, equipment	80,095	637
Struck by object	43,100	383
Struck against object	23,293	33
Caught in object, equipment, material	8,528	215
Fall to lower level	20,121	553
Fall on same level	63,002	145
Slips, trips	14,975	—
Overexertion	135,903	19
Overexertion in lifting	74,613	11
Repetitive motion	17,435	
Exposed to harmful substance	20,782	720
Transportation accidents	20,438	3,047
Fires, explosions	529	221
Assault, violent act	13,919	2,234
by person	12,222	1,644
by other	1,698	590
All other	47,196	89

Source: National Safety Council tabulations of Bureau of Labor Statistics data.
Note: Because of rounding and data exclusion of nonclassifiable responses, data may not sum to the totals. Dashes indicate data that do not meet publication guidelines.
[a] Days away from work include those that result in days away from work with or without restricted work activity.
[b] Includes Finance, Insurance, and Real Estate.
[c] Includes ages 15 and younger.

Government includes workers at all levels from federal civilian and military to state, county, and municipal.

Government employment totaled 20,118,000 in 1999. From 1992 through 1999, Government employment averaged 19,721,000 per year.

NUMBER OF NONFATAL OCCUPATIONAL INJURIES AND ILLNESSES INVOLVING DAYS AWAY FROM WORKa AND FATAL OCCUPATIONAL INJURIES BY SELECTED WORKER AND CASE CHARACTERISTICS, UNITED STATES, GOVERNMENT

Characteristic	Nonfatal Casesb, 1999	Fatalities, 1992–1999
Total	**(b)**	**3,706**
Sex		
Men		3,370
Women		336
Age		
Under 14		—
14 to 15		9c
16 to 19		104
20 to 24		430
25 to 34		1,130
35 to 44		908
45 to 54		646
55 to 64		347
65 and over		123
Occupation		
Managerial and professional		478
Technical, sales, and administrative support		354
Service		1,606
Farming, forestry, and fishing		51
Precision production, craft, and repair		210
Operators, fabricators, and laborers		264
Military occupations		727
Race or ethnic origin		
White, non-Hispanic		2,603
Black, non-Hispanic		370
Hispanic		210
Asian or Pacific Islander		51
American Indian or Alaskan Native		26
Not reported		446
Nature of injury, illness		
Sprains, strains		10
Fractures		27
Cuts, lacerations, punctures		798
Bruises, contusions		—
Heat burns		82
Chemical burns		—
Amputations		—
Carpal tunnel syndrome		—
Tendonitis		—
Multiple injuries		1,243
Soreness, pain		—
Back pain		—
All other		1,543

Characteristic	Nonfatal Casesb, 1999	Fatalities, 1992–1999
Part of body affected		
Head		895
Eye		—
Neck		79
Trunk		587
Back		61
Shoulder		—
Upper extremities		6
Finger		—
Hand, except finger		—
Wrist		—
Lower extremities		32
Knee		5
Foot, toe		—
Body systems		458
Multiple		1,600
All other		49
Source of injury, illness		
Chemicals, chemical products		46
Containers		20
Furniture, fixtures		8
Machinery		80
Parts and materials		76
Worker motion or position		—
Floor, ground surfaces		156
Hand tools		28
Vehicles		2,010
Health care patient		—
All other		1,279
Event or exposure		
Contact with object, equipment		188
Struck by object		122
Struck against object		—
Caught in object, equipment, material		62
Fall to lower level		118
Fall on same level		33
Slips, trips		—
Overexertion		—
Overexertion in lifting		—
Repetitive motion		—
Exposed to harmful substance		194
Transportation accidents		2,011
Fires, explosions		195
Assault, violent act		928
by person		729
by other		199
All other		35

Source: National Safety Council tabulations of Bureau of Labor Statistics data.
Note: Because of rounding and data exclusion of nonclassifiable responses, data may not sum to the totals. Dashes indicate data that do not meet publication guidelines.
a Days away from work include those that result in days away from work with or without restricted work activity.
b Data for government entities not collected in the BLS national Survey of Occupational Injuries and Illnesses.
cIncludes ages 15 and younger.

OCCUPATIONAL
HEALTH

OCCUPATIONAL HEALTH

Approximately 372,300 occupational illnesses were recognized or diagnosed in 1999 according to the Bureau of Labor Statistics (BLS). Disorders associated with repeated trauma were the most common illness with 246,700 new cases, followed by skin diseases and disorders (nearly 45,000), and respiratory conditions due to toxic agents (16,500).

The overall incidence rate of occupational illness for all workers was 41.2 per 10,000 full-time workers. Of the major industry divisions, manufacturing had the highest rate in 1999, 120.3 per 10,000 full-time workers. Workers in manufacturing also had the highest rates for disorders associated with repeated trauma, respiratory conditions due to toxic agents, disorders due to physical agents, and poisoning. Agriculture had the second

highest incidence rate, 34.8, although agricultural workers had the highest rate of all the industry divisions for skin diseases and disorders. Mining had the highest incidence rate for dust diseases of the lungs.

The table below shows the number of occupational illnesses and the incidence rate per 10,000 full-time workers as measured by the 1999 BLS survey. To convert these to incidence rates per 100 full-time workers, which are comparable to other published BLS rates, divide the rates in the table by 100. The BLS survey records illnesses only for the year in which they are recognized or diagnosed as work-related. Since only recognized cases are included, the figures underestimate the incidence of occupational illness.

NUMBER OF OCCUPATIONAL ILLNESSES AND INCIDENCE RATES BY INDUSTRY AND TYPE OF ILLNESS, UNITED STATES, 1999

Occupational Illness	Private Sector[a]	Agriculture[a, b]	Mining[b]	Construction	Manufacturing	Trans. & Pub. Util.	Trade[b]	Finance[b]	Services
Number of Illnesses (in thousands)									
All Illnesses	372.3	5.0	1.2	8.4	222.9	19.6	33.0	14.9	67.3
Disorders associated with repeated trauma	246.7	1.0	0.7	3.1	172.4	11.3	19.1	11.5	27.7
Skin diseases, disorders	44.6	2.2	(c)	1.7	20.3	2.3	3.7	0.7	13.6
Respiratory conditions due to toxic agents	16.5	0.3	(c)	0.6	6.6	1.8	1.7	0.5	5.0
Disorders due to physical agents	15.1	0.5	(c)	0.6	7.8	0.6	1.6	0.3	3.5
Poisoning	4.4	0.1	(c)	0.2	2.0	0.4	0.3	0.3	1.0
Dust diseases of the lungs	2.2	(c)	0.1	0.1	0.9	0.3	0.1	0.1	0.5
All other occupational diseases	42.9	0.8	0.2	2.0	12.9	2.9	6.4	1.5	16.0
Incidence Rate per 10,000 Full-Time Workers									
All Illnesses	41.2	34.8	20.8	14.3	120.3	30.6	13.9	22.1	24.8
Disorders associated with repeated trauma	27.3	6.9	12.3	5.3	93.0	17.6	8.0	17.0	10.2
Skin diseases, disorders	4.9	15.5	0.7	3.0	11.0	3.6	1.6	1.0	5.0
Respiratory conditions due to toxic agents	1.8	1.8	0.6	1.0	3.6	2.8	0.7	0.8	1.9
Disorders due to physical agents	1.7	3.7	0.7	1.1	4.2	1.0	0.7	0.5	1.3
Poisoning	0.5	1.0	0.1	0.3	1.1	0.7	0.1	0.5	0.4
Dust diseases of the lungs	0.2	0.2	2.2	0.1	0.5	0.5	0.1	0.1	0.2
All other occupational diseases	4.7	5.7	4.2	3.5	7.0	4.6	2.7	2.3	5.9

Source: Bureau of Labor Statistics, U.S. Department of Labor. Components may not add to totals due to rounding.
[a] Private sector includes all industries except government, but excludes farms with less than 11 employees.
[b] Agriculture includes forestry and fishing; mining includes quarrying and oil and gas extraction; trade includes wholesale and retail; finance includes insurance and real estate.
[c] Fewer than 50 cases.

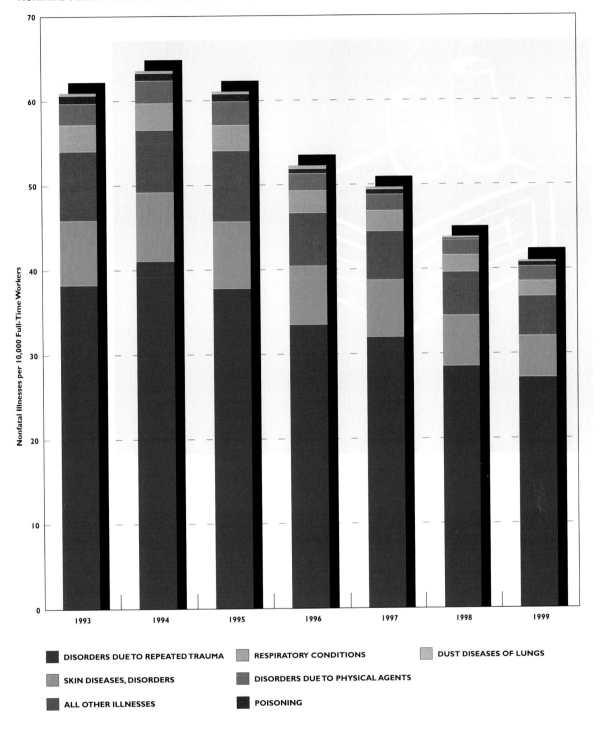

DISORDERS DUE TO REPEATED TRAUMA **RESPIRATORY CONDITIONS** **DUST DISEASES OF LUNGS**

SKIN DISEASES, DISORDERS **DISORDERS DUE TO PHYSICAL AGENTS**

ALL OTHER ILLNESSES **POISONING**

CARPAL TUNNEL SYNDROME

The contribution of various medical conditions such as diabetes mellitus, thyroid disease, wrist osteoarthritis, joint or tendon inflammation, and obesity to the development of carpal tunnel syndrome (CTS) was recently examined by Atcheson et al. (1998). The authors examined 297 patients who were medically certified with a work-related upper extremity industrial illness for concurrent medical diseases and evaluated four separate sets of clinical criteria for CTS diagnoses.

Concurrent medical conditions were common among all 297 patients, not just those with CTS. There were 109 separate diseases or illnesses capable of causing arm pain, CTS, or median neuropathy identified in 98 patients (33%). Only 35 patients (11.8%) were aware that they had any of these conditions. The two most prevalent conditions were the metabolic diseases of hypothyroidism and diabetes mellitus, with either or both present in 33 patients.

Each CTS case definition was tested for associations with medical disease, obesity, age, sex, and each of nine job categories, using those not diagnosed as having CTS as internal controls. Medical diseases and obesity were significantly correlated with CTS diagnoses. Combining medical disease or obesity into one variable produced striking associations with all four ways of diagnosing CTS. Medical diseases were 40% to 75% more common in those with CTS than in the control groups. In the number of prior CTS diagnoses and NIOSH criteria groups, about two thirds of the patients with CTS had a concurrent medical disease or were obese. Of 213 patients fitting at least one of the four CTS definitions, 40% were found to have a metabolic, inflammatory, or degenerative condition that might have caused the symptoms. In contrast, none of the 23 patients with acute trauma had a concurrent medical disease.

The study confirmed the hypothesis that patients diagnosed as having work-related CTS have a high prevalence of concurrent medical conditions capable of causing CTS without respect to any particular occupation. The results also suggest that treating or consulting physicians should seek nonoccupational explanations for CTS.

Atcheson, S.G., Ward, J.R., & Lowe, W. (July 27, 1998). Concurrent Medical Disease in Work-Related Carpal Tunnel Syndrome. Archives of Internal Medicine, 158 (14), 1506–1512.

ASSOCIATED DISEASE IN 297 PATIENTS DIAGNOSED AS HAVING WORK-RELATED ARM PAIN OR CARPAL TUNNEL SYNDROME

Disease	Diseases Known to All Patients (n=297)	Diseases Finally Diagnosed in All Patients (n=297)	Diseases in Those Meeting the NIOSH CTS Case Definition (n=193)	Diseases in Those Meeting Paired Clinical CTS Definition (n=96)
Metabolic	25 (8.4)	41 (13.8)	31 (16.1)	17 (17.7)
Hypothyroidism	5 (1.7)	18 (6.1)	12 (6.2)	7 (7.2)
Diabetes mellitus	16 (5.4)	17 (5.7)	14 (7.3)	9 (9.3)
Gout	3 (1.0)	3 (1.0)	2 (1.0)	—
Other	1 (0.3)	3 (1.0)	3 (1.6)	1 (1.0)
Inflammatory	8 (2.6)	33 (11.1)	24 (12.4)	15 (15.6)
Unclassified	—	12 (4.0)	10 (5.1)	5 (5.2)
Spondyloarthropathy	3 (1.0)	7 (2.4)	4 (2.1)	3 (3.1)
Rheumatoid arthritis	—	5 (1.7)	3 (1.6)	2 (2.1)
Seronegative arthritis	2 (0.6)	5 (1.7)	3 (1.6)	2 (2.1)
Raynaud phenomenon	3 (1.0)	4 (1.3)	4 (2.1)	3 (3.1)
Osteoarthritis/degenerative	2 (0.6)	35 (11.7)	23 (11.9)	14 (4.5)
Wrist	1 (0.3)	18 (6.1)	12 (6.2)	8 (8.3)
Finger	—	7 (2.4)	4 (2.1)	3 (3.1)
Cervical spine	—	4 (1.3)	2 (1.0)	2 (2.1)
Elbow	—	3 (1.0)	2 (1.0)	—
Other	—	3 (1.0)	3 (1.6)	1 (1.0)
Acute trauma/RSD[a]	—	29 (9.8)	9 (4.6)	4 (4.2)
Wrist	—	15 (5.1)	7 (3.6)	3 (3.1)
Hand/forearm/elbow	—	8 (2.7)	—	—
RSD (5 w/acute trauma)	—	6 (2.0)	2 (1.0)	1 (1.0)
Total Medical Diseases[b]	**35 (11.8)**	**109 (36.7)**	**78 (40.4)**	**46 (47.9)**

[a] RSD = reflex sympathetic dystrophy.
[b] Does not include trauma or RSD.

ILLNESS, MEDICAL TREATMENT, AND PRODUCTIVITY

Daily metrics of work output for nearly 6,000 individuals with similar job descriptions in the workforce of a large U.S. insurance company were studied by Cockburn et. al. (1999) to determine how illness and medical treatment can affect measurable performance at work. The initial test of the hypothesis that illness, possibly in conjunction with medical treatment, has a measurable impact on an individual's ability to function at work was evaluated using data from 682 individuals who filled prescriptions for antihistamine medications.

The most common medical condition defined as a treatment target was allergic rhinitis. Over half (55%) of the prescriptions were for one of three recent generation H_1-antagonist medications described as nonsedating antihistamines. The remaining 45% of the prescriptions were for a portfolio of older generation medicines that have well-documented sedating effects.

The output of claims processors was measured by tracking via computer the number of claims processed per day. About 94% of the daily output observations were from female subjects, with an average age of slightly over 32 years. Most were married and about three-quarters completed their formal education upon graduation from high school. Job tenure averaged more than five years, with a minimum of one day and a maximum of over 25 years. Almost 98% of observations were from full-time employees, with just under 2% having part-time status. The test of the impact of antihistamine use on productivity at work was formed by estimates of the effect on output of observations falling into brief before-and-after time periods surrounding the date on which the employee filled a prescription for an antihistamine drug. The tests were repeated for periods of 3, 5, 7, 10, and 14 days.

The results indicated that during the three days after filling a prescription for a sedating antihistamine, employees were 7.8% less productive than average, whereas those who filled a nonsedating antihistamine prescription were 5.2% more productive. The before effect was very small and statistically insignificant, indicating that if untreated, the condition for which the drugs are being prescribed seemed to have little impact on productivity. However, the choice of treatment had a very substantial impact with regard to at-work productivity.

Cockburn, I.M., Bailit, H.L., Berndt, E.R., & Finkelstein, S.N. (1999). Loss of work productivity due to illness and medical treatment. *Journal of Occupational and Environmental Medicine, 41 (11), 948–953.*

ANTIHISTAMINE PRESCRIPTIONS BY DRUG FOR 682 EMPLOYEES OF A LARGE U.S. INSURANCE COMPANY, 1993–1995

Drugs	Frequency
Nonsedating	
Astemizole	161
Loratidine	292
Loratidine with pseudoephedrine	84
Terfenadine	274
Terfenadine with pseudoephedrine	236
Total	*1,047*
Sedating	
Azatidine with pseudoephedrine	56
Brompheniramine, alone and in combination with pseudoephedrine	46
Carbinoxamine with pseudoephedrine	47
Chlorpheniramine alone or in combination with phenylephirine, phenylpropanolamine, phenyltoloxamine, and/or pseudoephedrine	332
Clemastine	12
Diphenhydramine	13
Pheniramine with phenyltoloxamine, pyrilamine and phenylpropanolamine	45
Promethazine	244
Promethazine with phenylephirine	48
Total	*843*
Total drugs	**1,890**

MOTOR VEHICLE

MOTOR VEHICLE, 2000

Between 1912 and 2000, motor-vehicle deaths per 10,000 registered vehicles were reduced 94%, from 33 to about 2. In 1912, there were 3,100 fatalities when the number of registered vehicles totaled only 950,000. In 2000, there were 43,000 fatalities, but registrations soared to 224 million.

While mileage data were not available in 1912, the 2000 mileage death rate of 1.60 per 100,000,000 vehicle miles was unchanged from 1999 and the lowest rate on record. Disabling injuries in motor-vehicle accidents totaled 2,300,000 in 2000, and total motor-vehicle costs were estimated at $201.5 billion. Costs include wage and productivity losses, medical expenses, administrative expenses, motor-vehicle property damage, and employer costs.

Motor-vehicle deaths were unchanged from 1999 to 2000 and down 1% from 1998. Miles traveled was

down about 0.1%, the number of registered vehicles increased 2%, and the population increased 1%. As a result, the mileage death rate was unchanged, the registration death rate was down 2%, and the population death rate decreased 1% from 1998 to 1999.

Compared with 1990, 2000 motor-vehicle deaths decreased by about 8%. However, mileage, registration, and population death rates were all sharply lower in 1999 compared to 1989 (see chart on opposite page).

The word "accident" may be used in this section as well as the word "crash." When used, "accident" has a specific meaning as defined in the *Manual on Classification of Motor Vehicle Traffic Accidents,* ANSI D16.2-1996. "Crash" is generally used by the National Highway Traffic Safety Administration to mean the same as accident, but it is not formally defined.

Deaths 43,000
Disabling injuries 2,300,000
Cost . . . . $201.5 billion
Motor-vehicle mileage . . . . 2,688 billion
Registered vehicles in the United States 224,000,000
Licensed drivers in the United States 189,800,000
Death rate per 100,000,000 vehicle miles 1.60
Death rate per 10,000 registered vehicles 1.92
Death rate per 100,000 population 15.6

ACCIDENT AND VEHICLE TOTALS, 2000

Severity of Accident	Number of Accidents	Drivers (Vehicles) Involved
Fatal	38,800	61,400
Disabling injury	1,500,000	2,900,000
Property damage and nondisabling injury[a]	11,900,000	22,100,000
Total (rounded)	13,400,000	25,100,000

[a] *Estimating procedures for these figures were revised beginning with the 1990 edition.*

TRAVEL DEATHS AND DEATH RATES, UNITED STATES, 1925–2000

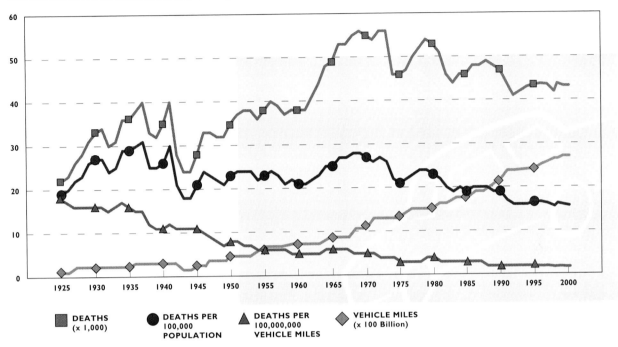

DEATHS DUE TO MOTOR-VEHICLE ACCIDENTS, 2000

TYPE OF ACCIDENT AND AGE OF VICTIM

All Motor-Vehicle Accidents

Includes deaths involving mechanically or electrically powered highway-transport vehicles in motion (except those on rails), both on and off the highway or street.

	Total	Change from 1999	Death Rate[a]
Deaths	43,000	0%	15.6
Nonfatal injuries	2,300,000		

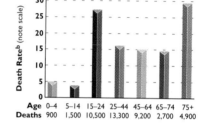

Collision Between Motor Vehicles

Includes deaths from collisions of two or more motor vehicles. Motorized bicycles and scooters, trolley buses, and farm tractors or road machinery traveling on highways are motor vehicles.

	Total	Change from 1999	Death Rate[a]
Deaths	20,600	+3%	7.5
Nonfatal injuries	1,830,000		

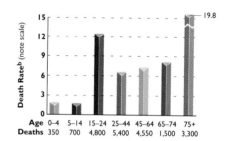

Collision with Fixed Object

Includes deaths from collisions in which the first harmful event is the striking of a fixed object such as a guardrail, abutment, impact attenuator, etc.

	Total	Change from 1999	Death Rate[a]
Deaths	11,200	−1%	4.1
Nonfatal injuries	240,000		

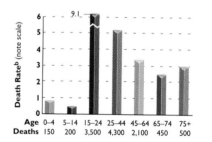

Pedestrian Accidents

Includes all deaths of persons struck by motor vehicles, either on or off a street or highway, regardless of the circumstances of the accident.

	Total	Change from 1999	Death Rate[a]
Deaths	5,300	−9%	1.9
Nonfatal injuries	85,000		

See footnotes on page 85.

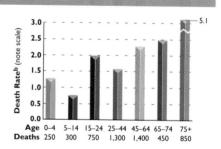

Noncollision Accidents

Includes deaths from accidents in which the first injury or damage-producing event was an overturn, jackknife, or other type of noncollision.

	Total	Change from 1999	Death Rate[a]
Deaths	4,600	-2%	1.7
Nonfatal injuries	80,000		

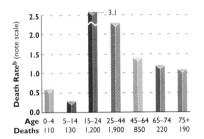

Age	0–4	5–14	15–24	25–44	45–64	65–74	75+
Deaths	110	130	1,200	1,900	850	220	190

Collision with Pedalcycle

Includes deaths of pedalcyclists and motor-vehicle occupants from collisions between pedalcycles and motor vehicles on streets, highways, private driveways, parking lots, etc.

	Total	Change from 1999	Death Rate[a]
Deaths	800	0%	0.3
Nonfatal injuries	54,000		

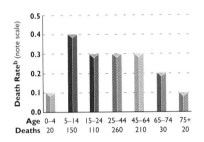

Age	0–4	5–14	15–24	25–44	45–64	65–74	75+
Deaths	20	150	110	260	210	30	20

Collision with Railroad Train

Includes deaths from collisions of motor vehicles (moving or stalled) and railroad vehicles at public or private grade crossings. In other types of accidents, classification requires motor vehicle to be in motion.

	Total	Change from 1999	Death Rate[a]
Deaths	400	+33%	0.1
Nonfatal injuries	1,000		

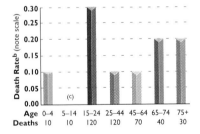

Age	0–4	5–14	15–24	25–44	45–64	65–74	75+
Deaths	10	10	120	120	70	40	30

Other Collision

Includes deaths from motor-vehicle collisions not specified in other categories above. Most of the deaths arose out of accidents involving animals or animal-drawn vehicles.

	Total	Change from 1999	Death Rate[a]
Deaths	100	0%	(c)
Nonfatal Injuries	10,000		

Note: Procedures and benchmarks for estimating deaths by type of accident and age were changed in 1990. Estimates for 1987 and later years are not comparable to earlier years. The noncollision and fixed object categories were most affected by the changes.
[a] Deaths per 100,000 population.
[b] Deaths per 100,000 population in each age group.
[c] Death rate was less than 0.05.

TYPE OF MOTOR-VEHICLE ACCIDENT

Although motor-vehicle deaths occur more often in collisions between motor vehicles than any other type of accident, this type represents only about 48% of the total. Collisions between a motor vehicle and a fixed object were the next most common type, with about 26% of the deaths, followed by pedestrian accidents and noncollisions (rollovers, etc.).

While collisions between motor vehicles accounted for less than half of motor-vehicle fatalities, this accident type represented 80% of injuries, 72% of injury accidents, and 72% of all accidents. Single-vehicle accidents involving collisions with fixed objects, pedestrians, and noncollisions, on the other hand,

accounted for a greater proportion of fatalities and fatal accidents compared to less serious accidents. These three accident types made up 49% of fatalities and 53% of fatal accidents, but less than 25% of injuries, injury accidents, or all accidents.

Of collisions between motor vehicles, angle collisions cause the greatest number of deaths, about 10,300 in 2000, and the greatest number of nonfatal injuries as well as fatal, injury, and all accidents. The table below shows the estimated number of motor-vehicle deaths, injuries, fatal accidents, injury accidents, and all accidents, for various types of accidents.

MOTOR-VEHICLE DEATHS AND INJURIES AND NUMBER OF ACCIDENTS BY TYPE OF ACCIDENT, 2000

Type of Accident	Deaths	Nonfatal Injuries	Fatal Accidents	Injury Accidents	All Accidents
Total	**43,000**	**2,300,000**	**38,800**	**1,500,000**	**13,400,000**
Collision with—					
Pedestrian	5,300	85,000	5,100	75,000	180,000
Other motor vehicle	20,600	1,830,000	16,800	1,080,000	9,600,000
Angle collision	*10,300*	*928,000*	*8,700*	*525,000*	*4,280,000*
Head-on collision	*6,800*	*94,000*	*5,100*	*44,000*	*230,000*
Rear-end collision	*2,700*	*726,000*	*2,300*	*460,000*	*3,990,000*
Sideswipe and other two-vehicle collisions	*800*	*82,000*	*700*	*51,000*	*1,100,000*
Railroad train	400	1,000	400	1,000	4,000
Pedalcycle	800	54,000	800	40,000	110,000
Animal, animal-drawn vehicle	100	10,000	100	10,000	490,000
Fixed object	11,200	240,000	11,100	230,000	2,646,000
Noncollision	**4,600**	**80,000**	**4,500**	**64,000**	**370,000**

Source: National Safety Council estimates, based on reports from state traffic authorities. Procedures for estimating the number of accidents by type were changed for the 1998 edition and are not comparable to estimates in previous editions (see Technical Appendix).

ESTIMATING MOTOR-VEHICLE CRASH COSTS

There are two methods currently used to measure the costs of motor-vehicle crashes. One is the *economic cost* framework and the other is the *comprehensive cost* framework.

Economic costs may be used by a community or state to estimate the economic impact of motor-vehicle crashes that occurred within its jurisdiction in a given time period. It is a measure of the productivity lost and expenses incurred because of the crashes. Economic costs, however, should not be used for cost-benefit analysis because they do not reflect what society is willing to pay to prevent a statistical fatality or injury.

There are five economic cost components: (a) wage and productivity losses, which include wages, fringe benefits, household production, and travel delay; (b) medical expenses including emergency service costs; (c) administrative expenses, which include the administrative cost of private and public insurance plus police and legal costs; (d) motor-vehicle damage including the value of damage to property; and (e) employer costs for crashes to workers.

The information below shows the average economic costs in 2000 per death (*not* per fatal crash), per injury (*not* per injury crash), and per property damage crash.

ECONOMIC COSTS, 2000

Death	**$1,000,000**
Nonfatal disabling injury	**$35,300**
Incapacitating injury[a]	$47,900
Nonincapacitating evident injury[a]	$16,000
Possible injury[a]	$9,100
Property damage crash (including minor injuries)	**$6,500**

Comprehensive costs include not only the economic cost components, but also a measure of the value of lost quality of life associated with the deaths and injuries, that is, what society is willing to pay to prevent them. The values of lost quality of life were obtained through empirical studies of what people actually pay to reduce their safety and health risks, such as through the purchase of air bags or smoke detectors. Comprehensive costs should be used for cost-benefit analysis, but because the lost quality of life represents only a dollar equivalence of intangible qualities, they do not represent real economic losses and should not be used to determine the economic impact of past crashes.

The information below shows the average comprehensive costs in 2000 on a per person basis.

COMPREHENSIVE COSTS, 2000

Death	**$3,214,290**
Incapacitating injury[a]	$159,449
Nonincapacitating evident injury[a]	$41,027
Possible injury[a]	$19,528
No injury	**$1,861**

Source: National Safety Council estimates (see the Technical Appendix) and Children's Safety Network Economics and Insurance Resource Center, Pacific Institute for Research and Evaluation.
[a] Committee on Motor Vehicle Traffic Accident Classification. (1997). Manual on Classification of Motor Vehicle Traffic Accidents, ANSI D16.1-1996 (6th ed.). Itasca, IL: National Safety Council.
Note: The National Safety Council's cost estimating procedures were extensively revised for the 1993 edition. New components were added, new benchmarks adopted and a new discount rate assumed. The costs are not comparable to those of prior years.

STATE LAWS

Currently all states and the District of Columbia have 21-year-old drinking age and child safety seat laws. Breath alcohol ignition interlock device laws are currently in effect in 40 states. Mandatory belt use laws are in effect in 49 states plus the District of Columbia. Graduated licensing is in effect in some form in 41 states and the District of Columbia.

STATE LAWS

State	Alcohol Laws				Mandatory Belt Use Law		Graduated Licensing Laws				
	Administrative License Revocation[a]	BAC Limit[b]	Zero Tolerance Limit[c] for Minors	Alcohol Ignition Interlock Device[d]	Enforcement	Seating Positions Covered by Law	Minimum Instructional Permit Period[e]	Minimum Hours of Supervised Driving[f]	Passenger Restriction	Nighttime Driving Restrictions	Unrestricted License Minimum Age[g]
Alabama	1996	0.08	0.02	no	standard	front	none	none	none	no	16 yrs.
Alaska	1983	0.10	0.00	yes	secondary	all	6 mo.	none	none	no	16 yrs.
Arizona	1992	0.10	0.00	yes	secondary	front	5 mo.	25/5	none	no	16 yrs.
Arkansas	1995	0.10	0.02	yes	secondary	front	6 mo.	none	none	no	16 yrs.
California	1989	0.08	0.01	yes[h]	standard	all	6 mo.	50/10	yes	yes	17 yrs.
Colorado	1983	0.10	0.02	yes[h]	secondary	front	6 mo.	50/10	none	yes	17 yrs.
Connecticut	1990	0.10	0.02	no	standard	front[i]	6 mo.	none	none	no	16 yrs. & 4 mo.
Delaware	yes	0.10	0.02	yes[h]	secondary	front	6 mo.	none[j]	yes	yes	16 yrs. & 10 mo.
District of Columbia	yes	0.08	0.00	no	standard	all	6 mo.	40[k]	yes	yes	18 yrs.
Florida	1990[p]	0.08	0.02	yes	secondary	front	12 mo.	50/10	none	yes	18 yrs.
Georgia	1995	0.10	0.02	yes[h]	standard	front[i]	12 mo.	40/6	yes	yes	18 yrs.
Hawaii	1990	0.08	0.00	no	standard	front[i]	3 mo.	none	no	no	16 yrs.
Idaho	1994	0.08	0.02	yes	secondary	front	4 mo.	50/10	none	yes	16 yrs.
Illinois	1986	0.08	0.00	yes[h]	secondary	front	3 mo.	25/–	yes	yes	17 yrs.
Indiana	yes	0.10	0.02	yes	standard	front	2 mo.	none	yes	yes	18 yrs.
Iowa	1982	0.10	0.02	yes	standard	front	6 mo.	20/2	none	yes	17 yrs.
Kansas	1988	0.08	0.02	yes	secondary	front	none	50/10	none	no	16 yrs.
Kentucky	no	0.08	0.02	yes[h]	secondary	all	6 mo.	none	none	yes	16 yrs. & 6 mo.
Louisiana	1984	0.10	0.02	yes	standard	front[l]	3 mo.	none	none	yes	17 yrs.
Maine	1984	0.08	0.00	yes[h]	secondary	all	3 mo.	35/5	yes	no	16 yrs. & 3 mo.
Maryland	1989	0.08[m]	0.00	yes	standard	front[i, n]	4 mo.	40/–	none	yes	17 yrs. & 7 mo.
Massachusetts	1994	0.08	0.02	no	secondary	all	6 mo.	12/–	yes	yes	18 yrs.
Michigan	no	0.10	0.02	yes	standard	front[i]	6 mo.	50/10	none	yes	17 yrs.
Minnesota	1976	0.10	0.01	no	secondary	front[i]	6 mo.	30/10	none	no	17 yrs.
Mississippi	1983	0.10	0.02	yes[h]	secondary	front	6 mo.	none	none	yes	16 yrs.
Missouri	1987	0.10	0.02	yes[h]	secondary	front[i]	6 mo.	20/–	none	yes	18 yrs.
Montana	no	0.10	0.02	yes	secondary	all	none	none	none	no	15 yrs.
Nebraska	1993	0.08	0.02	yes	secondary	front[i]	none	50/–[k]	none	yes	17 yrs.
Nevada	1983	0.10	0.02	yes[h]	secondary	all	none	50/–	none	no	16 yrs.
New Hampshire	1993	0.08	0.02	no	none	—	3 mo.	20/–	none	yes	18 yrs.
New Jersey	no	0.10	0.01	yes[h]	standard	front	6 mo.	none	yes	yes	17 yrs. & 6 mo.
New Mexico	1984	0.08	0.02	yes[h]	standard	all[o]	6 mo.	50/10	yes	yes	16 yrs. & 6 mo.
New York	1994[p]	0.10[m]	0.02	yes[h]	standard	front[i]	none	none	none	yes	17 yrs.
North Carolina	1983	0.08	0.00	yes[h]	standard	front[i]	12 mo.	none	none	yes	16 yrs. & 6 mo.
North Dakota	1983	0.10	0.02	yes[h]	secondary	front	6 mo.	none	none	no	16 yrs.
Ohio	1993	0.10	0.02	yes	secondary	front	6 mo.	50/10	none	yes	17 yrs.
Oklahoma	1983	0.10	0.00	yes	standard	front	none	none	none	no	16 yrs.
Oregon	1983	0.08	0.00	yes	standard	all	6 mo.	50/–	yes	yes	17 yrs.
Pennsylvania	no	0.10	0.02	yes[h]	secondary	front	6 mo.	50/–	none	yes	17 yrs.
Rhode Island	no	0.08	0.02	yes[h]	secondary	all	6 mo.	none	none	yes	17 yrs. & 6 mo.
South Carolina	1998	0.10	0.02	no	secondary	front[i, q]	3 mo.	none	none	yes	16 yrs. & 3 mo.
South Dakota	no	0.10	0.02	no	secondary	front	6 mo.[r]	none	none	yes	16 yrs.
Tennessee	no	0.10	0.02	yes	secondary	front[i]	6 mo.	50/10	yes	yes	17 yrs.
Texas	1995	0.08	0.00	yes[h]	standard	front	none	none	none	no	16 yrs.
Utah	1983	0.08	0.00	yes	secondary[s]	all	none	30/10	yes	yes	17 yrs.
Vermont	1969[p]	0.08	0.02(<18)	no	secondary	all	12 mo.	40/10	yes	no	16 yrs. & 6 mo.
Virginia	1995	0.08	0.02	yes	secondary	front	9 mo.	40/10	yes	yes	18 yrs.
Washington	1998	0.08	0.02	yes[h]	secondary	all	6 mo.	50/10	yes	yes	17 yrs.
West Virginia	1981	0.10	0.02	yes	secondary	front[i]	6 mo.	30/–[k]	yes	yes	17 yrs.
Wisconsin	1988	0.10[t]	0.00 (<19)	yes[h]	secondary	front[q]	6 mo.	30/10	yes	yes	16 yrs. & 9 mo.
Wyoming	1973	0.10	0.02	no	secondary	all	10 days	none	none	no	16 yrs.

Source: Offices of State Governor's Highway Safety Representatives (survey of state laws as of May 2001). Graduated licensing data adapted from Insurance Institute Highway Safety: U.S. Licensing Systems for Young Drivers, © 2001, used by permission.
Dash (—) indicates data not available.
[a] *Year original law became effective, not when grandfather clauses expired.*
[b] *Blood alcohol concentration that constitutes the threshold of legal intoxication.*
[c] *Blood alcohol concentration that constitutes "zero tolerance" threshold for minors (<21 years of age unless otherwise noted).*
[d] *Legislation for instruments designed to prevent drivers from starting their cars when breath alcohol content is at or above a set point.*
[e] *Minimum instructional periods often include time spent in driver's education classes.*
[f] *Figures shown as follows: Total hours/Nighttime hours. For example, 25/5 means 25 hours of supervised driving, 5 of which must be at night.*
[g] *Minimum age to obtain unrestricted license provided driver is crash and violation free. Alcohol restrictions still apply at least until 21.*
[h] *Primarily for repeat offenders (CA, CO, DE, GA, IL, KY, ME, MS, MO, NV, NJ, NM, NY, NC, ND, PA, RI, TX, WI). Under certain circumstances, a judge may order interlock installation.*
[i] *Required for certain ages at all seating positions.*
[j] *No minimum amount of supervised driving but with level 1 permit driving has to be supervised at all times for the first 6 months.*
[k] *DC: 40 hours of supervised driving during learner's stage; 10 hours at night during intermediate stage. NE, WV: none if driver's education course completed.*
[l] *Front for all occupants and back seat occupants 17 and under in FL and HI, and through age 12 in LA.*
[m] *BAC of 0.07 is prima facie evidence of DUI (MD). BAC of 0.05–0.10 constitutes driving while ability impaired (NY).*
[n] *Excluding front center seat. Required for all seats for occupants under 16.*
[o] *Legislation pending governor's signature.*
[p] *Revocation by judicial action (NY) or Department of Motor Vehicles (VT).*
[q] *Belt use required in rear seat if lap/shoulder belt is available.*
[r] *Three-month instructional period with driver's education.*
[s] *Secondary for 19 and older, standard for under 19.*
[t] *0.08 after second DUI conviction.*

Young drivers between the ages of 15 and 20 years of age represent about 7% of all licensed drivers in the United States, yet they are involved in 15% of all fatal crashes and 18% of all police-reported crashes. Motor-vehicle crashes were the leading cause of death for 15–20 year olds in 1998 (see page 30). Key risk factors for deaths among the young driver group include driver inexperience, male gender, speeding, low rates of safety belt use, driving at night, and alcohol or drug use.

Since experience level is an important factor—the fatality rate decreases sharply after the second year of driving—many states have developed graduated licensing systems to help provide teenagers with sufficient opportunity to acquire the necessary experience and develop good driving skills while protecting them from high-risk situations. A full graduated licensing system consists of three tiers: a learner's permit; a provisional license, usually awarded after six months of infraction-free driving; and a full license, usually awarded after two years of infraction-free driving. During the learner's permit phase, teenagers may drive only when accompanied by an adult, and not at night. During the provisional phase, driving with a parent or adult is not required, but the number and/or ages of other passengers is often restricted to avoid distractions. Each phase includes zero alcohol tolerance and mandatory safety belt use.

An evaluation of the full graduated licensing program in the state of Florida for drivers less than 18 years of age found a 9% reduction in the fatal and injury crash involvement rate during 1997, the first full year of the program, compared with 1995, the last full year without graduated licensing. Crash rate ratios were derived by dividing the crash rate for each target age group by the rate for 25–54-year-old drivers, employed as a reference group. On a percentage basis, crash rate ratios declined 19% among 15-year-olds, 11% among 16-year-olds, and 7% among 17-year-olds. No difference in crash reduction was observed for males compared with females. However, there was a larger reduction among white than nonwhite teenagers and in urban versus rural areas. In addition, nighttime crash involvement declined on a percentage basis more than daytime crashes. Reductions were not seen among a comparison group of Alabama teenagers not subject to a graduated licensing law, nor were they seen among 18-year-olds in Florida.

A survey of parents of 15-year-olds in Connecticut and Florida and graduating seniors in Connecticut and three other northeastern states revealed strong support for graduated licensing in all six populations. The Connecticut and Florida parents endorsed their new licensing systems even though there was recognition that they and their children would be inconvenienced by its provisions, and many indicated a desire for even tougher licensing provisions.

Source: National Center for Statistics and Analysis. (2000). Traffic Safety Facts 1999—Young Drivers. *Washington, DC: National Highway Traffic Safety Administration. Schieber, R. A., Gilchrist, J., Sleet, D. A. (2000). Legislative and regulatory strategies to reduce childhood unintentional injuries.* The Future of Children, 10 (1), 111-136. Ulmer, R. G. et al. (2000). Effect of Florida's graduated licensing program on the crash rate of teenage drivers. Accident Analysis and Prevention, 32 (4), 527-532. Williams, A. F. et al. (1998). Views of parents of teenagers about graduated licensing systems. *Journal of Safety Research, 29 (1), 1-7.*

CHANGES IN CRASH RATE RATIOS FOLLOWING IMPLEMENTATION OF GRADUATED LICENSING (GDL) PROGRAM

Driver Age	Percent Change 1997 vs. 1995	
	Florida	Alabama
15	-19	-7
16	-11	2
17	-7	2
18	0	0

Ulmer, R.G. et al. (2000). Effect of Florida's graduated licensing program on the crash rate of teenage drivers. Accident Analysis and Prevention; 32 (4), 527–532.

ALCOHOL

According to studies conducted by the National Highway Traffic Safety Administration (NHTSA), about 38% of all traffic fatalities in 1999 involved an intoxicated or alcohol-impaired driver or nonmotorist. In 1999, 30% of all traffic fatalities occurred in crashes where at least one driver or nonoccupant was intoxicated (blood alcohol concentration [BAC] of 0.10 or greater). Of the 12,321 people killed in such crashes, 70% were themselves intoxicated. The other 30% were passengers, nonintoxicated drivers, or nonintoxicated nonoccpants. The following data summarizes the extent of alcohol involvement in motor-vehicle crashes:

• Traffic fatalities in alcohol-related crashes fell by 1% from 1998 to 1999 and declined by 30% from 1989 to 1999. (See corresponding chart.) In 1989, alcohol-related fatalities accounted for 49% of all traffic deaths.

• According to NHTSA, alcohol was involved in 38% of fatal crashes and 7% of all crashes, both fatal and nonfatal, in 1999.

• Approximately 1.4 million drivers were arrested in 1998 for driving under the influence of alcohol or narcotics.

• About 3 in every 10 Americans will be involved in an alcohol-related crash at some time in their lives.

• There were 15,786 alcohol-related traffic fatalities in 1999, an average of one alcohol-related fatality every 33 minutes. An average of one person every 2 minutes is injured in a crash where alcohol is present.

• In 1999, alcohol was present in 29% of all fatal crashes on weekdays, compared to 51% on weekends. The rate of alcohol involvement in fatal crashes during the day is 17%, compared to 60% at night.

PERCENT OF TOTAL TRAFFIC FATALITIES WITH ALCOHOL PRESENT, BY STATE, 1999

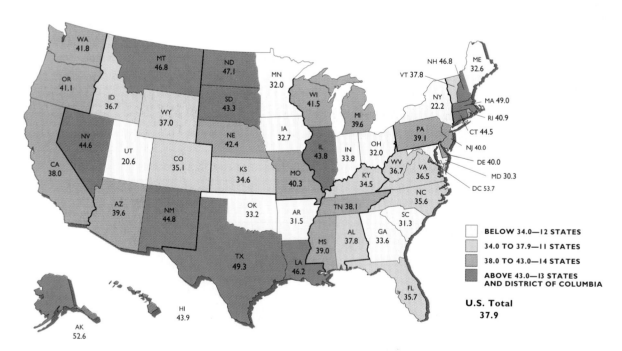

- From 1989 to 1999, intoxication rates decreased for drivers of all age groups. The greatest decrease was for 16-to-20-year-old drivers (30%). NHTSA estimates that 19,121 lives have been saved by 21-year-old minimum drinking age laws since 1975. All states and the District of Columbia now have such laws.

- Safety belts were used by about 19% of fatally injured intoxicated drivers, compared to 30% of fatally injured alcohol-impaired drivers and 48% of fatally injured sober drivers.

- The driver, pedestrian, or both were intoxicated in 38% of all fatal pedestrian traffic accidents in 1999. In these crashes, the intoxication rate for pedestrians was more than double the rate for drivers.

- The cost of alcohol-related motor-vehicle accidents is estimated by the National Safety Council at $29.1 billion in 2000.

Source: National Center for Statistics and Analysis. (2000). Traffic Safety Facts 1999—Alcohol. Washington, DC: National Highway Traffic Safety Administration.

PERCENT OF ALL TRAFFIC FATALITIES THAT OCCURRED IN ALCOHOL-RELATED CRASHES, 1989–1999

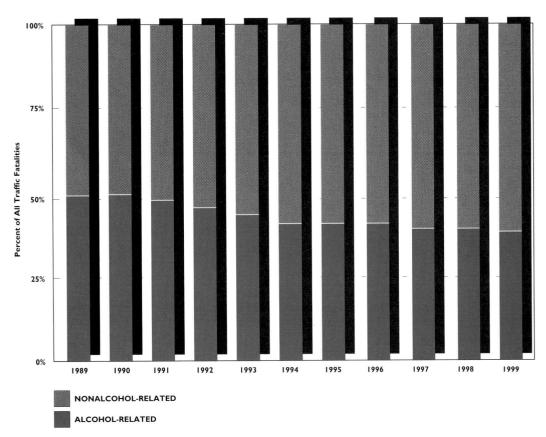

NONALCOHOL-RELATED

ALCOHOL-RELATED

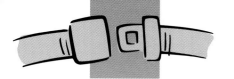

OCCUPANT PROTECTION

Safety Belts

- When used, lap/shoulder safety belts reduce the risk of fatal injury to front seat passenger car occupants by 45% and reduce the risk of moderate-to-critical injury by 50%.

- For light truck occupants, safety belts reduce the risk of fatal injury by 60% and moderate-to-critical injury by 65%.

- Forty-nine states and the District of Columbia have mandatory belt use laws in effect, the only exception being New Hampshire. Thirty-three of the states with belt use laws in effect in 1999 specified secondary enforcement (i.e., police officers are permitted to write a citation only after a vehicle is stopped for some other traffic infraction). Sixteen states and the District of Columbia had laws that allowed primary enforcement, enabling officers to stop vehicles and write citations whenever they observe violations of the belt law.

- Safety belts saved an estimated 11,197 lives in 1999 among passenger vehicle occupants over 4 years old. An *additional* 9,553 lives could have been saved in 1999 if all passenger vehicle occupants over age 4 wore safety belts. From 1975 through 1999, an estimated 123,213 lives were saved by safety belts.

- Safety belts provide the greatest protection against occupant ejection. Among crashes in which a fatality occurred in 1999, only 1% of restrained passenger car occupants were ejected, compared to 22% of unrestrained occupants.

- The results of a 1995 study by the National Highway Traffic Safety Administration suggest that belt use among fatally injured occupants was at least 15% higher in states with primary enforcement laws.

Air Bags

- Air bags, combined with lap/shoulder belts, offer the best available protection for passenger vehicle occupants. The overall fatality-reducing effectiveness for air bags is estimated at 11% over and above the benefits from using safety belts alone.

- Lap/shoulder belts should always be used, even in a vehicle with an air bag. Air bags are a supplemental form of protection and are not designed to deploy in crashes that are not severe.

- Children in rear-facing child seats should not be placed in the front seat of vehicles equipped with passenger-side air bags. The impact of the deploying air bag could result in injury to the child.

- An estimated 1,263 lives were saved by air bags in 1999 and a total of 4,969 lives were saved from 1987 through 1999.

- Beginning September 1997, all new passenger cars were required to have driver and passenger side air bags. In 1998, the same requirement went into effect for light trucks.

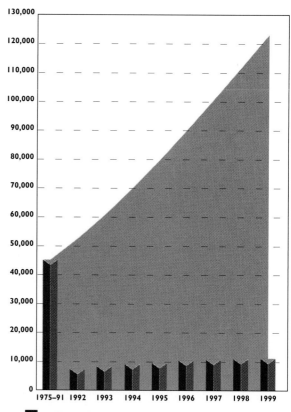

ESTIMATED LIVES SAVED BY SAFETY BELT USE, 1975–1999

- ■ LIVES SAVED—SAFETY BELTS
- ▨ CUMULATIVE LIVES SAVED—SAFETY BELTS

Child Restraints

- Child restraints saved an estimated 307 lives in 1999 among children under the age of 5. Of the 307 lives saved, 277 were attributed to the use of child safety seats while 30 lives were spared with the use of adult belts.

- At 100% child safety seat use for children under the age of 5, an estimated additional 162 lives could have been saved in 1999.

- All states and the District of Columbia have had child restraint use laws in effect since 1985.

- Research has shown that child safety seats reduce fatal injury in passenger cars by 71% for infants (less than 1 year old), and by 54% for toddlers (1–4 years old). For infants and toddlers in light trucks, the corresponding reductions are 58% and 59%, respectively.

- In 1999, there were 550 occupant fatalities among children less than 5 years of age. Of these, an estimated 53% were totally unrestrained.

- An estimated 4,500 lives have been saved by child restraints from 1975 through 1999.

Motorcycle Helmets

- Motorcycle helmets are estimated to be 29% effective in preventing fatal injuries to motorcyclists.

- Helmets saved the lives of 551 motorcyclists in 1999. An additional 326 lives could have been saved if all motorcyclists had worn helmets.

- According to the latest observational survey by the National Highway Traffic Safety Administration (NHTSA), helmet use was at 67% in 1998. Previous NHTSA surveys have reported helmet use to be essentially 100% in areas with helmet use laws governing all riders, compared to 34% to 54% at sites with no helmet use laws or laws limited to minors. Reported helmet use rates for fatally injured motorcyclists in 1999 were 55% for operators and 47% for passengers, compared with 54% and 45%, respectively, in 1998.

- In 1999, 21 states, the District of Columbia, and Puerto Rico required helmet use by all motorcycle operators and passengers. In another 26 states, only persons under 18 were required to wear helmets. Three states had no laws requiring helmet use.

Source: National Center for Statistics and Analysis. (2000). Traffic Safety Facts 1999–Occupant Protection; Traffic Safety Facts 1999–Motorcycles. *Washington, DC: National Highway Traffic Safety Administration.*

ESTIMATED LIVES SAVED BY CHILD RESTRAINTS AND AIR BAGS, 1975–1999

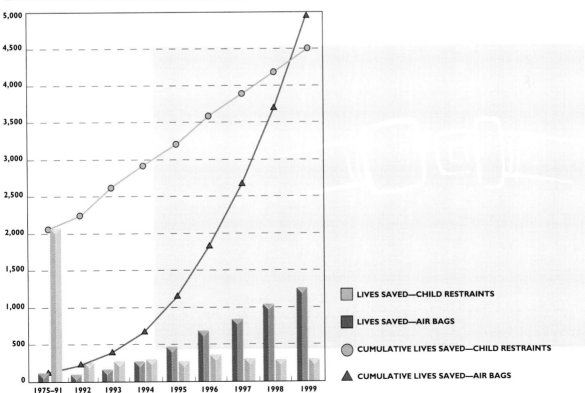

DEATHS AND DEATH RATES
BY DAY AND NIGHT

About 55% of all motor-vehicle deaths in 2000 occurred during the day, while the remainder occurred at night. Death rates based on mileage, however, were nearly two and one-half times higher at night than during the day with vehicle miles traveled by night representing only 25% of the total.

Source: State traffic authorities and the Federal Highway Administration.

DEATH RATES BY DAY AND NIGHT, 2000

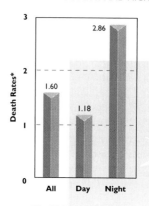

Per 100,000,000 vehicle miles

DEATHS AND MILEAGE DEATH RATES
BY MONTH

Motor-vehicle deaths in 2000 were at their lowest level in February and increased to their highest level in July. In 2000, the highest monthly mileage death rate of 1.75

deaths per 100,000,000 vehicle miles occurred in January. The overall rate for the year was 1.60.

Source: Deaths—National Safety Council estimates. Mileage—Federal Highway Administration, Traffic Volume Trends.

MOTOR-VEHICLE DEATHS AND MILEAGE DEATH RATES BY MONTH, 2000

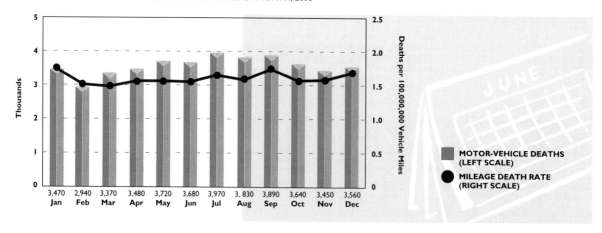

MOTOR-VEHICLE ACCIDENTS
BY TIME OF DAY AND DAY OF WEEK

More fatal accidents occurred on Saturday than any other day of the week in 2000, according to reports from state traffic authorities. Over 18% of fatal accidents occurred on Saturday, compared to about 12% each on Tuesdays and Wednesdays. For all accidents, Friday had the highest percentage with about 17%.

Patterns by hour of day for fatal accidents show peaks during afternoon rush hour for weekdays and, especially, late night for weekends. For all accidents, peaks occur during both morning and afternoon rush hour.

PERCENT OF WEEKLY ACCIDENTS BY HOUR OF DAY AND DAY OF WEEK, UNITED STATES, 2000

Time of Day	Fatal Accidents								All Accidents							
	Total	Mon.	Tues.	Wed.	Thurs.	Fri.	Sat.	Sun.	Total	Mon.	Tues.	Wed.	Thurs.	Fri.	Sat.	Sun.
All Hours	100.0%	12.7%	12.0%	12.0%	13.1%	15.5%	18.4%	16.4%	100.0%	14.2%	14.3%	14.5%	14.7%	16.9%	14.0%	11.5%
Midnight–3:59 A.M.	15.1%	1.4%	1.3%	1.2%	1.5%	1.9%	4.0%	3.7%	6.5%	0.6%	0.5%	0.6%	0.6%	0.8%	1.7%	1.7%
4:00–7:59 A.M.	11.9%	1.5%	1.5%	1.5%	1.7%	1.8%	1.9%	2.0%	10.1%	1.6%	1.7%	1.7%	1.7%	1.6%	0.9%	0.8%
8:00–11:59 A.M.	13.5%	2.1%	1.8%	1.8%	2.0%	2.0%	2.0%	1.8%	17.9%	2.8%	2.8%	2.7%	2.8%	2.8%	2.3%	1.6%
Noon–3:59 P.M.	18.3%	2.5%	2.4%	2.4%	2.7%	2.7%	2.8%	2.8%	25.8%	3.8%	3.7%	3.8%	3.7%	4.5%	3.5%	2.8%
4:00–7:59 P.M.	22.2%	3.1%	2.9%	3.0%	2.7%	3.4%	3.7%	3.4%	26.9%	3.9%	4.0%	4.1%	4.1%	4.8%	3.2%	2.8%
8:00–11:59 P.M.	19.1%	2.1%	2.0%	2.2%	2.6%	3.7%	4.0%	2.6%	12.7%	1.5%	1.5%	1.6%	1.7%	2.4%	2.3%	1.7%

Source: Based on reports from nine state traffic authorities.
Note: Column and row totals may not equal sums of parts due to rounding.

PERCENT OF ACCIDENTS BY TIME OF DAY AND DAY OF WEEK, 2000

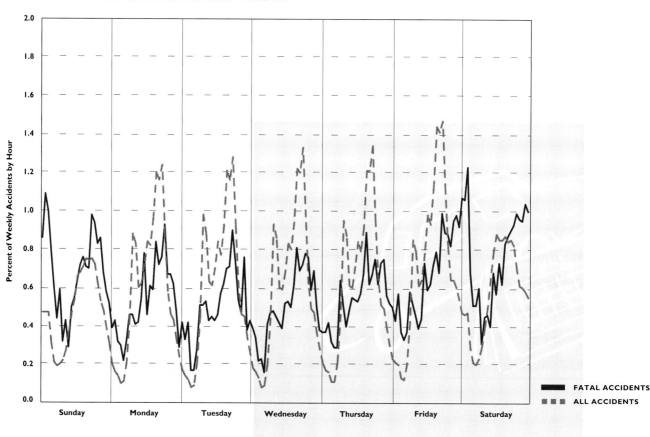

TYPE OF MOTOR VEHICLE

The types of vehicles listed in the table below are classified by body style, not by vehicle use. The light truck category includes both commercial and noncommercial trucks under 10,000 pounds gross vehicle weight. It also includes minivans and sport-utility vehicles. The medium/heavy truck category includes truck tractors with or without semi-trailers.

Passenger Cars

In 2000, passenger cars comprised about 60% of the registered vehicles and were involved in more than their share of motor-vehicle accidents (63.4%). Approximately three fifths of all motor-vehicle occupant fatalities are passenger car occupants. (See corresponding chart.)

Trucks

Light trucks represent about 35% of all motor-vehicle registrations and about 35% of vehicles involved in fatal accidents. Medium and heavy trucks account for over 2% of registered vehicles and about 8% of vehicles involved in fatal accidents. Medium and heavy truck occupants as well as light truck occupants are slightly under-represented in motor-vehicle occupant fatalities compared to their proportion of registrations. Medium and heavy truck occupants account for only about 2%

of all motor-vehicle occupant fatalities and light truck occupants account for 31%.

There were 847,000 light truck occupants and 33,000 large truck occupants injured in 1999, according to the National Highway Traffic Safety Administration.

Motorcycles

The number of registered motorcycles in the United States totaled about 4,100,000 in 2000, compared to approximately 4,300,000 a decade earlier. Although motorcycles accounted for less than 2% of the total 224,000,000 vehicle registrations in 2000, they were over-represented in the distribution of fatalities by type of vehicle. Of the 36,800 occupant deaths in motor-vehicle accidents in 2000, about 3,400 (9%) were motorcycle riders. Approximately 50,000 riders and passengers were injured in 1999 according to the National Highway Traffic Safety Administration.

Motorcycles traveled an estimated 10.9 billion miles in 2000. The 2000 mileage death rate for motorcycle riders is estimated to be about 31 occupant deaths per 100,000,000 miles of motorcycle travel, about 24 times the mileage death rate for occupants of other types of vehicles (passenger autos, trucks, buses, etc.).

TYPES OF MOTOR VEHICLES INVOLVED IN ACCIDENTS, 2000

Type of Vehicle	In Fatal Accidents		In All Accidents		Percent of Total Vehicle Registrations[a]	No. of Occupant Fatalities
	Number	Percent	Number	Percent		
All Types	**61,400**	**100.0%**	**25,100,000**	**100.0%**	**100.0%**	**36,800[b]**
Passenger cars	30,200	49.2	15,920,000	63.4	60.1	20,500
Trucks	26,400	43.0	8,800,000	35.0	37.7	11,840
Light trucks	21,300	34.7	7,940,000	31.6	35.4	11,100
Medium/heavy trucks	5,100	8.3	860,000	3.4	2.4	740
Farm tractor, equipment	100	0.2	7,000	[c]	[d]	40
Buses, commercial	200	0.3	95,000	0.4	0.1	50
Buses, school	100	0.2	77,000	0.3	0.3	10
Motorcycles	3,400	5.5	130,000	0.5	} 1.9	3,400
Motor scooters, motor bikes	100	0.2	3,000	[c]		100
Other	900	1.5	68,000	0.3	[d]	860

Source: Based on reports from 14 state traffic authorities. Vehicle registrations based on data from Federal Highway Administration. Estimating procedures were changed for the 1998 edition and are not comparable to estimates in previous editions.
[a] Percentage figures are based on numbers of vehicles and do not reflect miles traveled or place of travel, both of which affect accident experience. Percents may not add due to rounding.
[b] In addition to these occupant fatalities, there were 5,300 pedestrian, 800 pedalcyclist, and 100 other deaths.
[c] Less than 0.05%.
[d] Data not available.

REGISTRATIONS, INVOLVEMENTS, AND OCCUPANT FATALITIES BY TYPE OF VEHICLE, 2000

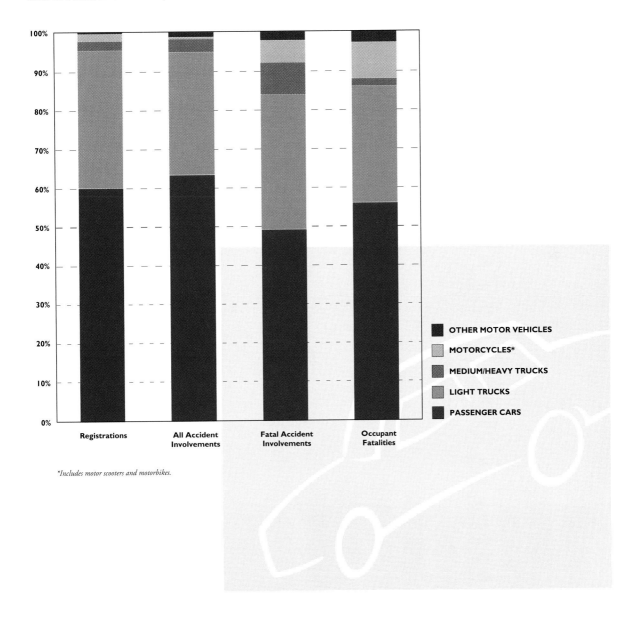

*Includes motor scooters and motorbikes.

School bus-related crashes killed 164 persons and injured an estimated 18,000 persons nationwide in 1999, according to data from the National Highway Traffic Safety Administration's (NHTSA) Fatality Analysis Reporting System (FARS) and General Estimates System (GES).

A school bus-related crash is defined by NHTSA to be any crash in which a vehicle, regardless of body design, used as a school bus is directly or indirectly involved, such as a crash involving school children alighting from a vehicle.

Over the past six years, about 70% of the deaths in fatal school bus-related crashes were occupants of vehicles other than the school bus and 20% were pedestrians. About 4% were school bus passengers and 2% were school bus drivers.

Of the pedestrians killed in school bus-related crashes over this period, approximately 77% were struck by the school bus.

Out of the people injured in school bus-related crashes from 1994 through 1999, about 44% were school bus passengers, 9% were school bus drivers, and another 43% were occupants of other vehicles. The remainder were pedestrians, pedalcyclists, and other or unknown type persons.

Characteristics of school bus transportation
School Bus Fleet (www.schoolbusfleet.com/stats.cfm) found that in the 1997–1998 school year, 44 states reported about 21.3 million public school pupils were transported at public expense and 29 states reported another 0.9 million private school pupils were transported at public expense. This compares to estimates from the U.S. Department of Education of enrollments in grades K–12 of about 46.8 million public school pupils and 5.9 million private school pupils nationwide. About 442,000 school buses were reported in use in 49 states and the District of Columbia and the buses in 40 states traveled about 3.2 billion route miles.

FATALITIES IN SCHOOL BUS-RELATED CRASHES, U.S., 1990–1999

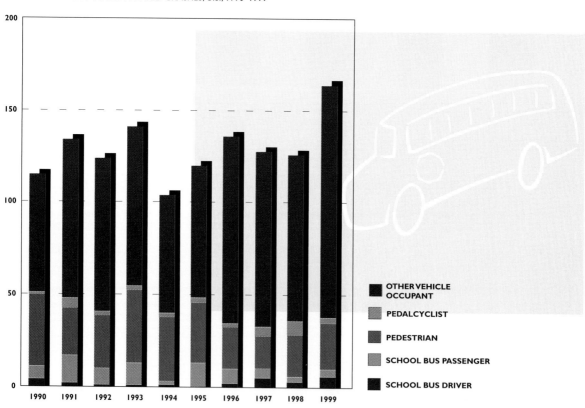

DEATHS AND INJURIES IN SCHOOL BUS-RELATED CRASHES, U.S., 1994–1999

	1994	1995	1996	1997	1998	1999
Deaths						
Total	104	121	136	128	126	164
School bus driver	1	0	2	5	3	6
School bus passenger	2	13	8	5	3	4
Pedestrian	35	33	23	18	23	25
Pedalcyclist	2	3	2	5	7	3
Occupant of other vehicle	64	71	101	95	90	126
Other or Unknown	0	1	0	0	0	0
Injuries						
Total	18,000	18,000	15,000	19,000	17,000	18,000
School bus driver	1,000	2,000	1,000	2,000	2,000	1,000
School bus passenger	8,000	7,000	7,000	10,000	6,000	8,000
Pedestrian	1,000	(a)	(a)	(a)	(a)	(a)
Pedalcyclist	(a)	(a)	(a)	(a)	(a)	(a)
Occupant of other vehicle	7,000	8,000	6,000	7,000	9,000	8,000
Other or Unknown	(a)	(a)	(a)	(a)	(a)	(a)

Source: National Highway Traffic Safety Administration. Traffic Safety Facts, 1994-1999 editions. Washington, DC: Author.
a Less than 500.

PEDESTRIAN DEATHS IN SCHOOL BUS-RELATED CRASHES, U.S., 1994–1999

		Age Group			
	All Ages	**Under 5**	**5–9**	**10–15**	**16 and older**
1994	35	2	15	8	10
Struck by bus	27	2	9	7	9
1995	33	3	12	7	11
Struck by bus	23	3	7	2	11
1996	23	1	11	3	8
Struck by bus	16	0	7	1	8
1997	18	0	8	3	7
Struck by bus	16	0	6	3	7
1998	23	3	9	1	10
Struck by bus	20	3	6	1	10
1999	25	0	13	4	8
Struck by bus	19	0	10	2	7

Source: National Highway Traffic Safety Administration. Traffic Safety Facts, 1994-1999 editions. Washington, DC: Author.

AGE OF DRIVER

The table below shows the total number of licensed drivers and drivers involved in accidents by selected ages and age groups. The figures in the last two columns indicate the frequency of accident involvement on the basis of the number of drivers in each age group. The fatal accident involvement rates per 100,000 drivers in each age group ranged from a low of 22 for drivers 55 to 64 years of age to a high of 89 for drivers 19 and under. The all accident involvement rates per 100 drivers in each age group ranged from 8 for drivers in the 65 to 74 and 75 and over age groups to 42 for drivers 19 and under.

On the basis of miles driven by each age group, however, involvement rates (not shown in the table) are highest for young and old drivers. For drivers aged 16 to 19, the fatal involvement rate per 100 million vehicle miles traveled was 9.2 in 1990, about three times the overall rate for all drivers in passenger vehicles, 3.0. The rate for drivers aged 75 and over was 11.5, the highest of all age groups. The same basic "U"-shaped curve is found for injury accident involvement rates.[a]

[a] Massie, D., Campbell, K., & Williams, A. (1995). Traffic accident involvement rates by driver age and gender. Accident Analysis and Prevention, 27 (1), 73-87.

AGE OF DRIVER—TOTAL NUMBER AND NUMBER IN ACCIDENTS, 2000

| Age Group | Licensed Drivers | | Drivers in Accidents | | | | | |
| | Number | Percent | Fatal | | All | | Per No. of Drivers | |
			Number	Percent	Number	Percent	Fatal[a]	All[b]
Total	**189,800,000**	**100.0%**	**61,400**	**100.0%**	**25,100,000**	**100.0%**	**32**	**13**
Under 16	31,000	([c])	600	1.0	180,000	0.7	([d])	([d])
16	1,448,000	0.8	1,600	2.6	840,000	3.3	110	58
17	2,310,000	1.2	2,000	3.3	1,030,000	4.1	87	45
18	2,849,000	1.5	2,300	3.7	1,020,000	4.1	81	36
19	2,986,000	1.6	2,100	3.4	960,000	3.8	70	32
19 and under	9,624,000	5.1	8,600	14.0	4,030,000	16.1	89	42
20	3,251,000	1.7	2,000	3.3	870,000	3.5	62	27
21	3,191,000	1.7	1,600	2.6	480,000	1.9	50	15
22	3,173,000	1.7	1,300	2.1	440,000	1.8	41	14
23	3,284,000	1.7	1,300	2.1	400,000	1.6	40	12
24	3,182,000	1.7	1,000	1.6	370,000	1.5	31	12
20–24	16,081,000	8.5	7,200	11.7	2,560,000	10.2	45	16
25–34	35,915,000	18.9	11,600	18.9	5,540,000	22.1	32	15
35–44	41,815,000	22.0	12,200	19.9	5,240,000	20.9	29	13
45–54	36,573,000	19.3	9,300	15.1	3,690,000	14.7	25	10
55–64	22,778,000	12.0	5,000	8.1	1,960,000	7.8	22	9
65–74	15,741,000	8.3	3,700	6.0	1,190,000	4.7	24	8
75 and over	11,273,000	5.9	3,800	6.2	890,000	3.5	34	8

Source: National Safety Council estimates. Drivers in accidents based on reports from 13 state traffic authorities. Total licensed drivers from the Federal Highway Administration; age distribution by National Safety Council.
Note: Percents may not add to total due to rounding.
[a] Drivers in fatal accidents per 100,000 licensed drivers in each age group.
[b] Drivers in all accidents per 100 licensed drivers in each age group.
[c] Less than 0.05.
[d] Rates for drivers under age 16 are substantially overstated due to the high proportion of unlicensed drivers involved.

Of the estimated 189,800,000 licensed drivers in 2000, about 95,469,000 (50.3%) were males and 94,331,000 (49.7%) were females. Males account for about 63% of the miles driven each year, according to the latest estimates, and females for 37%. At least part of the difference in involvement rates, cited below, may be due to differences in the time, place, and circumstances of driving.

For fatal accidents, males have higher involvement rates than females. About 45,600 male drivers and 15,800 female drivers were involved in fatal accidents in 2000. The involvement rate per one billion miles driven was 27 for males and 16 for females. For all accidents, females have higher involvement rates than males. About 15,200,000 male drivers and 9,900,000 female drivers were involved in all accidents in 2000. Their involvement rates per 10 million miles driven were 90 and 100, respectively.

In most motor-vehicle accidents, factors are present relating to the driver, the vehicle, and the road, and it is the interaction of these factors that often sets up the series of events that results in an accident. The table below relates only to the driver, and shows the principal kinds of improper driving in accidents in 2000 as reported by police.

Exceeding the posted speed limit or driving at an unsafe speed was the most common error in fatal accidents. Right-of-way violations predominated in the injury and all accidents categories.

While some drivers were under the influence of alcohol or other drugs, this represents the driver's physical condition—not a driving error. See page 90 for a discussion of alcohol involvement in traffic accidents.

Correcting the improper practices listed below could reduce the number of accidents. This does not mean, however, that road and vehicle conditions can be disregarded.

IMPROPER DRIVING REPORTED IN ACCIDENTS, 2000

Kind of Improper Driving	Fatal Accidents	Injury Accidents	All Accidents
Total	**100.0%**	**100.0%**	**100.0%**
Improper driving	**61.6**	**60.3**	**57.8**
Speed too fast or unsafe	23.7	16.3	13.6
Right of way	18.6	19.9	20.1
Failed to yield	*10.1*	*15.0*	*12.7*
Disregarded signal	*4.6*	*3.6*	*5.3*
Passed stop sign	*3.8*	*1.3*	*2.2*
Drove left of center	8.2	1.1	1.0
Made improper turn	0.7	2.0	2.4
Improper overtaking	0.9	0.6	0.9
Followed too closely	0.5	4.3	5.7
Other improper driving	9.0	16.1	14.1
No improper driving stated	**38.4**	**39.7**	**42.2**

Source: Based on reports from seven state traffic authorities.

MOTOR-VEHICLE DEATHS BY STATE, UNITED STATES, 1997–2000

| | Motor-Vehicle Traffic Deaths (Place of Accident) | | | | Total Motor-Vehicle Deaths[a] (Place of Residence) | | | |
| | Number | | Mileage Rate[b] | | Number | | Population Rate[b] | |
State	2000	1999	2000	1999	1998[c]	1997	1998	1997
Total U.S.[a]	**43,000**	**43,000**	**1.6**	**1.6**	**43,501**	**43,458**	**16.1**	**16.2**
Alabama	990	1,107	1.8	2.0	1,103	1,211	25.4	28.0
Alaska	103	76	2.3	1.7	72	85	11.7	14.0
Arizona	1,036	1,024	2.2	2.2	941	971	20.2	21.3
Arkansas	652	602	2.2	2.1	680	692	26.8	27.4
California	3,730	3,204	1.2	1.1	3,779	3,749	11.6	11.6
Colorado	679	—	1.7	—	663	648	16.7	16.7
Connecticut	342	301	1.1	1.0	341	337	10.4	10.3
Delaware	128	103	1.5	1.2	116	142	15.6	19.3
Dist. of Columbia	52	46	1.5	1.4	56	87	10.7	16.5
Florida	2,998	2,920	2.1	2.1	2,941	2,840	19.7	19.3
Georgia	1,548	1,514	1.6	1.5	1,657	1,618	21.7	21.6
Hawaii	133	98	1.6	1.2	124	138	10.4	11.6
Idaho	275	278	2.0	2.0	269	283	21.9	23.4
Illinois	1,414	1,456	1.4	1.4	1,521	1,261	12.6	10.5
Indiana	892	1,019	1.3	1.5	1,046	960	17.7	16.3
Iowa	445	489	1.5	1.7	462	484	16.1	17.0
Kansas	461	532	1.7	1.9	550	487	20.8	18.6
Kentucky	824	819	1.7	1.7	823	845	20.9	21.6
Louisiana	937	923	2.3	2.2	983	963	22.5	22.1
Maine	167	179	1.2	1.3	180	201	14.4	16.1
Maryland	617	598	1.3	1.2	647	627	12.6	12.3
Massachusetts	433	414	0.8	0.8	485	486	7.9	7.9
Michigan	1,382	1,386	1.4	1.4	1,472	1,472	15.0	15.0
Minnesota	625	626	1.2	1.2	674	565	14.3	12.1
Mississippi	949	926	2.7	2.7	963	892	35.0	32.7
Missouri	1,157	1,094	1.7	1.7	1,147	1,276	21.1	23.6
Montana	237	220	2.4	2.2	219	270	24.9	30.7
Nebraska	276	295	1.5	1.6	346	305	20.8	18.4
Nevada	325	350	1.9	2.0	349	400	20.0	23.9
New Hampshire	126	141	1.1	1.2	140	143	11.8	12.2
New Jersey	732	665	1.1	1.0	783	814	9.7	10.1
New Mexico	437	461	2.0	2.0	385	503	22.2	29.2
New York	1,353	1,473	1.1	1.2	1,686	1,719	9.3	9.5
North Carolina	1,563	1,506	1.8	1.7	1,672	1,588	22.2	21.4
North Dakota	86	119	1.2	1.6	118	126	18.5	19.7
Ohio	1,249	1,430	1.2	1.3	1,451	1,407	12.9	12.5
Oklahoma	658	740	1.5	1.7	777	852	23.3	25.7
Oregon	451	413	1.3	1.2	550	566	16.8	17.5
Pennsylvania	—	1,549	—	1.5	1,661	1,648	13.8	13.7
Rhode Island	81	88	1.0	1.1	86	91	8.7	9.2
South Carolina	1,061	1,064	2.4	2.4	992	917	25.8	24.2
South Dakota	173	150	2.1	1.8	165	155	22.6	21.2
Tennessee	1,235	1,282	1.9	2.0	1,223	1,445	22.5	26.9
Texas	3,519	3,517	1.7	1.7	3,769	3,736	19.1	19.3
Utah	376	360	1.7	1.7	395	403	18.8	19.5
Vermont	79	92	1.2	1.4	82	86	13.9	14.6
Virginia	930	877	1.3	1.2	942	962	13.9	14.3
Washington	630	637	1.2	1.2	750	704	13.2	12.6
West Virginia	410	395	2.2	2.1	375	406	20.7	22.4
Wisconsin	801	745	1.4	1.3	755	759	14.5	14.6
Wyoming	152	189	2.0	2.3	135	133	28.1	27.7

Source: Motor-Vehicle Traffic Deaths are provisional counts from state traffic authorities; Total Motor-Vehicle Deaths are from the National Center for Health Statistics (see also page 156).
[a] *Includes both traffic and nontraffic motor-vehicle deaths. See definitions of motor-vehicle traffic and nontraffic accidents on page 167.*
[b] *The mileage death rate is deaths per 100,000,000 vehicle miles; the population death rate is deaths per 100,000 population. Death rates are National Safety Council estimates.*
[c] *Latest year available. See Technical Appendix for comparability.*
Note: Dash (—) indicates data not reported.

MILEAGE DEATH RATES, 2000
MOTOR-VEHICLE TRAFFIC DEATHS PER 100,000,000 VEHICLE MILES

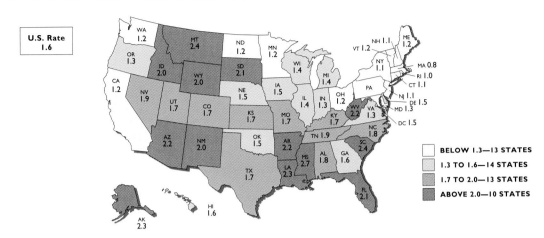

U.S. Rate
1.6

WA 1.2
MT 2.4
ND 1.2
MN 1.2
OR 1.3
ID 2.0
WY 2.0
SD 2.1
WI 1.4
MI 1.4
CA 1.2
NV 1.9
UT 1.7
CO 1.7
NE 1.5
IA 1.5
IL 1.4
IN 1.3
OH 1.2
PA
AZ 2.2
NM 2.0
KS 1.7
MO 1.7
KY 1.7
WV 2.2
VA 1.3
NC 1.8
OK 1.5
AR 2.2
TN 1.9
SC 2.4
TX 1.7
LA 2.3
MS 2.7
AL 1.8
GA 1.6
FL 2.1
AK 2.3
HI 1.6
VT 1.2
NH 1.1
ME 1.2
NY 1.1
MA 0.8
RI 1.0
CT 1.1
NJ 1.1
DE 1.5
MD 1.3
DC 1.5

BELOW 1.3—13 STATES
1.3 TO 1.6—14 STATES
1.7 TO 2.0—13 STATES
ABOVE 2.0—10 STATES

REGISTRATION DEATH RATES, 2000
MOTOR-VEHICLE TRAFFIC DEATHS PER 10,000 MOTOR VEHICLES

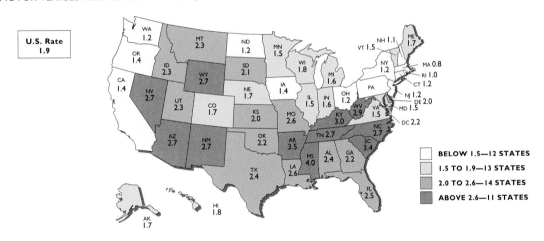

U.S. Rate
1.9

WA 1.2
MT 2.3
ND 1.2
MN 1.5
OR 1.4
ID 2.3
WY 2.7
SD 2.1
WI 1.8
MI 1.6
CA 1.4
NV 2.7
UT 2.3
CO 1.7
NE 1.7
IA 1.4
IL 1.5
IN 1.6
OH 1.2
PA
AZ 2.7
NM 2.7
KS 2.0
MO 2.6
KY 3.0
WV 2.9
VA 1.5
NC 2.7
OK 2.2
AR 3.5
TN 2.7
SC 3.4
TX 2.4
LA 2.6
MS 4.0
AL 2.4
GA 2.2
FL 2.5
AK 1.7
HI 1.8
VT 1.5
NH 1.1
ME 1.7
NY 1.2
MA 0.8
RI 1.0
CT 1.2
NJ 1.2
DE 2.0
MD 1.5
DC 2.2

BELOW 1.5—12 STATES
1.5 TO 1.9—13 STATES
2.0 TO 2.6—14 STATES
ABOVE 2.6—11 STATES

POPULATION DEATH RATES, 2000
MOTOR-VEHICLE TRAFFIC DEATHS PER 100,000 POPULATION

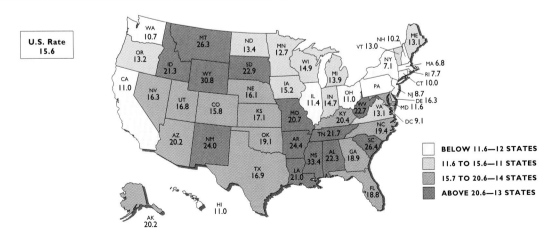

U.S. Rate
15.6

WA 10.7
MT 26.3
ND 13.4
MN 12.7
OR 13.2
ID 21.3
WY 30.8
SD 22.9
WI 14.9
MI 13.9
CA 11.0
NV 16.3
UT 16.8
CO 15.8
NE 16.1
IA 15.2
IL 11.4
IN 14.7
OH 11.0
PA
AZ 20.2
NM 24.0
KS 17.1
MO 20.7
KY 20.4
WV 22.7
VA 13.1
NC 19.4
OK 19.1
AR 24.4
TN 21.7
SC 26.4
TX 16.9
LA 21.0
MS 33.4
AL 22.3
GA 18.9
FL 18.8
AK 20.2
HI 11.0
VT 13.0
NH 10.2
ME 13.1
NY 7.1
MA 6.8
RI 7.7
CT 10.0
NJ 8.7
DE 16.3
MD 11.6
DC 9.1

BELOW 11.6—12 STATES
11.6 TO 15.6—11 STATES
15.7 TO 20.6—14 STATES
ABOVE 20.6—13 STATES

Source: Rates estimated by National Safety Council based on data from state traffic authorities, National Center for Health Statistics, Federal Highway Administration, and the U.S. Census Bureau.

PEDESTRIANS

In 2000, there were an estimated 5,300 pedestrian deaths and 85,000 injuries in motor-vehicle accidents. About half of these deaths and injuries occur when pedestrians cross or enter streets. Walking in the roadway accounted for about 8% of pedestrian deaths and injuries, with more cases occurring while walking with traffic than against traffic.

The distribution of pedestrian deaths and injuries by action varies for persons of different ages. While crossing or entering at or between intersections was the leading type for each age group, this type varied from a low of 47.6% of the total for those aged 0 to 4 years to a high of 61.1% for those aged 10 to 14 years (see corresponding chart).

DEATHS AND INJURIES OF PEDESTRIANS BY AGE AND ACTION, 2000

Actions	Total[a]	Age of Persons Killed or Injured							
		0–4	5–9	10–14	15–19	20–24	25–44	45–64	65 & Over
All Actions	*100.0%*	*3.6%*	*8.5%*	*10.9%*	*11.3%*	*8.1%*	*28.3%*	*18.7%*	*10.6%*
Totals	**100.0%**	**100.0%**	**100.0%**	**100.0%**	**100.0%**	**100.0%**	**100.0%**	**100.0%**	**100.0%**
Crossing or entering at or between intersections	54.0%	47.6%	58.7%	61.1%	51.7%	48.4%	49.6%	56.7%	59.3%
Walking in roadway	7.7%	3.7%	3.5%	7.8%	11.1%	7.4%	9.1%	7.1%	7.0%
with traffic	*5.1%*	*2.3%*	*2.0%*	*4.9%*	*7.3%*	*5.2%*	*6.3%*	*4.8%*	*3.9%*
against traffic	*2.7%*	*1.4%*	*1.5%*	*2.9%*	*3.8%*	*2.3%*	*2.8%*	*2.3%*	*3.1%*
Standing (or playing) in roadway	2.9%	3.7%	2.7%	2.5%	3.1%	4.5%	3.6%	2.5%	1.1%
Pushing/working on vehicle in roadway	0.7%	0.2%	0.2%	0.3%	0.7%	1.0%	0.9%	0.6%	0.7%
Other working in roadway	1.4%	0.2%	0.2%	0.1%	0.8%	2.4%	2.2%	2.0%	0.7%
Not in roadway	1.2%	1.2%	0.8%	0.8%	1.9%	1.1%	1.0%	1.2%	0.9%
Other action	29.5%	39.5%	31.8%	24.5%	27.7%	31.0%	31.2%	28.1%	28.9%
Not stated	2.7%	4.1%	2.1%	3.0%	2.8%	4.1%	2.4%	1.8%	1.3%

Source: Based on reports from nine state traffic authorities.
[a] Total includes "Age Unknown."

PEDESTRIAN DEATHS AND INJURIES BY AGE AND ACTION, 2000

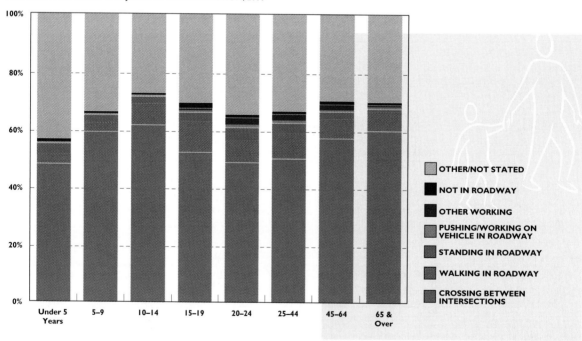

The estimated number of deaths from pedalcycle–motor-vehicle collisions increased from about 750 in 1940 to 1,200 in 1980, then declined to about 800 in 2000. Nonfatal disabling injuries were estimated to number 54,000 in 2000.

In 1998, 689 pedalcyclists died in motor-vehicle crashes and 120 in other accidents according to National Center for Health Statistics mortality data. Males accounted for more than 87% of all pedalcycle deaths, seven times the female fatalities.

Emergency-room-treated injuries associated with bicycles and bicycle accessories were estimated to total

595,679 in 1999, according to the U.S. Consumer Product Safety Commission (see also page 122). The CPSC reported that bike helmet use was 50% in 1998. About 38% of adults and 69% of children under 16 reported wearing bike helmets regularly. The Bicycle Helmet Safety Institute estimates that helmets reduce the risk of all head injuries by up to 85% and reduce the risk of severe head injuries by about one third. In 2001, 20 states and at least 83 localities had bicycle helmet laws.

Source: National Safety Council estimates and tabulations of National Center for Health Statistics mortality data. Rodgers, G.B., & Tinsworth, D. (1999). Bike Helmets. Consumer Product Safety Review, (4), *2-4.*

PEDALCYCLE FATALITIES BY SEX AND AGE GROUP, UNITED STATES, 1998

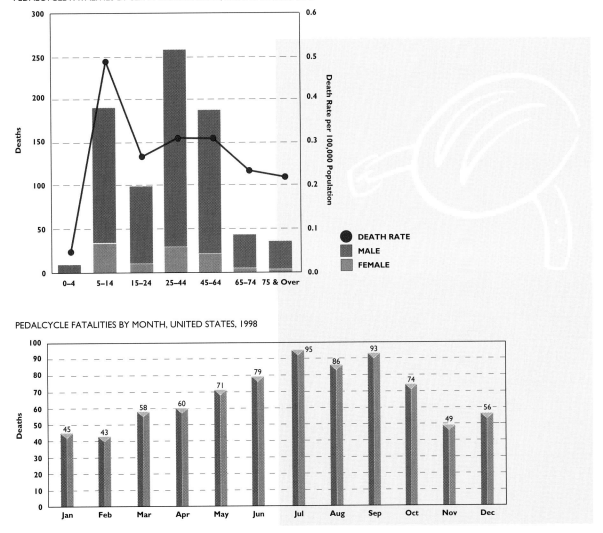

PEDALCYCLE FATALITIES BY MONTH, UNITED STATES, 1998

WORK ZONE DEATHS AND INJURIES

In 1999 there were 868 people killed and 49,557 people injured in work zone crashes (see table below). Compared to 1998, work zone fatalities and injuries increased 12% and 31%, respectively. Of the 868 people killed in work zones, 743 were in construction zones, 65 were in maintenance zones, 10 were in utility zones, and 50 were in an unknown type of work zone.

Over the eight years from 1992 through 1999, work zone deaths have ranged from 638 to 868 and averaged 755 per year.

Based on a National Safety Council survey in May 2001 of state governor's highway safety representatives, at least 41 states reported having either work zone speed laws in effect or special penalties for traffic violations in work zones, such as increased or doubled fines.

PERSONS KILLED AND INJURED IN WORK ZONES, UNITED STATES, 1999

	Total	Vehicle Occupants	Pedestrians	Pedalcyclists	Other Nonmotorists
Killed	868	735	122	7	4
Injured	49,557	47,786	1,342	400	29

Source: National Safety Council tabulations of data from National Highway Traffic Safety Administration—1999 Fatality Analysis Reporting System (FARS) and 1999 General Estimates Systems (GES).

EMERGENCY VEHICLES

CRASHES INVOLVING EMERGENCY VEHICLES, UNITED STATES, 1999

	Ambulance		Fire Truck/Car		Police Car	
	Total	Emergency Use[a]	Total	Emergency Use[a]	Total	Emergency Use[a]
Emergency vehicles in fatal crashes	15	8	17	13	65	26
Emergency vehicles in injury crashes	1,473	623	677	518	8,645	4,010
Emergency vehicles in all crashes	**5,050**	**2,382**	**6,839**	**3,608**	**29,419**	**11,558**
Emergency vehicle drivers killed	0	0	5	3	17	9
Emergency vehicle passengers killed	2	1	3	2	4	1
Other vehicle occupants killed	11	6	9	8	40	14
Nonmotorists killed	2	1	2	2	11	5
Total killed in crashes	**15**	**8**	**19**	**15**	**72**	**29**
Total injured in crashes	**2,659**	**1,434**	**1,130**	**914**	**15,230**	**7,293**

Source: National Safety Council tabulations of data from National Highway Traffic Safety Administration—1999 Fatality Analysis Reporting System (FARS) and 1999 General Estimates Systems (GES).
[a] Emergency lights and/or sirens in use.

FLEET ACCIDENT RATES BY TYPE OF VEHICLE

FLEET ACCIDENT RATES BY TYPE OF VEHICLE, 1998–2000, SUMMARIZED FROM THE NATIONAL FLEET SAFETY CONTEST

Type of Vehicle/Industry	2000			Accidents per 1,000,000 Vehicle Miles	
	No. of Fleets Reporting	No. of Vehicles	Vehicle Miles (Thousands)	2000	1998–2000
Trucks	**124**	**25,724**	**659,932**	**1.24**	**1.24**
Automobile Transporters	**7**	**4,072**	**252,708**	**5.14**	**5.41**
Government	**5**	**945**	**11,776**	**7.47**	**7.78**
Mail Contractors	**11**	**488**	**123,514**	**1.24**	**1.04**
Tractor-Trailers	6	376	117,718	1.24	1.01
Straight Truck	5	112	5,806	1.21	1.50
Postal Service	**43**	**3,505**	**27,346**	**12.07**	**13.90**
Intercity	4	155	2,397	5.84	6.50
City	4	371	3,902	7.18	11.16
Light Delivery Vehicles (LLV)	35	2,979	21,047	13.70	15.06
Trucks—Other Industries	**26**	**1,334**	**88,987**	**3.78**	**3.84**
Intercity	17	991	58,397	2.62	3.15
City	9	343	30,590	5.98	5.45
Utilities	**32**	**15,247**	**159,413**	**4.49**	**5.04**
Electric Utilities	13	10,050	90,396	4.03	4.84
Water Distribution Utilities	6	646	7,250	7.03	10.35
Communication Utilities	3	114	969	3.10	1.81
Gas Distribution Utilities	7	4,014	51,549	5.04	5.56
Gas Transmission Utilities	3	423	9,249	4.00	3.99
Buses	**36**	**2,315**	**64,759**	**4.09**	**13.80**
Intercity Bus	**6**	**344**	**21,746**	**4.09**	**3.82**
Scheduled Route Service	5	338	21,598	4.12	3.62
School Bus	**18**	**1,362**	**19,330**	**10.45**	**9.23**
Transit Bus	**12**	**600**	**23,683**	**33.02**	**27.08**
Cars	**9**	**311**	**2,502**	**12.39**	**12.20**
Emergency & Medical Response	**3**	**70**	**829**	**21.71**	**26.80**
Passenger Car—Other Industries	**5**	**115**	**1,509**	**5.30**	**5.00**
Postal Service	**1**	**120**	**147**	**27.30**	**4.93**

Source: Based upon reports of National Safety Council members participating in the National Fleet Safety Contest. The data should not be interpreted as representative of the industries listed or of Council members.

Definitions
Reportable Accident—Any incident involving death, injury or property damage, regardless of preventability of the incident or the cost of the property damage.
Intercity Operation—Includes fleets that travel more than 50 miles from their terminal.
City Operation—Includes fleets that travel less than 50 miles from their terminal.

Note: The totals for Trucks, Buses and Cars may include some other industries/types of operation that have not been listed separately.

MOTOR-VEHICLE DEATHS AND RATES

MOTOR-VEHICLE DEATHS AND RATES, UNITED STATES, 1913–2000

Year	No. of Deaths	Estimated No. of Vehicles (Millions)	Estimated Vehicle Miles (Billions)	Estimated No. of Drivers (Millions)	Death Rates		
					Per 10,000 Motor Vehicles	Per 100,000,000 Vehicle Miles	Per 100,000 Population
1913	4,200	1.3	(a)	2.0	33.38	(a)	4.4
1914	4,700	1.8	(a)	3.0	26.65	(a)	4.8
1915	6,600	2.5	(a)	3.0	26.49	(a)	6.6
1916	8,200	3.6	(a)	5.0	22.66	(a)	8.1
1917	10,200	5.1	(a)	7.0	19.93	(a)	10.0
1918	10,700	6.2	(a)	9.0	17.37	(a)	10.3
1919	11,200	7.6	(a)	12.0	14.78	(a)	10.7
1920	12,500	9.2	(a)	14.0	13.53	(a)	11.7
1921	13,900	10.5	(a)	16.0	13.25	(a)	12.9
1922	15,300	12.3	(a)	19.0	12.47	(a)	13.9
1923	18,400	15.1	85	22.0	12.18	21.65	16.5
1924	19,400	17.6	104	26.0	11.02	18.65	17.1
1925	21,900	20.1	122	30.0	10.89	17.95	19.1
1926	23,400	22.2	141	33.0	10.54	16.59	20.1
1927	25,800	23.3	158	34.0	11.07	16.33	21.8
1928	28,000	24.7	173	37.0	11.34	16.18	23.4
1929	31,200	26.7	197	40.0	11.69	15.84	25.7
1930	32,900	26.7	206	40.0	12.32	15.97	26.7
1931	33,700	26.1	216	39.0	12.91	15.60	27.2
1932	29,500	24.4	200	36.0	12.09	14.75	23.6
1933	31,363	24.2	201	35.0	12.96	15.60	25.0
1934	36,101	25.3	216	37.0	14.27	16.71	28.6
1935	36,369	26.5	229	39.0	13.72	15.88	28.6
1936	38,089	28.5	252	42.0	13.36	15.11	29.7
1937	39,643	30.1	270	44.0	13.19	14.68	30.8
1938	32,582	29.8	271	44.0	10.93	12.02	25.1
1939	32,386	31.0	285	46.0	10.44	11.35	24.7
1940	34,501	32.5	302	48.0	10.63	11.42	26.1
1941	39,969	34.9	334	52.0	11.45	11.98	30.0
1942	28,309	33.0	268	49.0	8.58	10.55	21.1
1943	23,823	30.9	208	46.0	7.71	11.44	17.8
1944	24,282	30.5	213	45.0	7.97	11.42	18.3
1945	28,076	31.0	250	46.0	9.05	11.22	21.2
1946	33,411	34.4	341	50.0	9.72	9.80	23.9
1947	32,697	37.8	371	53.0	8.64	8.82	22.8
1948	32,259	41.1	398	55.0	7.85	8.11	22.1
1949	31,701	44.7	424	59.3	7.09	7.47	21.3
1950	34,763	49.2	458	62.2	7.07	7.59	23.0
1951	36,996	51.9	491	64.4	7.13	7.53	24.1
1952	37,794	53.3	514	66.8	7.10	7.36	24.3
1953	37,956	56.3	544	69.9	6.74	6.97	24.0
1954	35,586	58.6	562	72.2	6.07	6.33	22.1
1955	38,426	62.8	606	74.7	6.12	6.34	23.4
1956	39,628	65.2	631	77.9	6.07	6.28	23.7
1957	38,702	67.6	647	79.6	5.73	5.98	22.7
1958	36,981	68.8	665	81.5	5.37	5.56	21.3
1959	37,910	72.1	700	84.5	5.26	5.41	21.5
1960	38,137	74.5	719	87.4	5.12	5.31	21.2
1961	38,091	76.4	738	88.9	4.98	5.16	20.8
1962	40,804	79.7	767	92.0	5.12	5.32	22.0
1963	43,564	83.5	805	93.7	5.22	5.41	23.1
1964	47,700	87.3	847	95.6	5.46	5.63	25.0
1965	49,163	91.8	888	99.0	5.36	5.54	25.4
1966	53,041	95.9	930	101.0	5.53	5.70	27.1
1967	52,924	98.9	962	103.2	5.35	5.50	26.8
1968	54,862	103.1	1,016	105.4	5.32	5.40	27.5
1969	55,791	107.4	1,071	108.3	5.19	5.21	27.7
1970	54,633	111.2	1,120	111.5	4.92	4.88	26.8
1971	54,381	116.3	1,186	114.4	4.68	4.57	26.3
1972	56,278	122.3	1,268	118.4	4.60	4.43	26.9
1973	55,511	129.8	1,309	121.6	4.28	4.24	26.3
1974	46,402	134.9	1,290	125.6	3.44	3.59	21.8
1975	45,853	137.9	1,330	129.8	3.33	3.45	21.3
1976	47,038	143.5	1,412	133.9	3.28	3.33	21.6

See source and footnotes on page 109.

MOTOR-VEHICLE DEATHS AND RATES, UNITED STATES, 1913–2000, Cont.

Year	No. of Deaths	Estimated No. of Vehicles (Millions)	Estimated Vehicle Miles (Billions)	Estimated No. of Drivers (Millions)	Death Rates		
					Per 10,000 Motor Vehicles	Per 100,000,000 Vehicle Miles	Per 100,000 Population
1977	49,510	148.8	1,477	138.1	3.33	3.35	22.5
1978	52,411	153.6	1,548	140.8	3.41	3.39	23.6
1979	53,524	159.6	1,529	143.3	3.35	3.50	23.8
1980	53,172	161.6	1,521	145.3	3.29	3.50	23.4
1981	51,385	164.1	1,556	147.1	3.13	3.30	22.4
1982	45,779	165.2	1,592	150.3	2.77	2.88	19.8
1983	44,452	169.4	1,657	154.2	2.62	2.68	19.0
1984	46,263	171.8	1,718	155.4	2.69	2.69	19.6
1985	45,901	177.1	1,774	156.9	2.59	2.59	19.3
1986	47,865	181.4	1,835	159.5	2.63	2.60	19.9
1987	48,290	183.9	1,924	161.8	2.63	2.51	19.9
1988	49,078	189.0	2,026	162.9	2.60	2.42	20.1
1989	47,575	191.7	2,107	165.6	2.48	2.26	19.3
1990	46,814	192.9	2,148	167.0	2.43	2.18	18.8
1991	43,536	192.5	2,172	169.0	2.26	2.00	17.3
1992	40,982	194.4	2,240	173.1	2.11	1.83	16.1
1993	41,893	198.0	2,297	173.1	2.12	1.82	16.3
1994	42,524	201.8	2,360	175.4	2.11	1.80	16.3
1995	43,363	205.3	2,423	176.6	2.11	1.79	16.5
1996	43,649	210.4	2,486	179.5	2.07	1.76	16.5
1997	43,458	211.5	2,562	182.7	2.05	1.70	16.2
1998[b]	43,501	215.0	2,632	185.2	2.02	1.65	16.1
1999[b]	43,000	220.5	2,691	187.2	1.95	1.60	15.8
2000[c]	43,000	224.0	2,688	189.8	1.92	1.60	15.6
Changes							
1990 to 2000	–8%	+16%	+25%	+14%	–21%	–27%	–17%
1999 to 2000	0%	+2%	([d])	+1%	–2%	0%	–1%

Source: Deaths from National Center for Health Statistics except 1964, 1999, and 2000, which are National Safety Council estimates based on data from state traffic authorities. See Technical Appendix for comparability. Motor-vehicle registrations, mileage and drivers estimated by Federal Highway Administration except 2000 registrations and drivers, which are National Safety Council estimates.
[a] Mileage data inadequate prior to 1923.
[b] Revised.
[c] Preliminary.
[d] Change less than 0.05%.

MOTOR-VEHICLE DEATH RATES BY POPULATION, VEHICLES, AND MILEAGE, UNITED STATES, 1990–2000

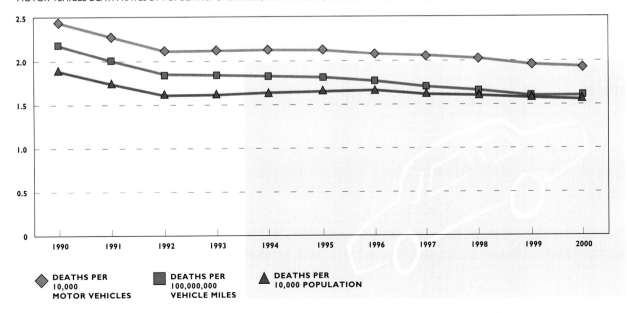

MOTOR-VEHICLE DEATHS BY TYPE OF ACCIDENT

MOTOR-VEHICLE DEATHS BY TYPE OF ACCIDENT, UNITED STATES, 1913–2000

Year	Total Deaths	Deaths from Collision with—							Deaths from Noncollision Accidents	Nontraffic Deaths[a]
		Pedestrians	Other Motor Vehicles	Railroad Trains	Streetcars	Pedalcycles	Animal-Drawn Vehicle or Animal	Fixed Objects		
1913	4,200	(b)	(b)	(b)	(b)	(b)	(b)	(b)	(b)	(c)
1914	4,700	(b)	(b)	(b)	(b)	(b)	(b)	(b)	(b)	(c)
1915	6,600	(b)	(b)	(b)	(b)	(b)	(b)	(b)	(b)	(c)
1916	8,200	(b)	(b)	(b)	(b)	(b)	(b)	(b)	(b)	(c)
1917	10,200	(b)	(b)	(b)	(b)	(b)	(b)	(b)	(b)	(c)
1918	10,700	(b)	(b)	(b)	(b)	(b)	(b)	(b)	(b)	(c)
1919	11,200	(b)	(b)	(b)	(b)	(b)	(b)	(b)	(b)	(c)
1920	12,500	(b)	(b)	(b)	(b)	(b)	(b)	(b)	(b)	(c)
1921	13,900	(b)	(b)	(b)	(b)	(b)	(b)	(b)	(b)	(c)
1922	15,300	(b)	(b)	(b)	(b)	(b)	(b)	(b)	(b)	(c)
1923	18,400	(b)	(b)	(b)	(b)	(b)	(b)	(b)	(b)	(c)
1924	19,400	(b)	(b)	1,130	410	(b)	(b)	(b)	(b)	(c)
1925	21,900	(b)	(b)	1,410	560	(b)	(b)	(b)	(b)	(c)
1926	23,400	(b)	(b)	1,730	520	(b)	(b)	(b)	(b)	(c)
1927	25,800	10,820	3,430	1,830	520	(b)	(b)	(b)	(b)	(c)
1928	28,000	11,420	4,310	2,140	570	(b)	(b)	540	8,070	(c)
1929	31,200	12,250	5,400	2,050	530	(b)	(b)	620	9,380	(c)
1930	32,900	12,900	5,880	1,830	480	(b)	(b)	720	9,970	(c)
1931	33,700	13,370	6,820	1,710	440	(b)	(b)	870	9,570	(c)
1932	29,500	11,490	6,070	1,520	320	350	400	800	8,500	(c)
1933	31,363	12,840	6,470	1,437	318	400	310	900	8,680	(c)
1934	36,101	14,480	8,110	1,457	332	500	360	1,040	9,820	(c)
1935	36,369	14,350	8,750	1,587	253	450	250	1,010	9,720	(c)
1936	38,089	15,250	9,500	1,697	269	650	250	1,060	9,410	(c)
1937	39,643	15,500	10,320	1,810	264	700	200	1,160	9,690	(c)
1938	32,582	12,850	8,900	1,490	165	720	170	940	7,350	(c)
1939	32,386	12,400	8,700	1,330	150	710	200	1,000	7,900	(c)
1940	34,501	12,700	10,100	1,707	132	750	210	1,100	7,800	(c)
1941	39,969	13,550	12,500	1,840	118	910	250	1,350	9,450	(c)
1942	28,309	10,650	7,300	1,754	124	650	240	850	6,740	(c)
1943	23,823	9,900	5,300	1,448	171	450	160	700	5,690	(c)
1944	24,282	9,900	5,700	1,663	175	400	140	700	5,600	(c)
1945	28,076	11,000	7,150	1,703	163	500	130	800	6,600	(c)
1946	33,411	11,600	9,400	1,703	174	450	130	950	8,900	(c)
1947	32,697	10,450	9,900	1,736	102	550	150	1,000	8,800	(c)
1948	32,259	9,950	10,200	1,474	83	500	100	1,000	8,950	(c)
1949	31,701	8,800	10,500	1,452	56	550	140	1,100	9,100	838
1950	34,763	9,000	11,650	1,541	89	440	120	1,300	10,600	900
1951	36,996	9,150	13,100	1,573	46	390	100	1,400	11,200	966
1952	37,794	8,900	13,500	1,429	32	430	130	1,450	11,900	970
1953	37,956	8,750	13,400	1,506	26	420	120	1,500	12,200	1,026
1954	35,586	8,000	12,800	1,289	28	380	90	1,500	11,500	1,004
1955	38,426	8,200	14,500	1,490	15	410	90	1,600	12,100	989
1956	39,628	7,900	15,200	1,377	11	440	100	1,600	13,000	888
1957	38,702	7,850	15,400	1,376	13	460	80	1,700	11,800	1,016
1958	36,981	7,650	14,200	1,316	9	450	80	1,650	11,600	929
1959	37,910	7,850	14,900	1,202	6	480	70	1,600	11,800	948
1960	38,137	7,850	14,800	1,368	5	460	80	1,700	11,900	995
1961	38,091	7,650	14,700	1,267	5	490	80	1,700	12,200	1,065
1962	40,804	7,900	16,400	1,245	3	500	90	1,750	12,900	1,029
1963	43,564	8,200	17,600	1,385	10	580	80	1,900	13,800	990
1964	47,700	9,000	19,600	1,580	5	710	100	2,100	14,600	1,123
1965	49,163	8,900	20,800	1,556	5	680	120	2,200	14,900	1,113
1966	53,041	9,400	22,200	1,800	2	740	100	2,500	16,300	1,108
1967	52,924	9,400	22,000	1,620	3	750	100	2,350	16,700	1,165
1968	54,862	9,900	22,400	1,570	4	790	100	2,700	17,400	1,061
1969	55,791	10,100	23,700	1,495	2	800	100	3,900[d]	15,700[d]	1,155
1970	54,633	9,900	23,200	1,459	3	780	100	3,800	15,400	1,140
1971	54,381	9,900	23,100	1,378	2	800	100	3,800	15,300	1,015
1972	56,278	10,300	23,900	1,260	2	1,000	100	3,900	15,800	1,064
1973	55,511	10,200	23,600	1,194	2	1,000	100	3,800	15,600	1,164
1974	46,402	8,500	19,700	1,209	1	1,000	100	3,100	12,800	1,088
1975	45,853	8,400	19,550	979	1	1,000	100	3,130	12,700	1,033
1976	47,038	8,600	20,100	1,033	2	1,000	100	3,200	13,000	1,026

See source and footnotes on page 111.

MOTOR-VEHICLE DEATHS BY TYPE OF ACCIDENT, UNITED STATES, 1913–2000, Cont.

Year	Total Deaths	Deaths from Collision with—							Deaths from Noncollision Accidents	Nontraffic Deaths[a]
		Pedestrians	Other Motor Vehicles	Railroad Trains	Streetcars	Pedal-cycles	Animal-Drawn Vehicle or Animal	Fixed Objects		
1977	49,510	9,100	21,200	902	3	1,100	100	3,400	13,700	1,053
1978	52,411	9,600	22,400	986	1	1,200	100	3,600	14,500	1,074
1979	53,524	9,800	23,100	826	1	1,200	100	3,700	14,800	1,271
1980	53,172	9,700	23,000	739	1	1,200	100	3,700	14,700	1,242
1981	51,385	9,400	22,200	668	1	1,200	100	3,600	14,200	1,189
1982	45,779	8,400	19,800	554	1	1,100	100	3,200	12,600	1,066
1983	44,452	8,200	19,200	520	1	1,100	100	3,100	12,200	1,024
1984	46,263	8,500	20,000	630	0	1,100	100	3,200	12,700	1,055
1985	45,901	8,500	19,900	538	2	1,100	100	3,200	12,600	1,079
1986	47,865	8,900	20,800	574	2	1,100	100	3,300	13,100	998
1987	48,290	7,500[e]	20,700	554	1	1,000[e]	100	13,200[e]	5,200[e]	993
1988	49,078	7,700	20,900	638	2	1,000	100	13,400	5,300	1,054
1989	47,575	7,800	20,300	720	2	900	100	12,900	4,900	989
1990	46,814	7,300	19,900	623	2	900	100	13,100	4,900	987
1991	43,536	6,600	18,200	541	1	800	100	12,600	4,700	915
1992	40,982	6,300	17,600	521	2	700	100	11,700	4,100	997
1993	41,893	6,400	18,300	553	3	800	100	11,500	4,200	994
1994	42,524	6,300	18,900	549	1	800	100	11,500	4,400	1,017
1995	43,363	6,400	19,000	514	(c)	800	100	12,100	4,400	1,032
1996	43,649	6,100	19,600	373	(c)	800	100	12,100	4,600	1,127
1997	43,458	5,900	19,900	371	(c)	800	100	12,000	4,400	1,118
1998[f]	43,501	5,900	19,700	309	(c)	700	100	12,200	4,600	1,310
1999[f]	43,000	5,800	20,000	300	(c)	800	100	11,300	4,700	1,300
2000[g]	43,000	5,300	20,600	400	(c)	800	100	11,200	4,600	1,100
Changes in Deaths										
1990 to 2000	−8%	−27%	+4%	−36%	—	−11%	0%	−15%	−6%	+11%
1999 to 2000	0%	−9%	+3%	+33%	—	0%	0%	−1%	−2%	−15%

Source: Total deaths from National Center for Health Statistics except 1964 and 1999-2000, which are National Safety Council estimates based on data from state traffic authorities. Most totals by type are estimated and may not add to the total deaths. See Technical Appendix for comparability.
[a] See definition, page 167. Nontraffic deaths are included in appropriate accident type totals in table; in 1998, 50% of the specified nontraffic deaths were pedestrians.
[b] Insufficient data for approximations.
[c] Data not available.
[d] 1969 through 1986 totals are not comparable to previous years.
[e] Procedures and benchmarks for estimating deaths for certain types of accidents were changed for the 1990 edition. Estimates for 1987 and later years are not comparable to earlier years.
[f] Revised.
[g] Preliminary.

MOTOR-VEHICLE DEATHS BY TYPE OF ACCIDENT, UNITED STATES, 2000

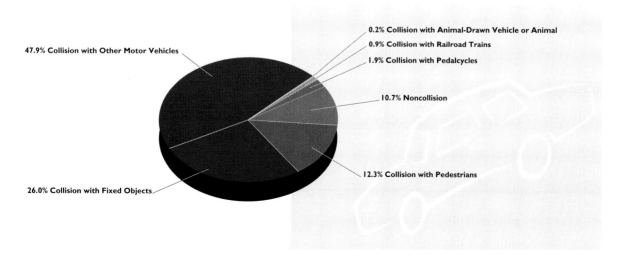

0.2% Collision with Animal-Drawn Vehicle or Animal
0.9% Collision with Railroad Trains
1.9% Collision with Pedalcycles
10.7% Noncollision
47.9% Collision with Other Motor Vehicles
12.3% Collision with Pedestrians
26.0% Collision with Fixed Objects

MOTOR-VEHICLE DEATHS BY AGE

MOTOR-VEHICLE DEATHS BY AGE, UNITED STATES, 1913–2000

Year	All Ages	Under 5 Years	5–14 Years	15–24 Years	25–44 Years	45–64 Years	65–74 Years	75 & Over[a]
1913	4,200	300	1,100	600	1,100	800	300	
1914	4,700	300	1,200	700	1,200	900	400	
1915	6,600	400	1,500	1,000	1,700	1,400	600	
1916	8,200	600	1,800	1,300	2,100	1,700	700	
1917	10,200	700	2,400	1,400	2,700	2,100	900	
1918	10,700	800	2,700	1,400	2,500	2,300	1,000	
1919	11,200	900	3,000	1,400	2,500	2,100	1,300	
1920	12,500	1,000	3,300	1,700	2,800	2,300	1,400	
1921	13,900	1,100	3,400	1,800	3,300	2,700	1,600	
1922	15,300	1,100	3,500	2,100	3,700	3,100	1,800	
1923	18,400	1,200	3,700	2,800	4,600	3,900	2,200	
1924	19,400	1,400	3,800	2,900	4,700	4,100	2,500	
1925	21,900	1,400	3,900	3,600	5,400	4,800	2,800	
1926	23,400	1,400	3,900	3,900	5,900	5,200	3,100	
1927	25,800	1,600	4,000	4,300	6,600	5,800	3,500	
1928	28,000	1,600	3,800	4,900	7,200	6,600	3,900	
1929	31,200	1,600	3,900	5,700	8,000	7,500	4,500	
1930	32,900	1,500	3,600	6,200	8,700	8,000	4,900	
1931	33,700	1,500	3,600	6,300	9,100	8,200	5,000	
1932	29,500	1,200	2,900	5,100	8,100	7,400	4,800	
1933	31,363	1,274	3,121	5,649	8,730	7,947	4,642	
1934	36,101	1,210	3,182	6,561	10,232	9,530	5,386	
1935	36,369	1,253	2,951	6,755	10,474	9,562	5,374	
1936	38,089	1,324	3,026	7,184	10,807	10,089	5,659	
1937	39,643	1,303	2,991	7,800	10,877	10,475	6,197	
1938	32,582	1,122	2,511	6,016	8,772	8,711	5,450	
1939	32,386	1,192	2,339	6,318	8,917	8,292	5,328	
1940	34,501	1,176	2,584	6,846	9,362	8,882	5,651	
1941	39,969	1,378	2,838	8,414	11,069	9,829	6,441	
1942	28,309	1,069	1,991	5,932	7,747	7,254	4,316	
1943	23,823	1,132	1,959	4,522	6,454	5,996	3,760	
1944	24,282	1,203	2,093	4,561	6,514	5,982	3,929	
1945	28,076	1,290	2,386	5,358	7,578	6,794	4,670	
1946	33,411	1,568	2,508	7,445	8,955	7,532	5,403	
1947	32,697	1,502	2,275	7,251	8,775	7,468	5,426	
1948	32,259	1,635	2,337	7,218	8,702	7,190	3,173	2,004
1949	31,701	1,667	2,158	6,772	8,892	7,073	3,116	2,023
1950	34,763	1,767	2,152	7,600	10,214	7,728	3,264	2,038
1951	36,996	1,875	2,300	7,713	11,253	8,276	3,444	2,135
1952	37,794	1,951	2,295	8,115	11,380	8,463	3,472	2,118
1953	37,956	2,019	2,368	8,169	11,302	8,318	3,508	2,271
1954	35,586	1,864	2,332	7,571	10,521	7,848	3,247	2,203
1955	38,426	1,875	2,406	8,656	11,448	8,372	3,455	2,214
1956	39,628	1,770	2,640	9,169	11,551	8,573	3,657	2,268
1957	38,702	1,785	2,604	8,667	11,230	8,545	3,560	2,311
1958	36,981	1,791	2,710	8,388	10,414	7,922	3,535	2,221
1959	37,910	1,842	2,719	8,969	10,358	8,263	3,487	2,272
1960	38,137	1,953	2,814	9,117	10,189	8,294	3,457	2,313
1961	38,091	1,891	2,802	9,088	10,212	8,267	3,467	2,364
1962	40,804	1,903	3,028	10,157	10,701	8,812	3,696	2,507
1963	43,564	1,991	3,063	11,123	11,356	9,506	3,786	2,739
1964	47,700	2,120	3,430	12,400	12,500	10,200	4,150	2,900
1965	49,163	2,059	3,526	13,395	12,595	10,509	4,077	3,002
1966	53,041	2,182	3,869	15,298	13,282	11,051	4,217	3,142
1967	52,924	2,067	3,845	15,646	12,987	10,902	4,285	3,192
1968	54,862	1,987	4,105	16,543	13,602	11,031	4,261	3,333
1969	55,791	2,077	4,045	17,443	13,868	11,012	4,210	3,136
1970	54,633	1,915	4,159	16,720	13,446	11,099	4,084	3,210
1971	54,381	1,885	4,256	17,103	13,307	10,471	4,108	3,251
1972	56,278	1,896	4,258	17,942	13,758	10,836	4,138	3,450
1973	55,511	1,998	4,124	18,032	14,013	10,216	3,892	3,236
1974	46,402	1,546	3,332	15,905	11,834	8,159	3,071	2,555
1975	45,853	1,576	3,286	15,672	11,969	7,663	3,047	2,640
1976	47,038	1,532	3,175	16,650	12,112	7,770	3,082	2,717

See source and footnotes on page 113.

MOTOR-VEHICLE DEATHS BY AGE, UNITED STATES, 1913–2000, Cont.

Year	All Ages	Under 5 Years	5–14 Years	15–24 Years	25–44 Years	45–64 Years	65–74 Years	75 & Over[a]
1977	49,510	1,472	3,142	18,092	13,031	8,000	3,060	2,713
1978	52,411	1,551	3,130	19,164	14,574	8,048	3,217	2,727
1979	53,524	1,461	2,952	19,369	15,658	8,162	3,171	2,751
1980	53,172	1,426	2,747	19,040	16,133	8,022	2,991	2,813
1981	51,385	1,256	2,575	17,363	16,447	7,818	3,090	2,836
1982	45,779	1,300	2,301	15,324	14,469	6,879	2,825	2,681
1983	44,452	1,233	2,241	14,289	14,323	6,690	2,827	2,849
1984	46,263	1,138	2,263	14,738	15,036	6,954	3,020	3,114
1985	45,901	1,195	2,319	14,277	15,034	6,885	3,014	3,177
1986	47,865	1,188	2,350	15,227	15,844	6,799	3,096	3,361
1987	48,290	1,190	2,397	14,447	16,405	7,021	3,277	3,553
1988	49,078	1,220	2,423	14,406	16,580	7,245	3,429	3,775
1989	47,575	1,221	2,266	12,941	16,571	7,287	3,465	3,824
1990	46,814	1,123	2,059	12,607	16,488	7,282	3,350	3,905
1991	43,536	1,076	2,011	11,664	15,082	6,616	3,193	3,894
1992	40,982	1,020	1,904	10,305	14,071	6,597	3,247	3,838
1993	41,893	1,081	1,963	10,500	14,283	6,711	3,116	4,239
1994	42,524	1,139	2,026	10,660	13,966	7,097	3,385	4,251
1995	43,363	1,004	2,055	10,600	14,618	7,428	3,300	4,358
1996	43,649	1,035	1,980	10,576	14,482	7,749	3,419	4,408
1997	43,458	933	1,967	10,208	14,167	8,134	3,370	4,679
1998[b]	43,501	921	1,868	10,026	14,095	8,416	3,410	4,765
1999[b]	43,000	900	1,800	10,200	12,900	8,800	3,300	5,100
2000[c]	43,000	900	1,500	10,500	13,300	9,200	2,700	4,900
Changes in Deaths								
1990 to 2000	–8%	–20%	–27%	–17%	–19%	+26%	–19%	+25%
1999 to 2000	0%	0%	–17%	+3%	+3%	+5%	–18%	–4%

Source: 1913 to 1932 calculated from National Center for Health Statistics data for registration states; 1933 to 1963, 1965 to 1998 are NCHS totals. All other figures are National Safety Council estimates. See Technical Appendix for comparability.
[a] Includes "age unknown." In 1998 these deaths numbered 30.
[b] Revised.
[c] Preliminary.

MOTOR-VEHICLE DEATHS BY AGE, UNITED STATES, 2000

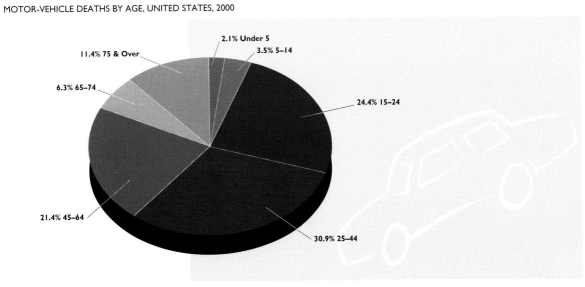

2.1% Under 5
3.5% 5–14
11.4% 75 & Over
6.3% 65–74
24.4% 15–24
21.4% 45–64
30.9% 25–44

MOTOR-VEHICLE DEATH RATES

MOTOR-VEHICLE DEATH RATES[a] BY AGE, UNITED STATES, 1913–2000

Year	All Ages	Under 5 Years	5–14 Years	15–24 Years	25–44 Years	45–64 Years	65–74 Years	75 & Over
1913	4.4	2.3	5.5	3.1	3.8	5.3	8.5	
1914	4.8	2.5	5.7	3.5	4.1	6.2	9.3	
1915	6.6	3.5	7.3	5.0	5.6	8.8	13.5	
1916	8.1	4.7	8.6	6.0	7.0	10.7	15.8	
1917	10.0	5.6	10.6	7.4	8.6	12.6	18.6	
1918	10.3	6.9	12.3	7.7	8.3	13.7	21.2	
1919	10.7	7.5	13.9	7.5	8.1	12.4	24.1	
1920	11.7	8.6	14.6	8.7	8.8	13.5	27.0	
1921	12.9	9.0	14.5	9.2	10.2	15.4	31.0	
1922	13.9	9.2	15.0	10.8	11.1	17.2	34.9	
1923	16.5	9.7	15.6	13.4	13.6	21.0	40.5	
1924	17.1	11.1	16.1	14.3	13.7	21.8	43.7	
1925	19.1	11.0	15.6	17.2	15.8	25.0	48.9	
1926	20.1	11.0	15.9	18.6	17.1	26.3	51.4	
1927	21.8	12.8	16.0	20.0	18.8	28.9	56.9	
1928	23.4	12.7	15.5	21.9	20.2	32.4	62.2	
1929	25.7	13.4	15.6	25.6	22.3	35.6	68.6	
1930	26.7	13.0	14.7	27.4	23.9	37.0	72.5	
1931	27.2	13.3	14.5	27.9	24.8	37.4	70.6	
1932	23.6	11.3	12.0	22.6	22.0	32.9	63.6	
1933	25.0	12.0	12.7	24.8	23.4	34.7	63.1	
1934	28.6	11.7	13.0	28.6	27.2	40.7	71.0	
1935	28.6	12.3	12.2	29.2	27.6	39.9	68.9	
1936	29.7	13.2	12.6	30.8	28.2	41.3	70.5	
1937	30.8	13.0	12.7	33.2	28.2	42.0	75.1	
1938	25.1	11.0	10.8	25.4	22.5	34.3	64.1	
1939	24.7	11.2	10.4	26.5	22.6	32.2	60.2	
1940	26.1	11.1	11.5	28.7	23.5	33.9	62.1	
1941	30.0	12.7	12.6	35.7	27.5	37.0	68.6	
1942	21.1	9.5	8.8	25.8	19.2	26.9	44.5	
1943	17.8	9.4	8.6	20.6	16.1	21.9	37.6	
1944	18.3	9.6	9.1	22.5	16.6	21.6	38.2	
1945	21.2	10.0	10.3	27.8	19.7	24.2	44.1	
1946	23.9	11.9	10.8	34.4	21.1	26.4	49.6	
1947	22.8	10.5	9.7	32.8	20.3	25.7	48.2	
1948	22.1	11.0	9.8	32.5	19.8	24.3	39.6	55.4
1949	21.3	10.7	9.0	30.7	19.9	23.4	37.8	53.9
1950	23.0	10.8	8.8	34.5	22.5	25.1	38.8	52.4
1951	24.1	10.9	9.2	36.0	24.7	26.5	39.5	53.0
1952	24.3	11.3	8.7	38.6	24.7	26.7	38.5	50.8
1953	24.0	11.5	8.5	39.1	24.5	25.8	37.7	52.6
1954	22.1	10.4	8.1	36.2	22.6	24.0	33.9	49.0
1955	23.4	10.2	8.0	40.9	24.5	25.2	35.1	47.1
1956	23.7	9.4	8.4	42.9	24.6	25.3	36.2	46.4
1957	22.7	9.2	8.0	39.7	23.9	24.8	34.4	45.5
1958	21.3	9.1	8.1	37.0	22.3	22.6	33.5	42.3
1959	21.5	9.1	7.9	38.2	22.2	23.2	32.3	41.8
1960	21.2	9.6	7.9	37.7	21.7	22.9	31.3	41.1
1961	20.8	9.2	7.6	36.5	21.8	22.5	30.7	40.5
1962	22.0	9.3	8.1	38.4	22.9	23.7	32.2	41.7
1963	23.1	9.8	8.0	40.0	24.3	25.2	32.6	44.3
1964	25.0	10.5	8.8	42.6	26.8	26.6	35.5	45.2
1965	25.4	10.4	8.9	44.2	27.0	27.0	34.6	45.4
1966	27.1	11.4	9.7	48.7	28.5	27.9	35.4	46.2
1967	26.8	11.2	9.5	48.4	27.8	27.1	35.6	45.4
1968	27.5	11.1	10.1	49.8	28.8	27.0	35.1	46.0
1969	27.7	12.0	9.9	50.7	29.1	26.6	34.3	42.0
1970	26.8	11.2	10.2	46.7	27.9	26.4	32.7	42.2
1971	26.3	10.9	10.5	45.7	27.4	24.7	32.4	41.3
1972	26.9	11.1	10.7	47.1	27.4	25.3	32.0	42.6
1973	26.3	11.9	10.5	46.3	27.2	23.6	29.4	39.1
1974	21.8	9.4	8.6	40.0	22.4	18.8	22.6	30.1
1975	21.3	9.8	8.6	38.7	22.1	17.5	21.9	30.1
1976	21.6	9.8	8.4	40.3	21.8	17.6	21.6	30.1

See source and footnotes on page 115.

MOTOR-VEHICLE DEATH RATES^a BY AGE, UNITED STATES, 1913–2000, Cont.

Year	All Ages	Under 5 Years	5–14 Years	15–24 Years	25–44 Years	45–64 Years	65–74 Years	75 & Over
1977	22.5	9.5	8.5	43.3	22.7	18.1	20.9	29.3
1978	23.6	9.9	8.6	45.4	24.6	18.2	21.5	28.7
1979	23.8	9.1	8.3	45.6	25.6	18.4	20.7	28.1
1980	23.4	8.7	7.9	44.8	25.5	18.0	19.1	28.0
1981	22.4	7.4	7.5	41.1	25.2	17.6	19.4	27.5
1982	19.8	7.5	6.7	36.8	21.5	15.5	17.5	25.2
1983	19.0	7.0	6.6	34.8	20.6	15.0	17.2	26.0
1984	19.6	6.4	6.7	36.4	21.0	15.6	18.2	27.7
1985	19.3	6.7	6.9	35.7	20.5	15.4	17.9	27.5
1986	19.9	6.6	7.0	38.5	21.0	15.2	18.1	28.3
1987	19.9	6.6	7.1	37.1	21.3	15.7	18.8	29.1
1988	20.1	6.7	7.1	37.8	21.2	15.9	19.5	30.2
1989	19.3	6.6	6.5	34.6	20.8	15.9	19.4	29.8
1990	18.8	6.0	5.8	34.2	20.4	15.7	18.5	29.7
1991	17.3	5.6	5.6	32.1	18.3	14.2	17.5	28.9
1992	16.1	5.2	5.2	28.5	17.1	13.6	17.6	27.8
1993	16.3	5.5	5.3	29.1	17.3	13.5	16.7	30.0
1994	16.3	5.8	5.4	29.5	16.8	13.9	18.1	29.4
1995	16.5	5.1	5.4	29.3	17.5	14.2	17.6	29.4
1996	16.5	5.4	5.2	29.2	17.3	14.4	18.3	29.0
1997	16.2	4.9	5.1	27.9	17.0	14.7	18.2	29.9
1998^b	16.1	4.9	4.8	26.9	16.9	14.7	18.5	29.8
1999^b	15.8	4.8	4.6	27.0	15.6	14.9	17.9	31.2
2000^c	15.6	4.8	3.8	27.3	16.2	15.0	14.8	29.4
Changes in Rates								
1990 to 2000	–17%	–20%	–34%	–20%	–21%	–4%	–20%	–1%
1999 to 2000	–1%	0%	–17%	+1%	+4%	+1%	–17%	–6%

Source: 1913 to 1932 calculated from National Center for Health Statistics data for registration states; 1933 to 1963, 1965 to 1998 are NCHS totals. All other figures are National Safety Council estimates. See Technical Appendix for comparability.
^a *Death rates are deaths per 100,000 population in each age group.*
^b *Revised.*
^c *Preliminary.*

CHANGE IN MOTOR-VEHICLE DEATH RATES BY AGE GROUP, UNITED STATES, 1990–2000

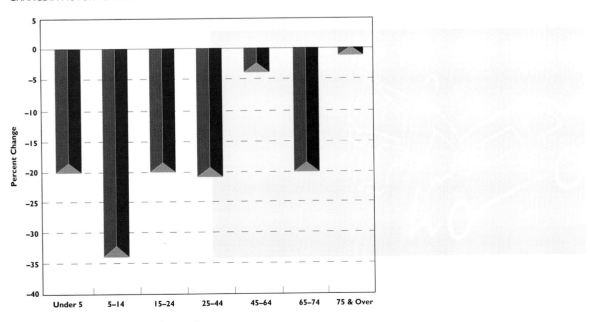

Rates based on deaths per 100,000 population in each age group.

HOME AND
COMMUNITY

PUBLIC, 2000

Between 1912 and 2000, public unintentional-injury deaths per 100,000 population were reduced 73% from 30 to 8. In 1912, an estimated 28,000 to 30,000 persons died from public nonmotor-vehicle injuries. In 2000, with a population nearly tripled, and travel and recreational activity greatly increased, only 22,100 persons died of public unintentional injuries and 7,300,000 suffered disabling injuries. The public class excludes deaths involving motor vehicles and persons at work or at home.

The number of public unintentional-injury deaths decreased by 1,400, or 6%, from the revised 1999 figure of 23,400. The death rate per 100,000 population decreased from 8.6 to 8.0, or 7%.

The 2000 standardized death rate of 6.4 per 100,000 population, adjusted to the age distribution of the

population in 1940, was 35% below the rate for 1950, despite an increase in deaths during the same period of 47%.

The Council adopted the Bureau of Labor Statistics' Census of Fatal Occupational Injuries count for work-related unintentional injuries retroactive to 1992 data. Because of the lower Work class total resulting from this change, several thousand unintentional-injury deaths that had been classified by the Council as work-related had to be reassigned to the Home and Public classes. For this reason, long-term historical comparisons for these three classes should be made with caution. See the Technical Appendix for an explanation of the methodological changes.

Deaths 22,000
Disabling injuries 7,300,000
Death rate per 100,000 population 8.0
Costs . . . . $82.6 billion

PUBLIC DEATHS AND DEATH RATES, UNITED STATES, 1992–2000

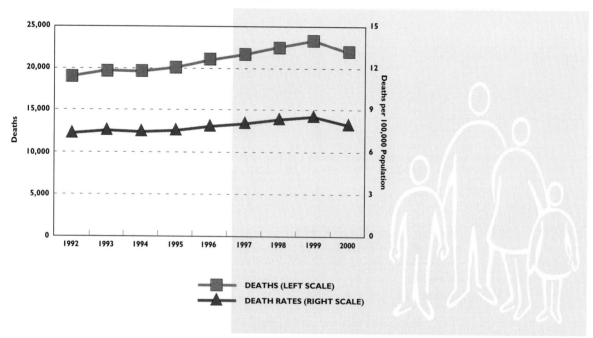

PRINCIPAL TYPES OF PUBLIC UNINTENTIONAL-INJURY DEATHS, UNITED STATES, 1950–2000

| Year | Total Public | Transport[a] | | | | | Nontransport | | | | |
| | | Total[b] | Air | Water | | Rail[d] | Total[b] | Falls | Drowning[c] | Firearms | Fires, Burns |
				Drowning[c]	Other						
1950	15,000	3,950	1,050	1,000	100	1,450	11,050	2,750	3,750	1,150	500
1955	15,500	3,600	1,300	1,000	100	950	11,900	3,200	4,300	950	450
1960	17,000	3,150	1,150	1,000[e]	100	700	13,850	3,700	4,350	1,100	750
1965	19,500	3,200	1,200	1,000	100	700	16,300	5,300	4,400	900	800
1970	23,500	3,300	1,200	1,200	100	600	20,200	5,000	5,200	900	700
1975	23,000	3,000	1,100	1,200	100	400	20,000	4,800	5,200	900	600
1980	21,300	2,900	1,100	1,100	100	400	18,400	4,500	4,700	700	600
1981	19,800	2,700	1,100	900	100	400	17,100	4,300	4,100	700	600
1982	19,500	2,900	1,200	1,000	100	400	16,600	4,100	4,000	700	500
1983	19,400	2,700	1,000	1,000	100	400	16,700	4,100	4,000	700	500
1984	18,300	2,400	900	800	100	400	15,900	4,100	3,300	700	500
1985	18,800	2,500	1,000	800	100	400	16,300	4,100	3,300	600	500
1986	18,700	2,300	800	800	100	400	16,400	3,900	3,600	600	500
1987	18,400	2,300	900	700	100	400	16,100	4,000	3,200	600	500
1988	18,400	2,100	700	700	100	400	16,300	4,100	3,100	600	500
1989	18,200	2,100	800	600	100	400	16,100	4,200	3,000	600	500
1990	17,400	2,100	700	700	100	400	15,300	4,300	2,800	500	400
1991	17,600	2,100	700	600	100	500	15,500	4,500	2,800	600	400
1992	19,000	2,300	700	600	100	600	16,700	4,400	2,500	400	200
1993	19,700	2,100	600	600	100	600	17,600	4,600	2,800	400	200
1994	19,600	2,000	600	500	100	600	17,600	4,700	2,400	400	200
1995	20,100	2,100	600	600	100	500	18,000	5,000	2,800	300	200
1996	21,000	2,000	700	500	100	500	19,000	5,300	2,500	300	200
1997	21,700	1,800	500	500	100	400	19,900	5,600	2,600	300	200
1998[f]	22,600	2,000	500	500	100	500	20,600	6,000	2,900	300	200
1999[f]	23,400	2,000	600	500	100	500	21,400	6,400	2,700	300	200
2000[g]	22,000	1,800	500	400	100	500	20,200	6,100	2,600	200	200

Source: National Safety Council estimates based on data from the National Center for Health Statistics and state vital statistics departments. The Council adopted the Bureau of Labor Statistics' Census of Fatal Occupational Injuries count for work-related unintentional injuries retroactive to 1992 data. Because of the lower Work class total resulting from this change, several thousand unintentional-injury deaths that had been classified by the Council as work-related had to be reassigned to the Home and Public classes. For this reason long-term historical comparisons for these three classes should be made with caution. See the Technical Appendix for an explanation of the methodological changes.
[a] *Transport is a primary classification but each class includes deaths from falls, drowning, burns, etc., occurring in connection with each type of transport.*
[b] *Includes some deaths not shown separately.*
[c] *Nontransport drownings are included in Total drownings in the tables on pages 40–43.*
[d] *Includes subways and elevateds.*
[e] *Data for this year and subsequent years not comparable with previous years due to classification changes.*
[f] *Revised.*
[g] *Preliminary.*

DEATHS DUE TO UNINTENTIONAL PUBLIC INJURIES, 2000

All Public

Includes deaths in public places or places used in a public way and not involving motor vehicles. Most sports, recreation, and transportation deaths are included. Excludes deaths in the course of employment.

	Total	Change from 1999	Death Rate[a]
Deaths	22,000	−6%	8.0

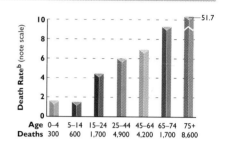

Age	0–4	5–14	15–24	25–44	45–64	65–74	75+
Deaths	300	600	1,700	4,900	4,200	1,700	8,600

Falls

Includes deaths from falls from one level to another or on the same level in public places. Excludes deaths from falls in moving vehicles.

	Total	Change from 1999	Death Rate[a]
Deaths	6,100	−5%	2.2

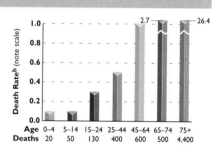

Age	0–4	5–14	15–24	25–44	45–64	65–74	75+
Deaths	20	50	130	400	600	500	4,400

Drowning

Includes drownings of persons swimming or playing in water, or falling into water, except on home premises or at work. Excludes drownings involving boats that are in water transportation.

	Total	Change from 1999	Death Rate[a]
Deaths	2,600	−4%	0.9

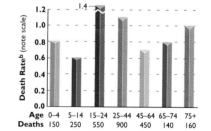

Age	0–4	5–14	15–24	25–44	45–64	65–74	75+
Deaths	150	250	550	900	450	140	160

Air Transport

Includes deaths in private flying, passengers in commercial aviation, and deaths of military personnel in the U.S. Excludes crews and persons traveling in the course of employment.

	Total	Change from 1999	Death Rate[a]
Deaths	500[c]	−17%	0.2

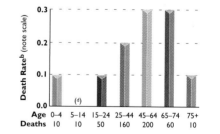

Age	0–4	5–14	15–24	25–44	45–64	65–74	75+
Deaths	10	10	50	160	200	60	10

Water Transport

Includes deaths in water transport accidents from falls, burns, etc., as well as drownings.

	Total	Change from 1999	Death Rate[a]
Deaths	500[c]	−17%	0.2

See footnotes on page 121.

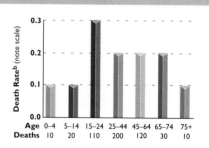

Age	0–4	5–14	15–24	25–44	45–64	65–74	75+
Deaths	10	20	110	200	120	30	10

Railroad

Includes deaths arising from railroad vehicles in motion (except those involving motor vehicles), subway and elevated trains, and persons boarding or alighting from standing trains.

	Total	Change from 1999	Death Rate[a]
Deaths	500[c]	0%	0.2

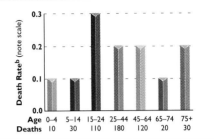

Firearms

Includes deaths from firearms injuries in public places, including hunting injuries. Excludes deaths from explosive materials.

	Total	Change from 1999	Death Rate[a]
Deaths	200	−33%	0.1

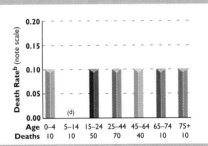

Fires, Burns, and Deaths Associated with Fires

Includes deaths from fires, burns, and injuries in conflagrations in public places—such as asphyxiation, falls, and struck by falling objects. Excludes burns from hot objects or liquids.

	Total	Change from 1999	Death Rate[a]
Deaths	200	0%	0.1

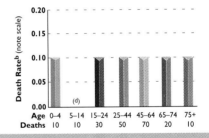

Other Transport

Includes deaths from injuries involving pedalcycles, animal-drawn vehicles, street cars, etc., except in collision with motor vehicles. Excludes trolley buses, subways, elevateds, and scooters.

	Total	Change from 1999	Death Rate[a]
Deaths	300[c]	0%	0.1

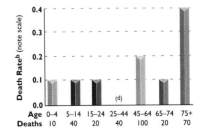

All Other Public

Most important types included are: medical and surgical complications and misadventures, suffocation by ingestion, poisoning by solids and liquids, and excessive heat or cold.

	Total	Change from 1999	Death Rate[a]
Deaths	11,100	−6%	4.0

[a] Deaths per 100,000 population.
[b] Deaths per 100,000 population in each age group.
[c] Excludes persons at work.
[d] Rate less than 0.05.

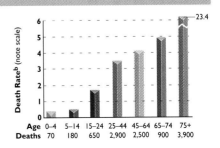

SPORTS INJURIES

The table below shows estimates of injuries treated in hospital emergency departments and participants associated with various sports. Differences between the two sources in methods, coverage, classification systems, and definitions can affect comparisons among sports. Because this list of sports is not complete, because the frequency and duration of participation is not known, and because the number of participants varies greatly, no inference should be made concerning the relative hazard of these sports or rank with respect to risk of injury. In particular, it is *not* appropriate to calculate injury rates from these data.

SPORTS PARTICIPATION AND INJURIES, UNITED STATES, 1999

Sport	Participants	Injuries	Percent of Injuries by Age				
			0–4	5–14	15–24	25–64	65 & Over
Archery	4,900,000	3,450	3.6	23.2	30.5	40.3	2.4
Baseball & softball	31,000,000	339,775	2.5	38.3	26.4	32.3	0.5
Basketball	29,600,000	597,224	0.4	32.4	45.8	21.4	0.1
Bicycle riding[a]	42,400,000	595,679	6.3	56.6	13.7	21.0	2.3
Billiards, pool	32,100,000	5,147	12.8	29.3	19.7	35.9	2.3
Bowling	41,600,000	22,639	9.8	16.2	17.5	47.1	9.2
Boxing	1,300,000	8,903	0.3	8.2	52.0	39.4	0.0
Exercise	(b)	160,141[c]	3.9	18.6	22.2	47.4	7.8
Fishing	46,700,000	70,514	2.9	24.5	12.6	52.1	7.9
Football[d]	19,800,000	372,380	0.3	46.2	43.2	10.1	0.1
Golf	27,000,000	47,386[e]	5.8	24.4	7.4	45.7	16.7
Gymnastics	5,000,000	32,749[f]	3.5	68.9	22.6	5.0	0.1
Hockey, street, roller & field	(b)	12,010[g, h]	0.0	39.7	43.9	16.4	0.0
Horseback riding	(b)	72,782	0.9	19.4	17.0	60.5	2.1
Horseshoe pitching	(b)	2,486	5.4	25.3	19.6	46.9	2.9
Ice hockey	1,900,000	19,835[h]	0.4	32.4	46.1	20.9	0.2
Ice skating	7,700,000	30,235[i]	1.5	53.8	17.4	25.3	2.0
Martial arts	5,100,000	24,970	0.8	29.5	26.5	42.6	0.6
Mountain climbing	(b)	3,104	2.8	5.5	42.9	48.8	0.0
Racquetball, squash & paddleball	32,000,000	9,363	0.1	3.7	20.5	70.2	4.8
Roller skating	32,300,000	140,362[i, j]	1.5	60.7	16.1	21.3	0.3
Rugby	(b)	8,921	0.0	0.5	67.2	32.3	0.0
Scuba diving	2,300,000	1,542	0.0	1.1	23.9	64.8	10.1
Skateboarding	7,000,000	59,964	1.7	53.8	35.1	9.4	0.0
Snowmobiling	3,400,000	14,107	1.3	9.2	35.0	54.5	0.0
Soccer	13,200,000	175,303	0.4	46.2	37.5	15.6	0.2
Swimming	57,900,000	99,691[k]	11.8	43.8	17.4	24.3	2.7
Tennis	10,900,000	25,181	0.6	13.4	17.5	54.8	13.7
Track & field	(b)	14,903	0.1	44.2	50.5	5.2	0.0
Volleyball	11,700,000	64,239	0.1	23.5	43.7	32.1	0.6
Water skiing	6,600,000	12,639	0.0	4.9	31.6	63.2	0.3
Weight lifting	(b)	65,347	4.7	12.6	34.4	46.4	1.8
Wrestling	3,800,000	51,164	0.4	36.4	54.2	8.7	0.1

Source: Participants—National Sporting Goods Association (NSGA); figures include those 7 years of age or older who participated more than once per year except for bicycle riding and swimming, which include those who participated six or more times per year. Injuries—Consumer Product Safety Commission (CPSC); figures include only injuries treated in hospital emergency departments.
[a] *Excludes mountain biking.*
[b] *Data not available.*
[c] *Includes exercise equipment (31,998 injuries) and exercise activity (128,143 injuries).*
[d] *Includes touch and tackle football.*
[e] *Excludes golf carts (9,249 injuries).*
[f] *Excludes trampolines (98,889 injuries).*
[g] *There were 2,938 injuries in street hockey, 4,298 in roller hockey, and 4,774 in field hockey.*
[h] *Excludes 39,711 injuries in hockey, unspecified.*
[i] *Excludes 20,484 injuries in skating, unspecified.*
[j] *Includes 2x2 (45,233 injuries) and in-line (95,129 injuries).*
[k] *Includes injuries associated with swimming, swimming pools, pool slides, diving or diving boards, and swimming pool equipment.*

Football

There were three fatalities directly related to football during the 2000 season compared to six in 1999. All three were associated with high school football. In both 1999 and 2000, there were 12 indirect fatalities caused by systemic failure as a result of exertion while participating in football activities or by a complication. In 2000, ten were associated with high school football and two with college football.

Source: Mueller, F.O., & Diehl, J.L. (2001). Annual Survey of Football Injury Research, 1931–2000. Overland Park, KS: National Collegiate Athletic Association.

Recreational Boating

Deaths associated with recreational boating numbered 734 in the United States and its territories in 1999 according to the United States Coast Guard. Drowning accounted for 517 of the deaths. The Coast Guard estimates that about 450 boaters who drowned could have been saved by wearing a life jacket. Alcohol was reported to be involved in 191 (26%) of the deaths.

Snowboarding and Alpine Skiing

According to the National Ski Areas Association, there were 30 skiing/snowboarding fatalities and about 44 serious injuries (e.g., paraplegics and head injuries) nationwide during the 1999–2000 season. Of the fatalities, 23 were skiers (19 male and 4 female) and 7 were snowboarders (6 male and 1 female). There were 52.2 million skier/snowboarder visits nationwide during the 1999–2000 season.

Scooters

According to data from the Consumer Product Safety Commission (CPSC), injuries associated with unpowered scooters soared in 2000 mainly due to the popularity of new, lightweight aluminum scooters. According to the National Sporting Goods Association, scooter sales skyrocketed from virtually zero in 1999 to 9.2 million units sold in 2000.

CPSC estimates that there were about 40,500 emergency room-treated injuries associated with scooters in 2000. Injuries increased almost 1,800% from May to September. August to October accounted for about 56% of the estimated total injuries. Each of these 3 months exceeded the 12-month totals for 1998 and 1999. About 85% of the injuries were to children under 15 years old. The most frequent injury was a fracture, usually to the arm or hand. CPSC knows of four deaths related to the new type of scooter. One adult and one child fell and struck their heads. Two children were struck by cars.

ESTIMATED NUMBER OF EMERGENCY ROOM-TREATED SCOOTER INJURIES BY MONTH, UNITED STATES, JANUARY 2000–APRIL 2001

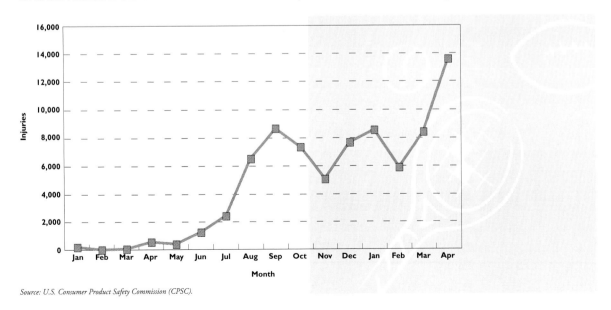

Source: U.S. Consumer Product Safety Commission (CPSC).

WEATHER

According to the National Weather Service[a], 5,148 injuries and 908 fatalities occurred due to severe weather in the United States in 1999, the latest year for which complete data are available. While 1999 weather-related injuries decreased from the 1998 total of 11,171, 1999 weather-related fatalities increased from the 1998 total of 687. In 1999, severe weather accounted for more than $12 billion in damage to crops and property.

Extreme Heat

Extreme heat was the number one weather-related killer accounting for 502 (55%) of the 908 weather-related deaths—nearly three times higher than 1998's fatality estimate of 173 and two and half times higher than the 10-year average of 194. A large portion of these fatalities occurred in Illinois with 138 deaths, Pennsylvania with 88, and Missouri with 77. The elderly are most at risk from heat. In 1999, 70- to 89-year-olds accounted for 47% of the 502 heat-related fatalities. Most deaths occurred in homes without air conditioning or adequate ventilation.

Tornadoes

Tornadoes were the second leading cause of weather-related deaths in 1999. There were 1,343 recorded tornadoes, a 6% decrease from the 1,425 tornadoes in 1998. Tornadoes accounted for 94 fatalities, 10% of the total weather-related fatalities. Most of the tornado

fatalities occurred in Oklahoma, which reported 42 fatalities in 1999. Of the 94 tornado deaths, 39 were in permanent homes and 34 were in mobile homes. Tornadoes accounted for 16% of the total damage to crops and property in 1999.

Floods

Floods, which include flash floods, river floods, and urban/small stream floods, accounted for 68 deaths, 7% of the total weather-related fatalities in 1999. This is 50% lower than the number of flood deaths in 1998. North Carolina recorded the highest number of flood fatalities with 24, followed by Pennsylvania and New Jersey with 6 fatalities each. Many of the deaths categorized as "in water" were due to being swept away by current after leaving a stalled vehicle. Flash floods accounted for 60 fatalities while river floods caused the remaining 8.

Lightning

Lightning was responsible for 46 deaths and 243 injuries in 1999. The 1999 fatalities were about 20% below the 10-year fatality average of 57. Florida ranked highest with five deaths in 1999, followed by North Carolina with four. Of those who died, 24 were outside, 9 were under a tree, and 6 were in boats.

[a] *National Weather Service.* Summary of Natural Hazard Statistics for 1999 in the United States *(based on data from National Climatic Data Center). Retrieved June 2001 from http://www.nws.noaa.gov/om/hazstats.htm.*

SEVERE WEATHER FATALITIES, UNITED STATES, 1990–1999

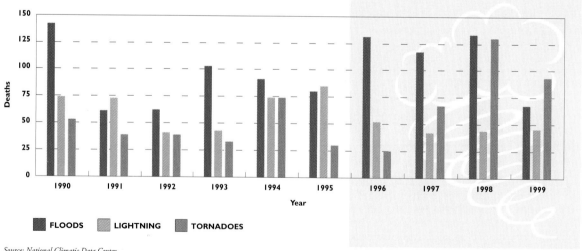

Source: National Climatic Data Center.

Unintentional firearms-related deaths fell
43% in 1998 from its 1993 high.

FIREARMS

Firearm-related deaths from unintentional, intentional, and undetermined causes totaled 30,708 in 1998, a decrease of 5.3% from 1997. Suicides accounted for nearly 57% of firearms deaths, about 38% were homicides, and almost 3% were unintentional deaths. Males dominate all categories of firearms deaths and accounted for more than 85% of the total.

The numbers of homicide, suicide, and unintentional deaths by firearms have decreased each of the last five years. Compared to 1993, homicides were down

35%, suicides were down 8%, and unintentional decreased 43%.

Hospital emergency department surveillance data indicate an estimated 13,698 nonfatal unintentional firearm-related injuries in 1998. For assault and legal intervention there were an estimated 46,365 nonfatal injuries and 4,421 intentionally self-inflicted nonfatal injuries.

Source: National Safety Council tabulation of National Center for Health Statistics data; Gotsch, K.E., Annest, J.L., Mercy, J.A., & Ryan, G.W. (2001). Surveillance for fatal and nonfatal firearm-related injuries—United States, 1993-1998. MMWR (CDC Surveillance Summaries), 50(SS-2), 1-34.

DEATHS INVOLVING FIREARMS, BY AGE AND SEX, UNITED STATES, 1998

Type & Sex	All Ages	Under 5 Years	5–14 Years	15–19 Years	20–24 Years	25–44 Years	45–64 Years	65–74 Years	75 & Over
Total Firearm Deaths	**30,708**	**83**	**529**	**3,180**	**4,240**	**11,999**	**6,137**	**2,081**	**2,459**
Male	26,189	51	371	2,817	3,791	10,012	5,084	1,834	2,229
Female	4,519	32	158	363	449	1,987	1,053	247	230
Unintentional	**866**	**19**	**102**	**141**	**119**	**280**	**140**	**34**	**31**
Male	762	15	81	130	113	242	123	32	26
Female	104	4	21	11	6	38	17	2	5
Suicides	**17,424**	**0**	**154**	**1,087**	**1,423**	**6,118**	**4,525**	**1,831**	**2,286**
Male	15,104	0	118	949	1,270	5,162	3,821	1,660	2,124
Female	2,320	0	36	138	153	956	704	171	162
Homicides	**11,798**	**63**	**251**	**1,870**	**2,614**	**5,311**	**1,365**	**202**	**122**
Male	9,771	36	152	1,662	2,334	4,347	1,049	129	62
Female	2,027	27	99	208	280	964	316	73	60
Legal Intervention	**304**	**0**	**3**	**28**	**47**	**179**	**41**	**4**	**2**
Male	298	0	1	27	47	178	39	4	2
Female	6	0	2	1	0	1	2	0	0
Undetermined[a]	**316**	**1**	**19**	**54**	**37**	**111**	**66**	**10**	**18**
Male	254	0	19	49	27	83	52	9	15
Female	62	1	0	5	10	28	14	1	3

[a]*Undetermined means the intentionality of the deaths (unintentional, suicide, homicide) was not determined.*

FIREARMS DEATHS BY INTENTIONALITY AND YEAR, UNITED STATES, 1989–1998

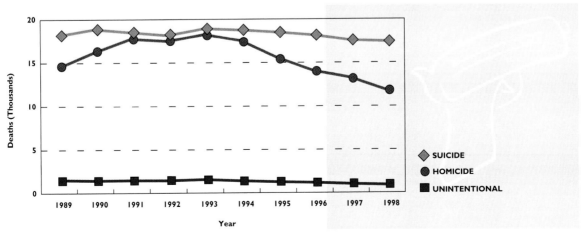

TRANSPORTATION ACCIDENT COMPARISONS

Passenger transportation incidents account for over one-fifth of all unintentional-injury deaths. But the risk of death to the passenger, expressed on a per mile basis, varies greatly by transportation mode. Automobile travel presents the greatest risk; air, rail, and bus travel have much lower death rates. The tables below show the latest information on passenger transportation deaths and death rates.

Passenger Automobiles and Taxis

Automobile occupants account for about 58% of all highway vehicle occupant deaths, and automobiles also represent about 58% of the total vehicle miles of highway travel. The automobile statistics shown in the tables below represent all passenger car usage, both intercity and local.

Buses

Intercity buses carried 359 million passengers and transit buses carried 5.6 billion passengers in 1999. School buses are not included in this comparison (see pages 98–99 for data on school bus fatalities and injuries).

Railroad Passenger Trains

In 1999, Amtrak accounted for about 37% of the railroad passenger miles. Railroads carried about 395 million passengers in 1999 and had 14 passenger deaths that year.

Scheduled Airlines

There were 17 passenger deaths in 1999 on scheduled service. Domestic certified airlines carried 589 million passengers in 1999.

TRANSPORTATION ACCIDENT DEATH RATES, UNITED STATES, 1997–1999

Kind of Transportation	1999			1997–1999 Average Death Rate
	Passenger Deaths	Passenger Miles (Billions)	Deaths per 100,000,000 Passenger Miles	
Passenger automobiles[a]	20,763	2,495.1	0.83	0.87
Buses[b]	39[c]	56.1	0.07	0.04
Transit buses	1	21.4	0.005	0.005
Intercity buses	29	34.7	0.08	0.04
Railroad passenger trains[d]	14	14.2	0.10	0.06
Scheduled airlines[e]	17	487.9	0.003	0.004

Source: Automobile and bus passenger deaths—Fatality Analysis Reporting System data. Railroad passenger deaths—Federal Railroad Administration. Airline passenger deaths—National Transportation Safety Board. Passenger miles for intercity buses, railroad, and airlines—Wilson, R. A. (2001). Transportation in America, 18th edition. Washington, DC: Eno Transportation Foundation, Inc. Passenger miles for transit buses—American Public Transit Association. All other figures—National Safety Council estimates.

[a] Includes taxi passengers. Drivers of passenger automobiles are considered passengers.
[b] Figures do not include school buses.
[c] Deaths include other and unknown bus types.
[d] Includes commutation.
[e] Includes large airlines and scheduled commuter airlines; excludes cargo service. Rates exclude suicide/sabotage deaths.

PASSENGER DEATHS AND DEATH RATES, UNITED STATES, 1989–1999

Year	Passenger Cars & Taxis		Buses[a]		Railroad Passenger Trains		Scheduled Airlines	
	Deaths	Rate[b]	Deaths	Rate[b]	Deaths	Rate[b]	Deaths	Rate[b]
1989	24,871	1.12	17	0.04	8	0.06	284	0.09
1990	23,924	0.99	16	0.04	3	0.02	11	0.003
1991	22,215	0.91	16	0.04	8	0.06	100	0.03
1992	21,257	0.83	17	0.04	3	0.02	38	0.01
1993	21,414	0.86	9	0.02	58	0.45	19	0.01
1994	21,813	0.91	13	0.03	5	0.04	245	0.06
1995	22,288	0.97	16	0.03	0	0.00	159	0.04
1996	22,359	0.96	10	0.02	12	0.09	329	0.08
1997	21,920	0.92	4	0.01	6	0.05	42	0.01
1998	21,099	0.86	26	0.05	4	0.03	0	0.00
1999	20,763	0.83	39	0.07	14	0.10	17	0.003

Source: See table above.
[a] Figures do not include school buses.
[b] Deaths per 100,000,000 passenger miles.

PASSENGER[a] DEATH RATES, UNITED STATES, 1997–1999

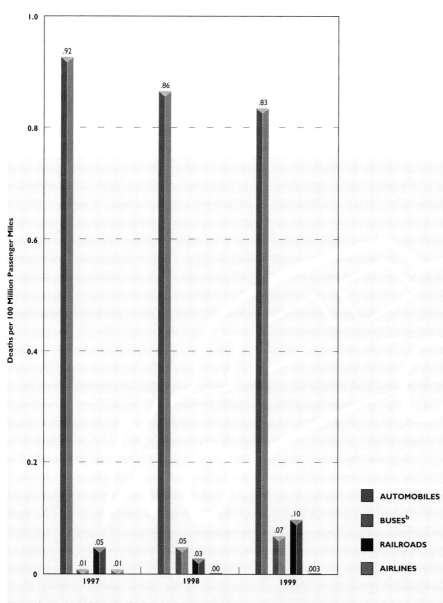

[a]Drivers of passenger automobiles are considered passengers.
[b]Figures do not include school buses.

AVIATION

Worldwide passenger deaths in scheduled air service totaled 755 in 2000, according to preliminary data from the International Civil Aviation Organization, a specialized United Nations agency with 185 member states. The death rate per 100 million passenger miles in 2000 was 0.04, up from 0.03 in 1999. Aircraft accidents involving a passenger fatality totaled 18. Passenger deaths per year averaged 795 for the last 10 years.

WORLDWIDE SCHEDULED AIR SERVICE ACCIDENTS, DEATHS, AND DEATH RATES, 1981–2000

Year	Aircraft Accidents[a]	Passenger Deaths	Death Rate[b]	Year	Aircraft Accidents[a]	Passenger Deaths	Death Rate[b]
1981	22	365	0.06	1991	24	518	0.05
1982	25	762	0.13	1992	24	978	0.09
1983	21	817	0.13	1993	31	806	0.07
1984	16	218	0.03	1994	23	962	0.08
1985	25	1,037	0.14	1995	20	541	0.04
1986	19	427	0.05	1996	21	1,125	0.08
1987	23	889	0.10	1997	25	867	0.05
1988	26	712	0.08	1998	20	904	0.06
1989	29	879	0.09	1999[c]	20	498	0.03
1990	23	473	0.05	2000[d]	18	755	0.04

Source: International Civil Aviation Organization. Figures exclude the USSR up to 1992 and the Commonwealth of Independent States thereafter.
[a] Involving a passenger fatality.
[b] Passenger deaths per 100 million passenger miles.
[c] Revised.
[d] Preliminary.

U.S. CIVIL AVIATION ACCIDENTS, DEATHS, AND DEATH RATES, 1996–2000

Year	Accidents Total	Accidents Fatal	Deaths[a]	Per 100,000 Flight-Hours Total	Per 100,000 Flight-Hours Fatal	Per Million Aircraft-Miles Total	Per Million Aircraft-Miles Fatal
Large Airlines[b]							
1996	32	3	342	0.247	0.023	0.0059	0.0006
1997	44	3	3	0.292	0.020	0.0069	0.0005
1998	43	1	1	0.270	0.006	0.0068	0.0002
1999	48	2	12	0.290	0.012	0.0072	0.0003
2000	49	3	92	0.285	0.017	0.0073	0.0004
Commuter Airlines[b]							
1996	11	1	14	0.399	0.036	0.0186	0.0017
1997	16	5	46	1.628	0.509	0.0636	0.0199
1998	8	0	0	2.262	—	0.1576	—
1999	13	5	12	2.876	1.106	0.1596	0.0614
2000	12	1	5	2.182	0.182	0.1071	0.0089
On-Demand Air Taxis[b]							
1996	90	29	63	4.44	1.43	—	—
1997	82	15	39	3.64	0.67	—	—
1998	77	17	45	2.80	0.62	—	—
1999	73	12	38	3.23	0.53	—	—
2000	80	22	71	3.29	0.91	—	—
General Aviation[b]							
1996	1,909	360	632	7.67	1.45	—	—
1997	1,851	352	641	7.27	1.38	—	—
1998	1,909	368	631	7.53	1.45	—	—
1999	1,913	342	630	6.49	1.16	—	—
2000	1,835	341	592	5.96	1.11	—	—

Source: National Transportation Safety Board: 2000 preliminary, 1996–1999 revised; exposure data for rates from Federal Aviation Administration.
[a] Includes passengers, crew members, and others.
[b] Civil aviation accident statistics collected by the National Transportation Safety Board are classified according to the Federal air regulations under which the flights were made. The classifications are (1) large airlines operating scheduled service under Title 14, Code of Federal Regulations, part 121 (14 CFR 121); (2) commuter carriers operating scheduled service under 14 CFR 135; (3) unscheduled, "on-demand" air taxis under 14 CFR 135; and (4) "general aviation," which includes accidents involving aircraft flown under rules other than 14 CFR 121 and 14 CFR 135. Suicide/sabotage is included in accident and fatality totals but excluded from rates. Not shown in the table is nonscheduled air carrier operations under 14 CFR 121 which experienced five accidents and no fatalities in 2000. Since 1997, Large Airlines includes aircraft with 10 or more seats, formerly operated as commuter carriers under 14 CFR 135.

DEATHS AND INJURIES IN RAILROAD ACCIDENTS AND INCIDENTS, UNITED STATES, 1991–2000

Year	Casualties Not at Grade Crossings	All Casualties					
		Total	Passengers on Trains[a]	Employees on Duty		Other Non-trespassers[a]	Trespassers
				Number	Rate[b]		
Deaths							
1991	586	1,194	8	35	0.013	484	663
1992	591	1,170	3	34	0.013	475	646
1993	653	1,279	58	47	0.018	489	675
1994	611	1,226	5	31	0.012	505	682
1995	567	1,146	0	34	0.013	443	660
1996	551	1,039	12	33	0.013	365	620
1997	602	1,063	6	37	0.015	362	646
1998	577	1,008	4	27	0.010	324	644
1999	530	932	14	31	0.012	302	572
2000	512	937	4	24	0.010	332	570
Nonfatal Injuries							
1991	21,374	23,468	382	19,626	7.40	2,110	769
1992	19,408	21,383	411	17,755	6.87	1,909	772
1993	17,284	19,121	559	15,363	5.91	1,856	733
1994	14,851	16,812	497	13,080	5.04	1,913	764
1995	12,546	14,440	573	10,777	4.22	1,869	700
1996	10,948	12,558	513	9,199	3.65	1,660	750
1997	10,227	11,767	601	8,295	3.29	1,517	728
1998	10,156	11,459	535	8,398	3.26	1,201	677
1999	10,304	11,700	481	8,622	3.38	1,307	650
2000	10,424	11,643	658	8,423	3.43	1,264	606

Source: Federal Railroad Administration. Includes train accidents, train incidents, and non-train incidents at both public and private grade crossings.
[a] Federal Railroad Administration definitions are "Persons on or getting on or off passenger-carrying trains under conditions not constituting trespass are designated as 'passengers on trains.' Other persons lawfully on railroad premises in connection with their journeys by railroads are designated 'other nontrespassers.'"
[b] The rates are the number of deaths or injuries per 200,000 hours worked. Because of differences in definitions, the injury rates are not comparable with those for other industries shown elsewhere in Injury Facts®.

RAIL-HIGHWAY GRADE-CROSSING DEATHS AND INJURIES, UNITED STATES, 1991–2000

Year	Deaths				Nonfatal Injuries			
	Total	Motor-Vehicle	Pedestrian	Other	Total	Motor-Vehicle	Pedestrian	Other
1991	608	535	52	21	2,094	2,029	30	35
1992	579	506	49	24	1,975	1,891	31	53
1993	626	554	48	24	1,837	1,760	28	49
1994	615	542	50	23	1,961	1,885	30	46
1995	579	508	47	24	1,894	1,825	28	41
1996	488	415	60	13	1,610	1,545	31	34
1997	461	419	38	4	1,540	1,494	33	13
1998	431	369	50	12	1,303	1,257	33	13
1999	402	345	45	12	1,396	1,338	35	23
2000	425	361	51	13	1,219	1,169	34	16

Source: Federal Railroad Administration data for public and private grade-crossing accidents.

HOME, 2000

Between 1912 and 2000, unintentional home injury deaths per 100,000 population were reduced 61% from 28 to 11. In 1912, when there were 21 million households, an estimated 26,000 to 28,000 persons were killed by unintentional home injuries. In 2000, with more than 103 million households and the population nearly tripled, home deaths numbered only 29,500.

The injury total of 7,100,000 means that 1 person in 39 in the United States was disabled one full day or more by unintentional injuries received in the home in 2000. Disabling injuries are more numerous in the home than in the workplace and in motor-vehicle crashes combined.

The National Health Interview Survey indicates that about 13,592,000 episodes of home injuries occurred in 1997 (the latest year available). This means that about 1 person in 20 incurred a home injury requiring medical attention. About 42% of all medically attended injuries occurred at home. See page 21 for definitions and numerical differences between National Health Interview Survey and National Safety Council figures.

The Council adopted the Bureau of Labor Statistics' Census of Fatal Occupational Injuries count for work-related unintentional injuries retroactive to 1992 data. Because of the lower Work class total resulting from this change, several thousand unintentional-injury deaths that had been classified by the Council as work-related had to be reassigned to the Home and Public classes. For this reason long-term historical comparisons for these three classes should be made with caution. See the Technical Appendix for an explanation of the methodological changes.

Deaths **29,500**
Disabling injuries **7,100,000**
Death rate per 100,000 population **10.7**
Costs . . . . **$111.9 billion**

HOME DEATHS AND DEATH RATES, UNITED STATES, 1992–2000

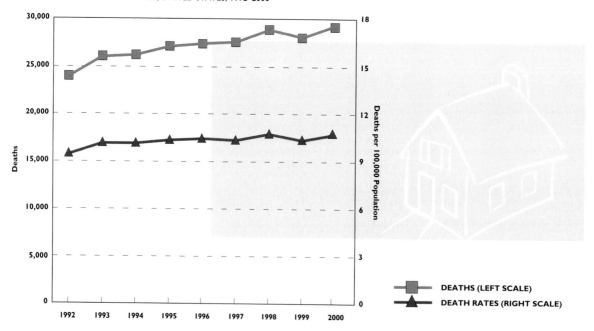

PRINCIPAL TYPES OF HOME UNINTENTIONAL-INJURY DEATHS, UNITED STATES, 1950–2000

Year	Total Home	Falls	Fires, Burns[a]	Suffocation, Ing. Obj.	Suffocation, Mech.	Drowning	Poison (Solid, Liquid)	Poison (Gas, Vapor)	Firearms	Other
1950	29,000	14,800	5,000	(b)	1,600	(b)	1,300	1,250	950	4,100
1955	28,500	14,100	5,400	(b)	1,250	(b)	1,150	900	1,100	4,600
1960	28,000	12,300	6,350	1,850	1,500	(b)	1,350	900	1,200	2,550
1965	28,500	11,700	6,100	1,300c	1,200	(b)	1,700	1,100	1,300	4,100c
1970	27,000	9,700	5,600	1,800c	1,100c	(b)	3,000	1,100	1,400c	3,300c
1975	25,000	8,000	5,000	1,800	800	(b)	3,700	1,000	1,300	3,400
1980	22,800	7,100	4,800	2,000	500	(b)	2,500	700	1,100	4,100d
1981	21,700	6,800	4,700	2,000	500	(b)	2,600	800	1,000	3,300
1982	21,200	6,500	4,300	2,100	600	(b)	2,700	800	1,000	3,200
1983	21,200	6,500	4,100	2,200	600	(b)	2,700	800	900	3,400
1984	21,200	6,400	4,100	2,300	600	(b)	3,000	700	900	3,200
1985	21,600	6,500	4,000	2,400	600	(b)	3,200	700	900	3,300
1986	21,700	6,100	4,000	2,500	600	(b)	3,700	600	800	3,400
1987	21,400	6,300	3,900	2,500	600	(b)	3,500	600	800	3,200
1988	22,700	6,600	4,100	2,600	600	(b)	4,300	500	800	3,200
1989	22,500	6,600	3,900	2,500	600	(b)	4,400	600	800	3,100
1990	21,500	6,700	3,400	2,300	600	(b)	4,000	500	800	3,200
1991	22,100	6,900	3,400	2,200	700	(b)	4,500	500	800	3,100
1992	24,000	7,700	3,700	1,500	700	900	4,800	400	1,000	3,300
1993	26,100	7,900	3,700	1,700	700	900	6,000	500	1,100	3,600
1994	26,300	8,100	3,700	1,600	800	900	6,300	500	900	3,500
1995	27,200	8,400	3,500	1,500	800	900	6,600	400	900	4,200
1996	27,500	9,000	3,500	1,500	800	900	6,800	500	800	3,700
1997	27,700	9,100	3,200	1,500	800	900	7,400	400	700	3,500
1998e	29,000	9,500	2,900	1,800	800	1,000	8,000	400	600	4,000
1999e	28,200	8,800	2,700	1,400	900	800	8,700	300	500	4,100
2000f	29,500	9,300	3,200	1,700	900	900	9,400	300	400	3,400

Source: National Safety Council estimates based on data from National Center for Health Statistics and state vital statistics departments. The Council adopted the Bureau of Labor Statistics' Census of Fatal Occupational Injuries count for work-related unintentional injuries retroactive to 1992 data. Because of the lower Work class total resulting from this change, several thousand unintentional-injury deaths that had been classified by the Council as work-related had to be reassigned to the Home and Public classes. For this reason long-term historical comparisons for these three classes should be made with caution. See the Technical Appendix for an explanation of the methodological changes.
a Includes deaths resulting from conflagration, regardless of nature of injury.
b Included in Other.
c Data for this year and subsequent years not comparable with previous years due to classification changes.
d Includes about 1,000 excessive heat deaths due to summer heat wave.
e Revised.
f Preliminary.

PRINCIPAL TYPES OF HOME UNINTENTIONAL-INJURY DEATHS, UNITED STATES, 2000

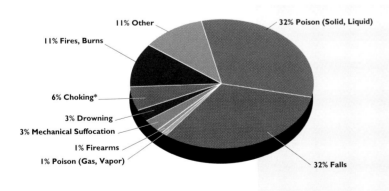

11% Other
11% Fires, Burns
6% Choking*
3% Drowning
3% Mechanical Suffocation
1% Firearms
1% Poison (Gas, Vapor)
32% Poison (Solid, Liquid)
32% Falls

Inhalation or ingestion of food or other object.

DEATHS DUE TO UNINTENTIONAL HOME INJURIES, 2000

TYPE OF EVENT AND AGE OF VICTIM

All Home

Includes deaths in the home and on home premises to occupants, guests, and trespassers. Also includes hired household workers but excludes other persons working on home premises.

	Total	Change from 1999	Death Rate[a]
Deaths	29,500	+5%	10.7

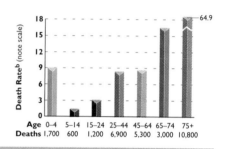

Poisoning by Solids and Liquids

Includes deaths from drugs, medicines, mushrooms, and shellfish, as well as commonly recognized poisons. Excludes poisonings from spoiled foods, salmonella, etc., which are classified as disease deaths.

	Total	Change from 1999	Death Rate[a]
Deaths	9,400	+8%	3.4

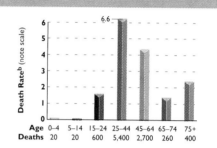

Falls

Includes deaths from falls from one level to another or on the same level in the home or on home premises.

	Total	Change from 1999	Death Rate[a]
Deaths	9,300	+6%	3.4

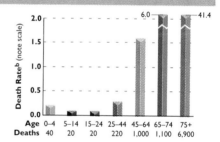

Fires, Burns, and Deaths Associated with Fires

Includes deaths from fires, burns, and injuries in conflagrations in the home—such as asphyxiation, falls, and struck by falling objects. Excludes burns from hot objects or liquids.

	Total	Change from 1999	Death Rate[a]
Deaths	3,200	+19%	1.2

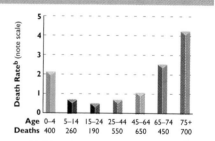

Suffocation by Ingested Object

Includes deaths from unintentional ingestion or inhalation of objects or food resulting in the obstruction of respiratory passages.

	Total	Change from 1999	Death Rate[a]
Deaths	1,700	+21%	0.6

See footnotes on page 133.

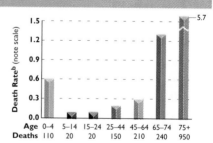

Drowning

Includes drownings of persons in or on home premises—such as in swimming pools and bathtubs. Excludes drowning in floods and other cataclysms.

	Total	Change from 1999	Death Rate[a]
Deaths	900	+13%	0.3

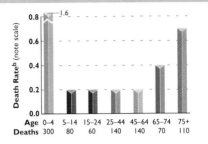

Age	0–4	5–14	15–24	25–44	45–64	65–74	75+
Deaths	300	80	60	140	140	70	110

Mechanical Suffocation

Includes deaths from smothering by bedclothes, thin plastic materials, etc.; suffocation by cave-ins or confinement in closed spaces; and mechanical strangulation.

	Total	Change from 1999	Death Rate[a]
Deaths	900	0%	0.3

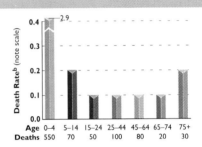

Age	0–4	5–14	15–24	25–44	45–64	65–74	75+
Deaths	550	70	50	100	80	20	30

Firearms

Includes firearms injuries in or on home premises—such as while cleaning or playing with guns. Excludes deaths from explosive materials.

	Total	Change from 1999	Death Rate[a]
Deaths	400	-20%	0.1

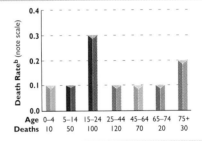

Age	0–4	5–14	15–24	25–44	45–64	65–74	75+
Deaths	10	50	100	120	70	20	30

Poisoning by Gases and Vapors

Principally carbon monoxide due to incomplete combustion, involving cooking stoves, heating equipment, and standing motor vehicles. Gas poisonings in conflagrations are classified as fire deaths.

	Total	Change from 1999	Death Rate[a]
Deaths	300	0%	0.1

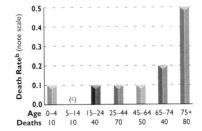

Age	0–4	5–14	15–24	25–44	45–64	65–74	75+
Deaths	10	10	40	70	50	40	80

All Other Home

Most important types included are: electric current; hot substances, corrosive liquids, and steam; and explosive materials.

	Total	Change from 1999	Death Rate[a]
Deaths	3,400	-17%	1.2

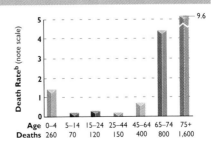

Age	0–4	5–14	15–24	25–44	45–64	65–74	75+
Deaths	260	70	120	150	400	800	1,600

[a] Deaths per 100,000 population.
[b] Deaths per 100,000 population in each age group.
[c] Death rate less than 0.05.

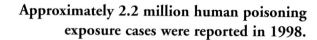

UNINTENTIONAL POISONINGS

Deaths from unintentional solid and liquid poisoning increased approximately 7% from 9,587 in 1997 to 10,255 in 1998, the latest year for which detailed tabulations are available. Deaths attributed to local anesthetics and other drugs acting on the central and autonomic nervous system, including cocaine, increased by about 15%, from 1,336 fatalities in 1997 to 1,540 in 1998.

Over the last 30 years, the number and circumstances of deaths from unintentional solid and liquid poisoning have changed greatly. Since 1968, the death rate per 100,000 population has nearly tripled from 1.3 to 3.8 in 1998. The 25 to 44 year age group had the greatest increase in death rate, from 1.8 in 1968 to 7.5 in 1998.

The death rate for the 0 to 4 year age group has fallen dramatically, from 1.6 in 1968 to 0.1 in 1998.

Due to classification system changes, death figures by type of poisoning are only comparable since 1979. The number of deaths from drugs, medicaments, and biologicals has increased steadily since 1979, while the number of deaths from other solid and liquid poisonings, including household chemicals, has decreased.

Total human poisoning exposure cases reported, both fatal and nonfatal, were estimated to be 2.2 million in 1998, according to the American Association of Poison Control Centers.

UNINTENTIONAL POISONING DEATHS BY TYPE AND AGE, UNITED STATES, 1998

Type of Poisoning	All Ages	Under 5 Years	5–14 Years	15–24 Years	25–44 Years	45–64 Years	65 Years & Over
Total Poisoning by Solids and Liquids, E850–E866	**10,255**	**26**	**20**	**779**	**6,224**	**2,650**	**556**
Rate (deaths per 100,000 population)	3.8	0.1	0.1	2.1	7.5	4.6	1.6
Male	7,497	15	11	627	4,667	1,931	246
Female	2,758	11	9	152	1,557	719	310
Drugs, medicaments, biologicals, E850–E858	**9,838**	**22**	**15**	**734**	**6,047**	**2,519**	**501**
Male	7,180	11	8	588	4,532	1,829	212
Female	2,658	11	7	146	1,515	690	289
Analgesics, antipyretics, antirheumatics, E850	3,141	8	7	273	1,937	848	68
Opiates, related narcotics, E850.0	2,718	6	7	251	1,702	722	30
Salicylates (incl. aspirin), E850.1	32	1	0	2	13	10	6
Other, unspecified analgesics, antipyretics, antirheumatics, E850.2–E850.5, E850.8, E850.9	391	1	0	20	222	116	32
Barbiturates, E851	16	1	0	0	6	8	1
Other sedatives, hypnotics, E852	8	0	0	0	3	5	0
Tranquilizers, E853	107	0	0	6	52	38	11
Other psychotropic agents, E854	334	1	3	19	185	107	119
Other drugs acting on central and autonomic nervous system (incl. local anesthetics), E855	1,540	4	1	113	1,032	359	31
Antibiotics, E856	39	0	0	2	2	16	19
Anti-infectives, E857	4	0	0	0	3	0	1
Other drugs, E858	4,649	8	4	321	2,827	1,138	351
Cardiovascular drugs, E858.3	194	2	0	1	4	23	164
Gastrointestinal drugs, E858.4	3	1	0	0	0	1	1
Other, unspecified drugs, E858.0–E858.2, E858.5–E858.9	4,452	5	4	320	2,823	1,114	186
Other solids and liquids, E860–E866	**417**	**4**	**5**	**45**	**177**	**131**	**55**
Male	317	4	3	39	135	102	34
Female	100	0	2	6	42	29	21
Alcohol, E860	300	1	1	28	148	100	22
Cleansing, polishing agents, disinfectants, paints, varnishes, E861	10	0	0	1	3	1	5
Petroleum products, other solvents and their vapors, E862	37	2	2	9	17	4	3
Agricultural, horticultural chemical, pharmaceutical preparations, E863	8	0	0	0	3	4	1
Corrosives, caustics, E864	5	0	0	1	0	2	2
Foodstuffs, poisonous plants, E865	3	0	0	0	0	1	2
Other, unspecified solids and liquids, E866	54	1	2	6	6	19	20
Total Poisoning by Gases and Vapors, E867–E869	**546**	**10**	**13**	**81**	**169**	**126**	**147**
Rate (deaths per 100,000 population)	0.2	0.1	(a)	0.2	0.2	0.2	0.4
Male	410	5	8	65	144	98	90
Female	136	5	5	16	25	28	57
Gas distributed by pipeline, E867	15	0	0	3	2	4	6
Other utility gas, other carbon monoxide, E868	444	9	12	65	140	98	120
Other gases and vapors, E869	87	1	1	13	27	24	21

Source: National Safety Council tabulations of National Center for Health Statistics mortality data. See pages 40–43 for earlier year totals and rates; see Technical Appendix for comparability.
[a] *Rate less than 0.05.*

UNINTENTIONAL POISONINGS, 1988–1998

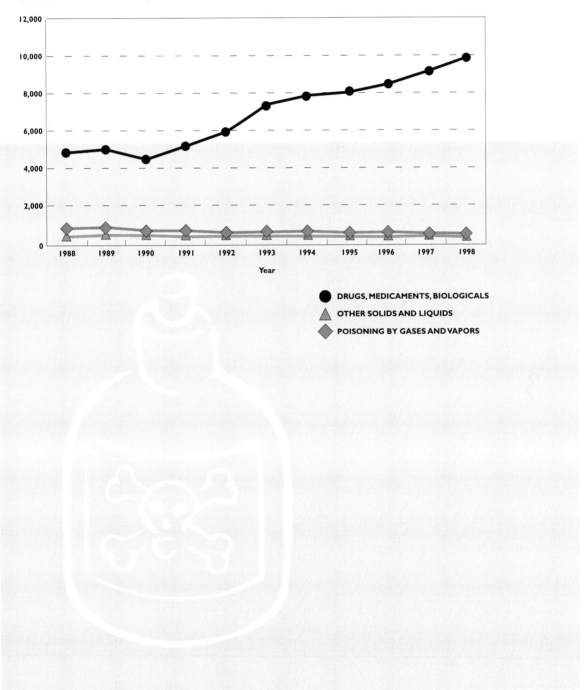

DRUGS, MEDICAMENTS, BIOLOGICALS

OTHER SOLIDS AND LIQUIDS

POISONING BY GASES AND VAPORS

INJURIES ASSOCIATED WITH CONSUMER PRODUCTS

The following list of items found in and around the home was selected from the U.S. Consumer Product Safety Commission's National Electronic Injury Surveillance System (NEISS) for 1999. The NEISS estimates are calculated from a statistically representative sample of hospitals in the United States. Injury totals represent estimates of the number of hospital emergency department-treated cases nationwide associated with various products. However, product involvement may or may not be the cause of the injury.

ESTIMATED HOSPITAL EMERGENCY DEPARTMENT VISITS RELATED TO SELECTED CONSUMER PRODUCTS, 1999
(excluding chemicals and most sports or sports equipment; see also page 122)

Description	Injuries[a]	Description	Injuries[a]
Home Workshop Equipment		Glass doors	38,755
Saws (hand or power)	96,658	Counters or countertops	38,597
Hammers	40,015	Poles	37,435
Power grinders, buffers & polishers	17,025	Fireplaces	19,143
Drills	17,994	Cabinet or door hardware	17,831
Welding & soldering equipment	18,039	Ramps or landings	16,736
Packaging and Containers, Household		**General Household Appliances**	
Bottles and jars	75,581	Refrigerators	28,408
Bags	28,189	Ranges	26,627
Household containers & packaging	19,611	Irons	15,762
Housewares		**Heating, Cooling, and Ventilating Equipment**	
Knives	446,225	Pipes (excluding smoking pipes)	28,050
Tableware and flatware (excluding knives)	112,665	Fans	15,560
Drinking glasses	99,847		
Cookware, bowls and canisters	31,118	**Home Communication and Entertainment Equipment**	
Scissors	30,162	Televisions	40,634
Waste containers, trash baskets, etc.	29,083	Sound recording and reproducing equipment	20,816
		Telephones or telephone accessories	16,663
Home Furnishings, Fixtures, and Accessories			
Beds	455,027	**Personal Use Items**	
Tables, n.e.c.[b]	304,758	Jewelry	65,127
Chairs	292,406	Razors and shavers	37,853
Bathtubs and showers	195,324	Coins	30,100
Ladders	163,138	Daywear	27,777
Sofas, couches, davenports, divans, etc.	120,653	Hair grooming equipment & accessories	23,434
Rugs and carpets	117,156	Other clothing[e]	19,974
Other furniture[c]	73,992	Luggage	15,826
Toilets	56,424		
Misc. decorating items	30,990	**Yard and Garden Equipment**	
Benches	24,391	Lawn mowers	70,640
Electric lighting equipment	24,042	Pruning, trimming & edging equipment	39,046
Sinks	23,140	Chainsaws	28,543
Mirrors or mirror glass	21,396	Other unpowered garden tools[f]	24,357
Stools	15,061		
		Sports and Recreation Equipment	
Home Structures and Construction Materials		Trampolines	98,889
Stairs or steps	1,029,418	All terrain vehicles	84,800
Floors or flooring materials	1,024,522	Swimming pools	81,809
Other doors[d]	331,344	Swings or swing sets	79,893
Ceilings and walls	259,301	Monkey bars or other playground climbing equipment	78,576
Household cabinets, racks, & shelves	240,629	Skateboards	59,964
Nails, screws, tacks or bolts	162,597	Slides or sliding boards	51,423
Porches, balconies, open-side floors	139,105	Other playground equipment[g]	28,060
Windows	129,276	Bleachers	22,063
Fences or fence posts	117,175	Grills	19,910
House repair and construction materials	73,542	Go-carts	18,772
Door sills or frames	43,082	BBs or pellets	14,910
Handrails, railings or banisters	39,574		

Source: U.S. Consumer Product Safety Commission, National Electronic Injury Surveillance System, Product Summary Report, All Products, CY1999. Not all product categories are shown. Products were selected for high injury frequency.

[a] *Estimated number of product-related injuries in the United States and territories that were treated in hospital emergency departments.*
[b] *Excludes baby changing and television tables or stands.*
[c] *Includes cabinets, racks, shelves, desks, bureaus, chests, buffets, etc.*
[d] *Excludes glass doors and garage doors.*
[e] *Excludes costumes, masks, daywear, footwear, nightwear, and outerwear.*
[f] *Includes cultivators, hoes, pitchforks, rakes, shovels, spades, and trowels.*
[g] *Excludes monkey bars, seesaws, slides and swings.*
n.e.c. = not elsewhere classified.

Residential fires in 1999 accounted for an estimated 383,000 or 73% of the total structure fires, virtually unchanged from 1998. Of these fires, 282,500 (74%) occurred in one- and two-family dwellings, 88,500 (23%) occurred in apartments, and 12,000 (3%) took place in other residential dwellings, including hotels and motels, college dormitories, and boarding houses.

An estimated 2,920 civilians died in residential fires in 1999, a decrease of 10.2% from 1998. There were 520 deaths in apartment fires, an increase of 16.9%. Another 2,375 fatalities occurred in one- and two-family dwellings, a decrease of 14.4% and the lowest number of civilian fire deaths in these structures since the National Fire Protection Association (NFPA) changed its survey methodology in 1977. Overall, about 81% of all fire deaths occurred in the home. An estimated 11,550 civilian injuries occurred in fires in one- and two-family dwellings, while an additional 4,500 occurred in apartment fires. These two figures together accounted for 98% of the total 16,425 civilian injuries in residential fires in 1999.

Residential property loss in 1999 from structure fires totaled nearly $5.1 billion, a significant increase of 16% from 1998. About $4.1 billion (81%) of the total resulted from fires in one- and two-family dwellings and about $842 million (17%) from fires

in apartments. These two figures represent significant increases of 13% and 33%, respectively, from 1998.

By region, the South had the highest fire incident rate for 1999 with 7.8 fires per thousand population, followed by the Northeast with a rate of 7.6. The South, with 15.1, also had the highest death rate per million population, followed by the North Central with 14.2. The Northeast (103.7) had the highest injury rate per million population, while the West had the lowest rate (65.2).

National estimates of fire-related deaths are made by the National Safety Council and the National Fire Protection Association (NFPA). The NFPA estimates include intentional deaths due to incendiary or suspicious fires (arson) and unintentional deaths due to fires in transport vehicles while in transit. The Council's estimate excludes deaths in incendiary or suspicious fires because such deaths are not unintentional. Deaths due to fires in transport vehicles are included in the appropriate transportation category.

Further differences may be due to the sources and methods employed. The Council's estimate is based on death certificate data from the National Center for Health Statistics and state vital statistics departments. NFPA estimates are based on a probability sample of fire departments.

Source: Karter, M. J., Jr. (2000, September). Fire loss in the United States during 1999. Quincy, MA: National Fire Protection Association.

CIVILIAN FIRE DEATH AND INJURY RATES BY REGION[a], 1999

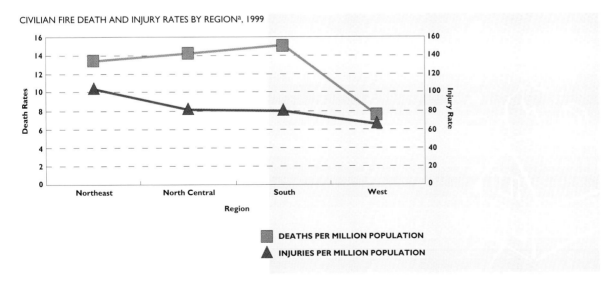

■ DEATHS PER MILLION POPULATION

▲ INJURIES PER MILLION POPULATION

[a]*The four regions are:* Northeast: *Connecticut, Maine, Massachusetts, New Hampshire, New Jersey, New York, Pennsylvania, Rhode Island, and Vermont.* North Central: *Illinois, Indiana, Iowa, Kansas, Michigan, Minnesota, Missouri, Nebraska, North Dakota, Ohio, South Dakota, and Wisconsin.* South: *Alabama, Arkansas, Delaware, District of Columbia, Florida, Georgia, Kentucky, Louisiana, Maryland, Mississippi, North Carolina, Oklahoma, South Carolina, Tennessee, Texas, Virginia, and West Virginia.* West: *Alaska, Arkansas, California, Colorado, Hawaii, Idaho, Montana, Nevada, New Mexico, Oregon, Utah, Washington, and Wyoming.*

FALLS

About 11 million fall-related episodes of injury were estimated to have occurred annually in 1997–1998 according to special tabulations of data from the National Health Interview Survey (NHIS) provided by the National Center for Health Statistics. The NHIS is a personal-interview household survey that collects health-related data from a member of the household.

The table below shows the estimated number of fall-related episodes by the type of fall for sex and age groups. More than one third (37.2%) of falls were on the floor or level ground and about 12.1% were falls on or down or from stairs or steps. Slightly fewer men fell on the floor or level ground (34.4%) and slightly more females (39.6%). Proportionately, women also fell more frequently than men down stairs or steps (14.7% vs. 8.9%, respectively) and on or from curbs and sidewalks (10.9% vs. 7.7%, respectively). (Percentages are based

on the number of fall episodes rather than the total number of types of falls mentioned. See footnote "b" below the table.)

Children under 12 years old fell most frequently on the floor or level ground (31.7%) and from furniture (14.7%) and from playground equipment (14.0%). Persons 12–64 years old most commonly fell on the floor or level ground (36.8%), down stairs or steps (13.2%), and from or on curbs or sidewalks (10.2%). The elderly (65 and older) followed the same pattern with 43.3% of falls on floors or level ground, 14.2% down stairs or steps, and 11.0% from or on curbs or sidewalks.

See also page 21 for general NHIS data and pages 22–23 for more data on falls.

AVERAGE ANNUAL NUMBER OF FALL-RELATED EPISODES BY TYPE OF FALL, SEX, AND AGE GROUP, UNITED STATES, 1997–1998

	Number of Episodes (in Thousands)					
	Both Sexes	Male	Female	0–11 Years	12–64 Years	65 Years or Over
All fall episodes	11,081	5,003	6,078	2,173	6,449	2,459
Type of fall						
All types of falls mentioned[b]	12,023	5,501	6,522	2,310	7,031	2,682
Floor/level ground	4,123	1,719	2,404	688	2,372	1,063
Stairs/step	1,340	446	894	138[a]	853	349
Curb/sidewalk	1,048	386	662	119[a]	658	271
Furniture	776	300	476	318	232	225
Playground equipment	465	270	196[a]	305	160[a]	—
Ladder/scaffolding	373	294	79[a]	25[a]	300	48[a]
Hole/opening	336	154[a]	182[a]	29[a]	256	51[a]
Other (specified)[c]	632	367	265	146[a]	364	122[a]
Other	2,780	1,483	1,297	524	1,749	507
Refused, Don't know	149[a]	(a)	(a)	(a)	(a)	(a)

Source: National Center for Health Statistics, Office of Analysis, Epidemiology, and Health Promotion.
[a] These data have a relative standard error of 20%–30%. Data not shown have a relative standard error greater than 30%. Dashes indicate zero.
[b] "All fall types mentioned" is greater than the total number of fall episodes because respondents could indicate up to two types of falls.
[c] Other (specified) type of fall includes escalator, building, tree, toilet, bathtub, and pool.

SCHOOL VIOLENCE

Approximately 322 persons died as a result of school-related violence during the school years 1992–1993 through 2000–2001, according to data compiled by the National School Safety Center. School-related violence includes homicides or suicides that occur while attending or on the way to or from a K–12 school or as a direct result of an official school-sponsored event.

About 75% of those who died in school-related violent incidents were shooting victims. Another 14% were stabbing/slashing victims, while a further 5% were the result of beating/kicking. Over three quarters (77%) of the victims were male.

Two thirds of the fatalities occurred in high school, while 16% took place in junior high school and 11% in elementary school. On campus and near school, with 25% and 22% respectively, accounted for nearly 50% of the deaths by location. Other locations associated with a large number of deaths included hallways (12%), parking lots (11%), and classrooms/offices (8%).

Forty-four or 86% of the states reported at least one school-related violent death. The state with the highest number of deaths was California with 74, followed by Texas (22), Florida (19), Georgia (17), and New York (16).

Although violent deaths at school receive national attention, a recent study (Kaufman et al., 2000) indicates that far greater numbers of school age children are murdered or commit suicide away from school. During the period from July 1, 1997 to June 30, 1998, 35 student murders and 7 student suicides occurred at school. For the same time period, there were 2,717 murders of youth ages 5 through 19 away from school, while for calendar year 1998 there were 2,054 suicides away from school among youth in the same age group.

Source: National School Safety Center, www.nssc1.org. Kaufman, P. et al. (2000). Indicators of school crime and safety, 2000 *(NCES 2001-017/NCJ-184176). Washington, DC: U.S. Departments of Education and Justice.*

SCHOOL-RELATED VIOLENT DEATHS BY REASON FOR DEATH, SCHOOL YEARS 1992/1993–2000/2001

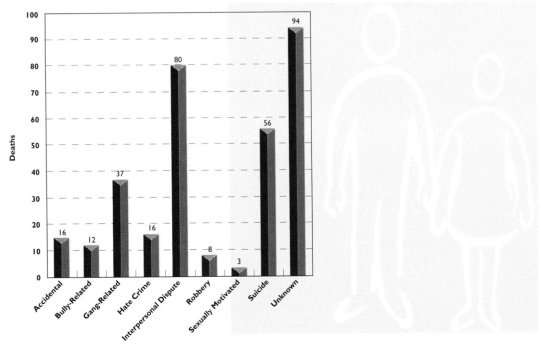

ENVIRONMENTAL
HEALTH

ENVIRONMENTAL HEALTH FACTS

Environmental hazards can harm health or cause deaths. The topics on this page and the following pages are some areas where personal behavior, corporate behavior, and public policy choices can make a difference in reducing unintentional death, disease, and injury associated with environmental causes.

Asthma

Asthma is a chronic, episodic inflammatory condition of the lungs that often affects people for most of their lives. Many different things can trigger asthma attacks including allergens and environmental pollutants like sulfur dioxide, dust mites, cockroaches, animal dander, tobacco smoke, and mold. Severe attacks, unless treated quickly, can be fatal.

The American Lung Association reports, from a 1998 survey by the National Center for Health Statistics, Centers for Disease Control and Prevention (CDC), that an estimated 26.3 million people had been diagnosed with asthma in their lifetime compared to the 25.7 million in the 1997 survey. In both 1997 and 1998, asthma was most prevalent in children ages 5 to 17. Between 1979 and 1998, the age-adjusted mortality rate for asthma increased 33% in males and 67% in females. In 1998, the female death rate was 25% greater than the rate among males.[a] Asthma caused 5,438 deaths in 1998, the latest year for which U.S. data are available. This is a 109% increase from the 2,598 deaths in 1979.[b]

Radon

Radon is an invisible, odorless gas released when uranium in soil decays. Radon can enter buildings through holes in the foundation made for plumbing or through cracks in the foundation. Radon gas entering homes and other buildings from soil under foundations can increase the risk for lung cancer over time if present at high levels.[c] According the National Cancer Institute, 10% of lung cancer cases a year are attributed to radon.[d]

Foodborne Illness

CDC reports that each year foodborne diseases cause approximately 76 million illnesses, 325,000 hospitalizations, and 5,000 deaths in the United States.[e]

The causes of foodborne illnesses include viruses, bacteria, parasites, toxins, metals, and prions. Symptoms can range from mild gastroenteritis to life-threatening neurologic, hepatic, and renal syndromes.

Known pathogens account for an estimated 38.3 million of all gastrointestinal illnesses each year (regardless of mode of transmission), including 5.2 million (14%) due to bacteria and 30.8 million (80%) due to viruses. Overall, CDC estimates that 13.6 million of the 38.3 million cases of acute gastroenteritis are caused by foodborne transmission. Among the illnesses due to foodborne transmission, about 4 million (30%) are caused by bacteria and about 6 million (67%) by viruses.

Waterborne disease

Today, since most of the U.S. population benefits from modern sewage treatment and drinking water purification, diarrheal diseases like cholera and typhoid are exceedingly rare.

During 1997–1998, a total of 13 U.S. states reported 17 outbreaks associated with drinking water (7 in 1997 and 10 in 1998). These outbreaks caused an estimated 2,038 persons to become ill, but no deaths were reported. Fifteen of the 17 outbreaks were linked to groundwater sources.

Thirty-two outbreaks from 18 states were attributed to recreational water exposure (swimming pools, lakes, and ponds) and affected over 2,000 people. Eighteen of the 32 were outbreaks of gastroenteritis. Ten of the 18 gastroenteritis outbreaks were associated with treated pools (e.g., chlorinated pools) and most of the outbreaks were related to human fecal contaminants.[f]

[a] Centers for Disease Control and Prevention. National Center for Health Statistics. (2000) National Vital Statistics Report, Deaths: Final data for 1998, v. 48, n. 11, table 10.
[b] American Lung Association, Epidemiology & Statistics Unit. (2001) Trends in Asthma Morbidity and Mortality. Retrieved from http://www.lungusa.org/data/asthma/asthmach_index.html#text
[c] American Cancer Society. (2000, June 21). Radon Gas Confirmed as Second Largest Risk Factor for Lung Cancer. ACS News Today. Retrieved from: http://www2.cancer.org/zine/index.cfm?sc=001&fn=001_06212000_0
[d] National Cancer Institute. (1998) Cancer Facts. Retrieved from: http://cis.nci.nih.gov/fact/3_52.htm
[e] Mead, P.S., Slutsker, L., Dietz, V., McCaig, L., Bresee, J., Shapiro, C., Griffin, P., Tauxe, R.V. (1999) Synopses: Food-Related Illness and Death in the United States. Emerging Infectious Diseases, 5(5).
[f] Centers for Disease Control and Prevention. (2000) Surveillance for Waterborne Disease Outbreaks—United States, 1997–1998. Morbidity and Mortality Weekly Report, 49(SS-04); 1–35.

Skin cancer comes in two major forms: melanoma and nonmelanoma. Melanoma skin cancers begin in the melanocytes, cells that produce skin coloring. Nonmelanoma skin cancers are the most common skin cancers and develop from basal and squamous cells rather than melanocytes. About 1.3 million cases of nonmelanoma skin cancers are diagnosed each year in the United States. Melanoma, also known as malignant melanoma, accounts for 4% of skin cancer cases but causes about 79% of skin cancer deaths. In 2001, the American Cancer Society estimates that there will be 51,400 new cases of melanoma in the United States and about 7,800 people will die from melanoma skin cancers.[a]

According to the National Cancer Institutes SEER program, from 1992 to 1998, the incidence rate for all races and both sexes for melanoma was 12.9 per 100,000 population in the United States. The death rate was 2.2 per 100,000 population. This is compared to the lung cancer incidence rate of 54.4 and the death rate of 49.1.[b] According to the American Cancer

Society, the survival rate for the period from 1989–1996 for melanoma was 88% compared to the lung cancer survival rate of 14%.[a] For nonmelanoma skin cancers, a cure is highly likely if the cancer is detected and treated early.

One of the risk factors for melanoma is fair skin. White males are over 16 times more likely to develop melanoma skin cancer than black males, and white females are over 17 times more likely to develop melanoma than black females.[b] Other risk factors for melanoma skin cancer include moles, family history, immune suppression, overexposure to ultraviolet (UV) radiation, and age. Moles are benign skin tumors and aren't present at birth but begin to appear in children and teenagers. Having an atypical mole makes a person more susceptible to developing melanoma.

[a] *American Cancer Society. (2001) Cancer Resource Center, Cancer Facts & Figures 2001. Retrieved from http://www3.cancer.org/cancerinfo/sitecenter.asp?ct=1&ctid=8&scp= 8.0.1.40000&scs=1&scss=1&scdoc=40051.*
[b] *Howe, H.L., Wingo, P.A., Thun, M.J., Ries, L.A.G., Rosenberg, H.M., Feigal, E.G., & Edwards, B.K. (2001). The Annual Report to the Nation on the Status of Cancer (1973 Through 1998), Featuring Cancers With Recent Increasing Trends. Journal of the National Cancer Institute 93(11):824-842. Retrieved from http://seer.cancer.gov/Publications/ ReportCard/.*

CANCER INCIDENCE AND DEATH RATES, AVERAGE ANNUAL RATES, UNITED STATES, 1992–1998

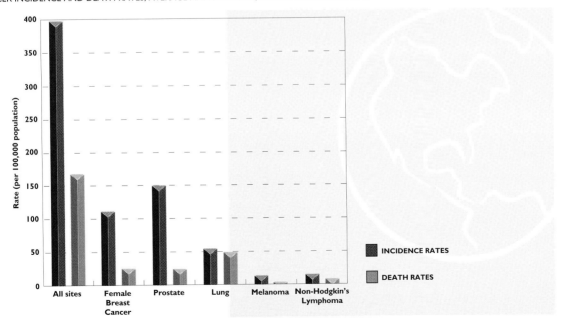

Source: Howe, H.L., Wingo, P.A., Thun, M.J., Ries, L.A.G., Rosenberg, H.M., Feigal, E.G., Edwards, B.K. (2001). The Annual Report to the Nation on the Status of Cancer (1973 Through 1998), Featuring Cancers With Recent Increasing Trends (Supplemental materials). Journal of the National Cancer Institute 93(11):824-842.

LUNG CANCER

Cancer is the second leading cause of death following heart disease. Lung cancer is the leading cause of cancer mortality in both men and women in the United States. According to the American Cancer Society[a], in 2001 lung cancer will strike a projected 169,500 people, accounting for 13% of the cancer diagnoses, and kill an estimated 157,400 people, accounting for 28% of all cancer deaths.

The incidence rate declined significantly among men, from a high of 86.5 per 100,000 in 1984 to 69.1 in 1997. In the 1990s, the increasing trend among women leveled off with incidence rates near the 1997 rate of 43.1 per 100,000. During 1990–1997, death rates declined significantly among men while rates for women continued to increase. Since 1987, more women have died each year of lung cancer than breast cancer, which had been the leading cause of cancer since the 1950s.[a]

According to a trend report by the American Lung Association, the number of deaths due to lung cancer increased 57% from 98,541 in 1979 to 154,561 in 1998. In 1998, 91,447 males and 63,114 females died from lung cancer. The overall mortality rate has increased from 33.6 per 100,000 in 1979 to 37.0 per

100,000 in 1998, an increase of 10.1%. While the mortality rate in males has fluctuated over the 20-year period, the rate reported in 1998 was 11.1% lower than that reported in 1979. However, over the same time period, the mortality rate among females increased steadily by over 65%. Even with this growth in the mortality rates for females, the mortality rate in males is still almost double the rate in females.[b]

Tobacco smoking is the leading cause of lung cancer, followed by radon gas. More than 80% of lung cancers are thought to result from smoking.[c] Cigar smoking and pipe smoking are almost as likely to cause lung cancer as cigarette smoking. There is no evidence that smoking low tar cigarettes reduces the risk of lung cancer. Death from lung cancer is about seven times more likely to occur among asbestos workers than among the general population. Asbestos workers who smoke are 50 to 90 times more likely to develop lung cancer than the general public.

[a] American Cancer Society. (2001) Cancer Facts and Figures 2001. Retrieved from http://www3.cancer.org/cancerinfo/sitecenter.asp?ct=1&ctid=8&scp=8.0.1.40000&scs=1&scss=1&scdoc=40051.
[b] American Lung Association, Epidemiology and Statistics Unit. (2000) Trends in Lung Cancer Morbidity and Mortality. Retrieved from http://www.lungusa.org/data/lc/lctrendsindex.html.
[c] American Cancer Society. Cancer Resource Center. Prevention and Risk Factors (for lung cancer). Retrieved June 2001 from http://www3.cancer.org/cancerinfo/load_cont.asp?st=pr&ct=26& language=english.

AGE-ADJUSTED MORTALITY RATES FOR CANCER OF THE TRACHEA, BRONCHUS AND LUNG BY SEX, UNITED STATES, 1979–1998[d]

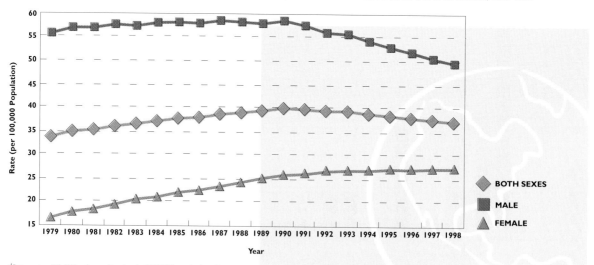

[d] Rates are per 100,000 and age-adjusted to the 1940 U.S. standard population.
Source data: American Lung Association, Epidemiology and Statistics Unit. (2000) Trends in Lung Cancer Morbidity and Mortality.

150,000 to 300,000 children will suffer respiratory effects from breathing secondhand smoke.

ENVIRONMENTAL TOBACCO SMOKE

Environmental tobacco smoke (ETS) is a mixture of particles that are emitted from the burning end of a cigarette, pipe, or cigar and from the smoke exhaled by the smoker. Tobacco smoke can contain any of more than 4,000 compounds, including carbon monoxide and formaldehyde. More than 40 of the compounds in tobacco smoke are known to cause cancer in humans or animals and many of them are strong irritants. ETS is also known as "secondhand smoke" and exposure to ETS is called "passive smoking."[a]

Secondhand smoke has been classified as a Group A carcinogen by the U.S. Environmental Protection Agency (EPA), a rating used only for substances proven to cause cancer in humans. A study conducted by the EPA in 1992 concluded that each year 3,000 lung cancer deaths in nonsmoking adults are attributable to ETS. Of these lung cancer deaths, the EPA estimates that 800 are due to secondhand smoke at home and 2,200 from exposure in work or social situations. Exposure to secondhand smoke also causes eye, nose, and throat irritation. It may affect the cardiovascular system and some studies have linked passive smoking with the onset of chest pain. ETS is an even greater threat to people who already have heart and lung illnesses.

The conclusion that secondhand smoke causes respiratory effects in children is widely shared and undisputed. EPA estimates that every year between 150,000 and 300,000 children under one and one-half years of age get bronchitis or pneumonia from breathing secondhand tobacco smoke, resulting in thousands of hospitalizations. In children under 18 years old, secondhand smoke exposure also results in more coughing and wheezing, a small but significant decrease in lung function, and an increase in fluid in the middle ear. Children with asthma have more frequent and more severe asthma attacks because of exposure to secondhand smoke, which is also a risk factor for onset of asthma in children who did not previously have symptoms.[b]

In 2000, the U.S. Department of Health and Human Services introduced an initiative entitled *Healthy People 2010* to address the problem of tobacco-related deaths. As part of the *Healthy People 2010* plan, goals have been set to reduce tobacco-related deaths by reducing exposure to ETS, decreasing tobacco-use initiation, and increasing tobacco-use cessation.[c]

[a] *National Safety Council's Environmental Health Center. Retrieved June 2001 from http://www.nsc.org/ehc/indoor/ets.htm*
[b] *U.S. Environmental Protection Agency. (1994, June). Setting the Record Straight: Secondhand Smoke is a Preventable Health Risk. Retrieved from http://www.epa.gov/iaq/pubs/strsfs.html*
[c] *Hopkins, D.P., Briss, P.A., Harris, J.R., Ricard, C., Rosenquist, J.N., Harria, K.W., Husten, C.G., McKenna, J.W., Sharp, D.J., Woollery, T.A., Sharma, N., & Pechacek, T.F. (2000). Strategies for Reducing Exposure to Environmental Tobacco Smoke, Increasing Tobacco-Use Cessation, and Reducing Initiation in Communities and Health Care Systems: A Report on Recommendations of the Task Force on Community Preventive Services. Morbidity and Mortality Weekly Report, 49, No. RR–12.*

HEALTHY PEOPLE 2010: OBJECTIVES FOR REDUCING TOBACCO USE AND EXPOSURE TO ETS

Targeted Condition	Targeted Population	Baseline % of Population	2010 Objective
Cigarette smoking	Adults	24% (1997)	Decrease to 12%
Tobacco use (past month)	Adolescents (grades 9–12)	43% (1997)	Decrease to 21%
Smoking cessation	Pregnant women	12% (1991)	Increase to 30%
Smoking cessation attempts	Adult smokers	43% (1997)	Increase to 75%
Smoking cessation attempts	Adolescent smokers	73% (1997)	Increase to 84%
Exposure to ETS	Nonsmokers	65% (1994)	Decrease to 45%
Exposure to ETS at home	Children	27% (1994)	Decrease to 10%

Source: U.S. Department of Health and Human Services.(2000) Healthy People 2010 (conference ed., in 2 vols.). Washington, DC: U.S. Department of Health and Human Services.
Note: The years in parentheses indicate when the data were analyzed to establish baseline estimates. Some estimates are age-adjusted to the year 2000 standard population.

AIR QUALITY

Air quality data are based on actual measurements of pollutant concentrations in the outside air at monitoring sites across the country. Emissions data are based on actual monitored readings or engineering calculations of the amounts and types of pollutants emitted by vehicles, factories, and other sources.

According to the Environmental Protection Agency (EPA), air quality levels in the United States measured at thousands of monitoring stations across the country have shown improvement from 1980 to 1999 for all six principal air pollutants—carbon monoxide, lead, nitrogen dioxide, ozone (formed from volatile organic compounds [VOCs] and nitrogen oxides), particulate matter (PM), and sulfur dioxide.

Between 1970 and 1999, total emissions of the six principal pollutants decreased 31%. This decrease occurred simultaneously with significant increase in economic growth and population. Since the 1970 Clean Air Act was signed, emissions of each of the principal pollutants decreased with the exception of nitrogen oxides. Still, over 150 million tons of air pollution were released into the air in 1999 in the United States and approximately 62 million people lived in counties where monitored data showed unhealthy air for one or more of the six principal pollutants.

From 1980–1999, carbon monoxide emissions decreased 22%, lead decreased 95%, VOCs 33%, particulate matter 55%, and sulfur dioxides 28%. Nitrogen oxides emissions actually increased 1% from 1980–1999 and 2% from 1990–1999. This increase has been attributed to heavy-duty diesel vehicles and coal-fired power plants. Emissions of nitrogen oxides contribute to the formation of ground level ozone. Nitrogen oxides and VOCs react in the presence of heat and sunlight to produce ground-level ozone or smog. VOCs are emitted from a variety of sources, including motor vehicles, chemical plants, refineries, and other industrial sources. Nitrogen oxides are emitted from motor vehicles, power plants, and other sources of combustion.

Short-term and prolonged exposures to atmospheric ozone have been linked to a number of health effects including respiratory infections, asthma, and premature aging of the lungs. Ozone also effects vegetation and ecosystems leading to decreased agricultural and commercial forest yields, and increased plant susceptibility to disease, pests, and other environmental stress like severe weather.

Source: U.S. Environmental Protection Agency, Office of Air Quality Planning and Standards. (2000). Latest findings on national air quality: 1999 status and trends. (EPA Document No. 454/F-00-002). Research Triangle Park, NC: U.S. Environmental Protection Agency. Retrieved from http://www.epa.gov/oar/aqtrnd99/brochure/brochure.pdf.

EMISSIONS OF PRINCIPAL POLLUTANTS, UNITED STATES 1970–1999

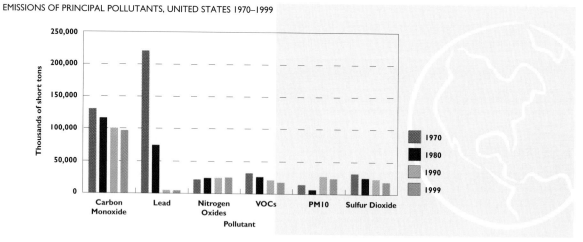

Source: U.S. Environmental Protection Agency, Office of Air Quality Planning and Standards, National Emission Inventory. (2001). Average Annual Emissions, All Criteria Pollutants Years Including 1970, 1975, 1980, 1985, 1989, 1990–1999. Retrieved July 2001 from http://www.epa.gov/ttn/chief/trends/trends99/tier3_yrsemis.pdf.
Note: PM10 refers to coarse particulate matter, meaning particulates with a diameter between 2.5 and 10 micrometers. VOCs = volatile organic compounds.

In 1998, 32% of U.S. waters were examined to determine if they met water quality standards. About 40% of the U.S. streams, lakes, and estuaries that were assessed were not clean enough to support uses such as fishing and swimming.

The EPA has defined several categories for water classification:[a]

- *Good/Fully Supporting:* These waters meet applicable water quality standards, both criteria and designated uses.[b]

- *Good but Threatened:* These waters currently meet water quality standards, but water quality may degrade in the near future.

- *Polluted/Impaired:* These waters do not meet water quality standards.

In 1998, 23% of the nation's 3.6 million miles of rivers and streams were tested to determine if they met water quality standards under the Clean Water Act. Of the assessed river and stream miles, 55% were rated good, 10% were rated good but threatened, and 35% were

rated polluted or impaired. Forty-two percent of the nation's 41.6 million acres of lakes, reservoirs, and ponds were assessed for water quality in 1998. Forty-six percent were rated good, 9% good but threatened, and 45% impaired or polluted. Ninety percent of the Great Lakes shorelines were assessed. Ninety-six percent of the assessed shorelines were impaired or polluted while 2% were good but threatened and only 2% rated good.

Primary water pollutants include nutrients (too many can poison a balanced ecosystem), silt, oxygen-depleting substances, metals, turbidity, suspended solids, organic chemicals, and pathogens. The primary sources of these pollutants include agricultural activities, hydromodification, urban runoff and storm sewers, atmospheric deposition, municipal and industrial point sources, land disposal, discharges from factory pipes no longer in use, contaminated sediments, and spills.

[a] *United States Environmental Protection Agency. Office of Water. (2000). The Quality of Our Nation's Waters: A Summary of the National Water Quality Inventory: 1998 Report to Congress. Retrieved from http://www.epa.gov/305b/98report/.*
[b] *Designated use: an element of water quality standards that describes what the waterbody is used for. The Clean Water Act envisions that all waters be able to provide for recreation and the protection and propagation of aquatic life.*

SUMMARY OF QUALITY OF ASSESSED WATERS IN THE UNITED STATES, 1998

Types of Waters	Amount Assessed (% of total)	Good (% of Assessed)	Good but Threatened (% of Assessed)	Polluted/ Impaired (% of Assessed)	Major Pollutants	Main Source of Pollutants
Rivers and streams **3,662,255 miles**	842,426 (23%)	463,411 (55%)	85,544 (10%)	291,264 (35%)	Silt Pathogens Nutrients	Agriculture Hydromodification Urban runoff/Storm sewers
Lakes, ponds, reservoirs **41,593,748 acres**	17,390,370 (42%)	7,927,486 (46%)	1,565,175 (9%)	7,897,110 (45%)	Nutrients Metals Silt	Agriculture Hydromodification Urban runoff/Storm sewers
Estuaries **90,465 sq. miles**	28,687 (32%)	13,439 (47%)	2,766 (10%)	12,482 (44%)	Pathogens (bacteria) O_2-depleting substances Metals	Municipal point sources Urban runoff/Storm sewers Atmospheric deposition
Great Lakes shorelines **5,521 miles**	4,950 (90%)	85 (2%)	103 (2%)	4,762 (96%)	Toxic organic chemicals Pesticides Nonpriority organic chemicals	Atmospheric deposition Discontinued discharge from pipes Contaminated sediments
Ocean shorelines **66,645 miles**	3,130 (5%)	2,496 (80%)	257 (8%)	377 (12%)	Pathogens Turbidity Nutrients	Urban runoff/Storm sewers Land disposal Municipal point sources

Source: United States Environmental Protection Agency. (2000) The Quality of Our Nation's Waters: A Summary of the National Water Quality Inventory: 1998.
Note: Percentages may not sum to 100 due to rounding.

NATIONAL SAFETY COUNCIL® INJURY FACTS® 2001 EDITION

STATE DATA

STATE DATA

Death rates for unintentional injuries (U-I) can vary greatly from one type of injury to the next and from state to state. The graph on the next page shows each state's death rates (per 100,000 population) for total unintentional-injury deaths and the four leading types of unintentional-injury deaths nationally—motor-vehicle crashes, falls, solid and liquid poisonings, and drownings (both transport and nontransport drownings).

The charts on pages 152 through 154 show (a) total unintentional-injury deaths and where U-I rank as a cause of death in each state, and (b) the five leading causes of U-I deaths in each state.

Unintentional injuries as a whole are the fifth leading cause of death in the United States and in 22 states. U-I are the third leading cause of death in Alaska and New Mexico and the fourth leading cause in 14 states plus the District of Columbia. U-I rank sixth in eight states and seventh in four states (Maryland, Massachusetts, New Jersey, and Rhode Island).

Motor-vehicle crashes are the leading cause of U-I deaths in every state and the District of Columbia. The second leading cause of U-I deaths is falls in 43 states, solid and liquid poisoning in 5 states and the District of Columbia, and drowning in 1 state (Alaska). The most

common third leading causes of U-I deaths are solid and liquid poisoning in 26 states, drowning in 9 states, falls in 6 states and the District of Columbia, and choking in 6 states. Drowning is the fourth leading cause of U-I deaths in 21 states, while the fourth ranking is choking in 10 states and solid and liquid poisoning in 7 states.

The table on page 155 consists of a 3-year state-by-state comparison of unintentional-injury deaths and death rates for 1998, 1997, and 1996. For the total United States, the U-I death rate per 100,000 population increased 1.1% from 1996 to 1998. Rates decreased in 23 states and increased in 27 states and the District of Columbia. Death rates in the District of Columbia and North Dakota showed the greatest increases, 31% and 24% respectively. The states with the greatest decreases in death rates were Hawaii (-21%) and Alaska (-19%).

The table on pages 156 and 157 shows the number of U-I deaths by state for the 17 most common types of injury events. State populations are also shown to facilitate computation of detailed death rates.

All of the state data shown on the following pages are National Safety Council tabulations of National Center for Health Statistics mortality data.

UNINTENTIONAL-INJURY DEATH RATES BY STATE, UNITED STATES, 1998

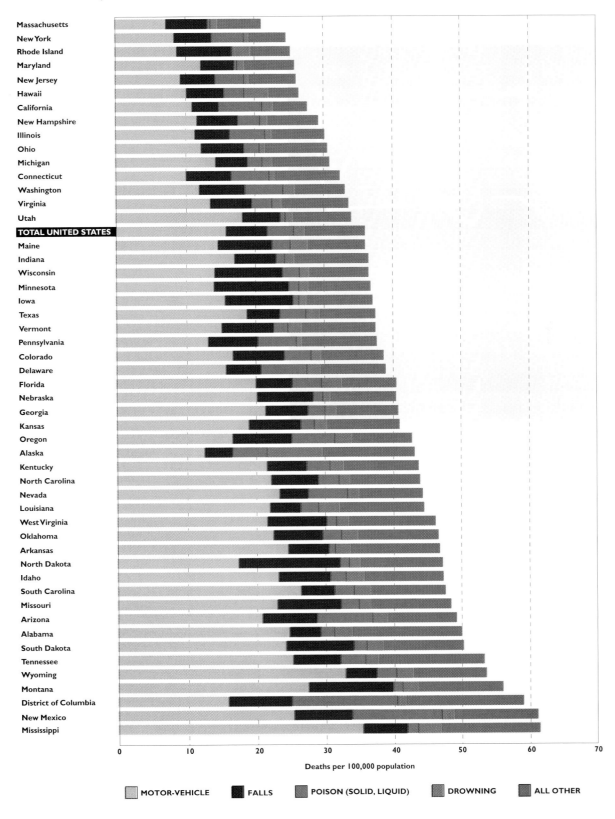

UNINTENTIONAL-INJURY DEATHS BY STATE

The following series of charts is a state-by-state ranking of the five leading causes of deaths due to unintentional injuries (U-I) based on 1998 data. The first line of each section gives the total number of U-I deaths, the rate of U-I deaths per 100,000 population, and the rank of unintentional-injury deaths among all causes of death. The following lines list the five leading types of unintentional-injury deaths along with the number and rate for each type.

TOTAL UNITED STATES

Rank	Cause	Deaths	Rate
5	All U-I	97,835	36.2
1	Motor-vehicle	43,501	16.1
2	Falls	16,274	6.0
3	S+L Poison[a]	10,255	3.8
4	Drowning[b]	4,406	1.6
5	Choking[c]	3,515	1.3

ALABAMA

Rank	Cause	Deaths	Rate
4	All U-I	2,181	50.1
1	Motor-vehicle	1,088	25.0
2	Falls	197	4.5
3	Drowning[b]	112	2.6
4	Choking[c]	103	2.4
5	Fires and burns	92	2.1

ALASKA

Rank	Cause	Deaths	Rate
3	All U-I	267	43.4
1	Motor-vehicle	79	12.8
2	Drowning[b]	49	8.0
3	S+L Poison[a]	31	5.0
4	Falls	25	4.1
5	Air transport	23	3.7

ARIZONA

Rank	Cause	Deaths	Rate
5	All U-I	2,314	49.6
1	Motor-vehicle	985	21.1
2	S+L Poison[a]	380	8.1
3	Falls	371	7.9
4	Drowning[b]	107	2.3
5	Natural, envir. factors	83	1.8

ARKANSAS

Rank	Cause	Deaths	Rate
5	All U-I	1,197	47.2
1	Motor-vehicle	632	24.9
2	Falls	150	5.9
3	Fires and burns	70	2.8
4	Drowning[b]	57	2.2
5	Choking[c]	56	2.2

CALIFORNIA

Rank	Cause	Deaths	Rate
6	All U-I	9,132	27.9
1	Motor-vehicle	3,665	11.2
2	S+L Poison[a]	2,067	6.3
3	Falls	1,267	3.9
4	Drowning[b]	532	1.6
5	Medical misadventures[d]	248	0.8

COLORADO

Rank	Cause	Deaths	Rate
5	All U-I	1,542	38.9
1	Motor-vehicle	674	17.0
2	Falls	296	7.5
3	S+L Poison[a]	152	3.8
4	Choking[c]	68	1.7
5	Drowning[b]	58	1.5

CONNECTICUT

Rank	Cause	Deaths	Rate
6	All U-I	1,063	32.5
1	Motor-vehicle	336	10.3
2	Falls	215	6.6
3	S+L Poison[a]	179	5.5
4	Choking[c]	74	2.3
5	Medical misadventures[d]	63	1.9

DELAWARE

Rank	Cause	Deaths	Rate
5	All U-I	292	39.2
1	Motor-vehicle	119	16.0
2	S+L Poison[a]	49	6.6
3	Falls	38	5.1
4	Drowning[b]	15	2.0
5	Choking[c]	9	1.2
5	Medical misadventures[d]	9	1.2

DISTRICT OF COLUMBIA

Rank	Cause	Deaths	Rate
4	All U-I	309	59.3
1	Motor-vehicle	84	16.1
2	S+L Poison[a]	80	15.3
3	Falls	48	9.2
4	Fires and burns	22	4.2
5	Medical misadventures[d]	16	3.1

FLORIDA

Rank	Cause	Deaths	Rate
5	All U-I	5,976	40.1
1	Motor-vehicle	2,977	20.0
2	Falls	833	5.6
3	S+L Poison[a]	633	4.2
4	Drowning[b]	441	3.0
5	Choking[c]	209	1.4

GEORGIA

Rank	Cause	Deaths	Rate
4	All U-I	3,140	41.1
1	Motor-vehicle	1,660	21.7
2	Falls	468	6.1
3	S+L Poison[a]	194	2.5
4	Drowning[b]	130	1.7
5	Choking[c]	126	1.6

HAWAII

Rank	Cause	Deaths	Rate
5	All U-I	319	26.8
1	Motor-vehicle	124	10.4
2	Falls	66	5.5
3	Drowning[b]	43	3.6
4	S+L Poison[a]	35	2.9
5	Choking[c]	9	0.8

IDAHO

Rank	Cause	Deaths	Rate
4	All U-I	585	47.5
1	Motor-vehicle	289	23.5
2	Falls	92	7.5
3	Drowning[b]	33	2.7
4	S+L Poison[a]	27	2.2
5	Air transport	18	1.5

ILLINOIS

Rank	Cause	Deaths	Rate
6	All U-I	3,668	30.4
1	Motor-vehicle	1,398	11.6
2	S+L Poison[a]	618	5.1
3	Falls	614	5.1
4	Choking[c]	146	1.2
5	Medical misadventures[d]	143	1.2

INDIANA

Rank	Cause	Deaths	Rate
5	All U-I	2,165	36.6
1	Motor-vehicle	1,022	17.3
2	Falls	360	6.1
3	Choking[c]	101	1.7
4	Medical misadventures[d]	95	1.6
5	Fires and burns	88	1.5

IOWA

Rank	Cause	Deaths	Rate
6	All U-I	1,068	37.3
1	Motor-vehicle	455	15.9
2	Falls	283	9.9
3	Choking[c]	40	1.4
4	Fires and burns	38	1.3
5	Drowning[b]	32	1.1

KANSAS

Rank	Cause	Deaths	Rate
5	All U-I	1,086	41.2
1	Motor-vehicle	509	19.3
2	Falls	199	7.5
3	Choking[c]	53	2.0
4	Drowning[b]	49	1.9
4	S+L Poison[a]	49	1.9

See footnotes on page 154.

KENTUCKY

Rank	Cause	Deaths	Rate
5	All U-I	1,728	43.9
1	Motor-vehicle	863	21.9
2	Falls	225	5.7
3	S+L Poison[a]	132	3.4
4	Drowning[b]	77	2.0
5	Choking[c]	64	1.6

LOUISIANA

Rank	Cause	Deaths	Rate
4	All U-I	1,955	44.8
1	Motor-vehicle	975	22.3
2	Falls	192	4.4
3	Drowning[b]	134	3.1
4	S+L Poison[a]	112	2.6
5	Fires and burns	99	2.3

MAINE

Rank	Cause	Deaths	Rate
6	All U-I	452	36.2
1	Motor-vehicle	186	14.9
2	Falls	99	7.9
3	S+L Poison[a]	32	2.6
4	Drowning[b]	31	2.5
5	Choking[c]	18	1.4

MARYLAND

Rank	Cause	Deaths	Rate
7	All U-I	1,334	26.0
1	Motor-vehicle	639	12.5
2	Falls	250	4.9
3	Medical misadventures[d]	77	1.5
4	Choking[c]	58	1.1
5	Drowning[b]	56	1.1

MASSACHUSETTS

Rank	Cause	Deaths	Rate
7	All U-I	1,311	21.3
1	Motor-vehicle	453	7.4
2	Falls	374	6.1
3	Choking[c]	91	1.5
4	Drowning[b]	63	1.0
5	Fires and burns	52	0.8

MICHIGAN

Rank	Cause	Deaths	Rate
5	All U-I	3,059	31.1
1	Motor-vehicle	1,434	14.6
2	Falls	460	4.7
3	S+L Poison[a]	210	2.1
4	Drowning[b]	146	1.5
5	Fires and burns	141	1.4

MINNESOTA

Rank	Cause	Deaths	Rate
4	All U-I	1,747	37.0
1	Motor-vehicle	675	14.3
2	Falls	514	10.9
3	Drowning[b]	66	1.4
4	S+L Poison[a]	65	1.4
5	Medical misadventures[d]	52	1.1

MISSISSIPPI

Rank	Cause	Deaths	Rate
4	All U-I	1,697	61.7
1	Motor-vehicle	980	35.6
2	Falls	182	6.6
3	Fires and burns	100	3.6
4	Drowning[b]	93	3.4
5	Choking[c]	86	3.1

MISSOURI

Rank	Cause	Deaths	Rate
5	All U-I	2,645	48.6
1	Motor-vehicle	1,266	23.3
2	Falls	499	9.2
3	S+L Poison[a]	143	2.6
4	Choking[c]	108	2.0
5	Drowning[b]	98	1.8

MONTANA

Rank	Cause	Deaths	Rate
5	All U-I	495	56.3
1	Motor-vehicle	244	27.7
2	Falls	109	12.4
3	Natural, envir. factors	21	2.4
3	Drowning[b]	21	2.4
5	Fires and burns	13	1.5

NEBRASKA

Rank	Cause	Deaths	Rate
5	All U-I	679	40.9
1	Motor-vehicle	341	20.5
2	Falls	135	8.1
3	Choking[c]	36	2.2
4	S+L Poison[a]	24	1.4
5	Drowning[b]	19	1.1

NEVADA

Rank	Cause	Deaths	Rate
5	All U-I	777	44.6
1	Motor-vehicle	414	23.7
2	S+L Poison[a]	99	5.7
3	Falls	71	4.1
4	Air transport	30	1.7
5	Drowning[b]	29	1.7

NEW HAMPSHIRE

Rank	Cause	Deaths	Rate
5	All U-I	349	29.4
1	Motor-vehicle	141	11.9
2	Falls	71	6.0
3	S+L Poison[a]	38	3.2
4	Choking[c]	17	1.4
5	Drowning[b]	13	1.1

NEW JERSEY

Rank	Cause	Deaths	Rate
7	All U-I	2,133	26.3
1	Motor-vehicle	769	9.5
2	Falls	412	5.1
3	S+L Poison[a]	341	4.2
4	Choking[c]	80	1.0
5	Medical misadventures[d]	77	1.0

NEW MEXICO

Rank	Cause	Deaths	Rate
3	All U-I	1,065	61.4
1	Motor-vehicle	444	25.6
2	S+L Poison[a]	230	13.3
3	Falls	146	8.4
4	Natural, envir. factors	32	1.8
5	Drowning[b]	31	1.8

NEW YORK

Rank	Cause	Deaths	Rate
6	All U-I	4,520	24.9
1	Motor-vehicle	1,569	8.6
2	Falls	990	5.5
3	S+L Poison[a]	854	4.7
4	Fires and burns	177	1.0
5	Medical misadventures[d]	176	1.0

NORTH CAROLINA

Rank	Cause	Deaths	Rate
4	All U-I	3,332	44.2
1	Motor-vehicle	1,701	22.5
2	Falls	515	6.8
3	S+L Poison[a]	223	3.0
4	Choking[c]	127	1.7
5	Drowning[b]	118	1.6

NORTH DAKOTA

Rank	Cause	Deaths	Rate
4	All U-I	303	47.5
1	Motor-vehicle	113	17.7
2	Falls	94	14.7
3	Machinery	11	1.7
4	Drowning[b]	10	1.6
5	Natural, envir. factors	9	1.4

OHIO

Rank	Cause	Deaths	Rate
6	All U-I	3,463	30.8
1	Motor-vehicle	1,402	12.5
2	Falls	708	6.3
3	S+L Poison[a]	249	2.2
4	Medical misadventures[d]	189	1.7
5	Choking[c]	161	1.4

OKLAHOMA

Rank	Cause	Deaths	Rate
5	All U-I	1,565	46.9
1	Motor-vehicle	760	22.8
2	Falls	237	7.1
3	S+L Poison[a]	91	2.7
4	Drowning[b]	80	2.4
5	Fires and burns	58	1.7

OREGON

Rank	Cause	Deaths	Rate
5	All U-I	1,411	43.0
1	Motor-vehicle	554	16.9
2	Falls	282	8.6
3	S+L Poison[a]	204	6.2
4	Drowning[b]	81	2.5
5	Medical misadventures[d]	36	1.1

See footnotes on page 154.

PENNSYLVANIA

Rank	Cause	Deaths	Rate
5	All U-I	4,563	38.0
I	Motor-vehicle	1,614	13.4
2	Falls	882	7.3
3	S+L Poison[a]	657	5.5
4	Medical misadventures[d]	318	2.6
5	Choking[c]	241	2.0

SOUTH DAKOTA

Rank	Cause	Deaths	Rate
4	All U-I	369	50.5
I	Motor-vehicle	179	24.5
2	Falls	72	9.9
3	Drowning[b]	18	2.5
4	S+L Poison[a]	14	1.9
5	Machinery	11	1.5
5	Struck by or against	11	1.5

UTAH

Rank	Cause	Deaths	Rate
4	All U-I	720	34.3
I	Motor-vehicle	389	18.5
2	Falls	115	5.5
3	Medical misadventures[d]	25	1.2
3	Natural, envir. factors	25	1.2
5	Drowning[b]	24	1.1

WASHINGTON

Rank	Cause	Deaths	Rate
5	All U-I	1,893	33.3
I	Motor-vehicle	694	12.2
2	Falls	381	6.7
3	S+L Poison[a]	312	5.5
4	Drowning[b]	97	1.7
5	Choking[c]	77	1.4

WYOMING

Rank	Cause	Deaths	Rate
4	All U-I	259	54.0
I	Motor-vehicle	159	33.1
2	Falls	22	4.6
3	S+L Poison[a]	14	2.9
4	Drowning[b]	12	2.5
5	Natural, envir. factors	8	1.7

RHODE ISLAND

Rank	Cause	Deaths	Rate
7	All U-I	252	25.5
I	Motor-vehicle	89	9.0
2	Falls	79	8.0
3	Drowning[b]	27	2.7
4	Choking[c]	16	1.6
5	Medical misadventures[d]	5	0.5

TENNESSEE

Rank	Cause	Deaths	Rate
4	All U-I	2,914	53.6
I	Motor-vehicle	1,387	25.5
2	Falls	377	6.9
3	S+L Poison[a]	195	3.6
4	Fires and burns	128	2.4
5	Choking[c]	119	2.2

VERMONT

Rank	Cause	Deaths	Rate
6	All U-I	223	37.8
I	Motor-vehicle	91	15.4
2	Falls	45	7.6
3	S+L Poison[a]	12	2.0
3	Drowning[b]	12	2.0
5	Fires and burns	11	1.9

WEST VIRGINIA

Rank	Cause	Deaths	Rate
5	All U-I	842	46.5
I	Motor-vehicle	397	21.9
2	Falls	155	8.6
3	Choking[c]	43	2.4
4	Fires and burns	35	1.9
5	Drowning[b]	32	1.8

SOUTH CAROLINA

Rank	Cause	Deaths	Rate
4	All U-I	1,841	47.9
I	Motor-vehicle	1,026	26.7
2	Falls	188	4.9
3	S+L Poison[a]	107	2.8
4	Drowning[b]	96	2.5
5	Choking[c]	87	2.3

TEXAS

Rank	Cause	Deaths	Rate
4	All U-I	7,426	37.7
I	Motor-vehicle	3,772	19.1
2	Falls	941	4.8
3	S+L Poison[a]	732	3.7
4	Drowning[b]	385	2.0
5	Fires and burns	259	1.3

VIRGINIA

Rank	Cause	Deaths	Rate
5	All U-I	2,295	33.8
I	Motor-vehicle	935	13.8
2	Falls	414	6.1
3	S+L Poison[a]	199	2.9
4	Drowning[b]	96	1.4
5	Choking[c]	95	1.4

WISCONSIN

Rank	Cause	Deaths	Rate
5	All U-I	1,914	36.7
I	Motor-vehicle	750	14.4
2	Falls	516	9.9
3	S+L Poison[a]	134	2.6
4	Drowning[b]	74	1.4
5	Fires and burns	63	1.2

Source: National Safety Council tabulations of National Center for Health Statistics mortality data for 1998.
[a]*Solid and liquid poisoning.*
[b]*Includes transport drownings.*
[c]*Inhalation or ingestion of food or other object.*
[d]*Medical and surgical complications and misadventures.*

UNINTENTIONAL-INJURY DEATHS BY STATE, UNITED STATES, 1996–1998

State	Deaths[a]			Death Rate[c]		
	1998[b]	1997	1996	1998	1997	1996
Total U.S.	**97,835**	**95,644**	**94,948**	**36.2**	**35.7**	**35.8**
Alabama	2,181	2,255	2,187	50.1	52.2	51.2
Alaska	267	286	325	43.4	47.0	53.5
Arizona	2,314	2,192	2,178	49.6	48.2	49.2
Arkansas	1,197	1,262	1,209	47.2	50.0	48.2
California	9,132	8,897	9,368	27.9	27.6	29.4
Colorado	1,542	1,476	1,452	38.9	37.9	40.0
Connecticut	1,063	980	996	32.5	30.0	30.4
Delaware	292	286	249	39.2	38.9	34.3
Dist. of Columbia	309	260	246	59.3	49.2	45.3
Florida	5,976	5,640	5,557	40.1	38.4	38.6
Georgia	3,140	3,091	3,010	41.1	41.3	40.9
Hawaii	319	365	403	26.8	30.7	34.0
Idaho	585	575	562	47.5	47.5	47.3
Illinois	3,668	3,176	3,436	30.4	26.4	29.0
Indiana	2,165	2,077	2,110	36.6	35.4	36.1
Iowa	1,068	1,060	1,059	37.3	37.1	37.1
Kansas	1,086	959	1,006	41.2	36.7	39.1
Kentucky	1,728	1,757	1,735	43.9	45.0	44.7
Louisiana	1,955	1,957	1,845	44.8	45.0	42.4
Maine	452	444	410	36.2	35.7	33.0
Maryland	1,334	1,326	1,363	26.0	26.0	26.9
Massachusetts	1,311	1,269	1,256	21.3	20.8	20.6
Michigan	3,059	3,081	3,006	31.1	31.5	31.3
Minnesota	1,747	1,681	1,621	37.0	35.9	34.8
Mississippi	1,697	1,570	1,448	61.7	57.5	53.3
Missouri	2,645	2,562	2,495	48.6	47.4	46.6
Montana	495	487	438	56.3	55.5	49.8
Nebraska	679	669	670	40.9	40.4	40.6
Nevada	777	722	693	44.6	43.1	43.2
New Hampshire	349	334	292	29.4	28.5	25.1
New Jersey	2,133	2,268	2,225	26.3	28.2	27.9
New Mexico	1,065	1,076	1,035	61.4	62.5	60.4
New York	4,520	4,803	4,706	24.9	26.5	25.9
North Carolina	3,332	3,128	3,197	44.2	42.1	43.7
North Dakota	303	274	247	47.5	42.8	38.4
Ohio	3,463	3,388	3,292	30.8	30.2	29.5
Oklahoma	1,565	1,600	1,526	46.9	48.3	46.2
Oregon	1,411	1,342	1,375	43.0	41.4	42.9
Pennsylvania	4,563	4,819	4,378	38.0	40.1	36.3
Rhode Island	252	227	211	25.5	23.0	21.3
South Carolina	1,841	1,708	1,687	47.9	45.1	45.6
South Dakota	369	311	365	50.5	42.6	49.9
Tennessee	2,914	2,847	2,872	53.6	52.9	54.0
Texas	7,426	7,148	7,290	37.7	36.9	38.1
Utah	720	734	663	34.3	35.5	33.2
Vermont	223	220	203	37.8	37.4	34.5
Virginia	2,295	2,279	2,220	33.8	33.9	33.3
Washington	1,893	1,865	1,890	33.3	33.3	34.2
West Virginia	842	797	793	46.5	43.9	43.4
Wisconsin	1,914	1,855	1,873	36.7	35.7	36.3
Wyoming	259	259	275	54.0	54.0	57.2

Source: National Safety Council estimates based on data from National Center for Health Statistics and U.S. Bureau of the Census. See Technical Appendix for comparability.
[a] *Deaths for each state are by place of occurrence. All death totals exclude nonresident aliens (1998—649 deaths, 1997—718 deaths, 1996—718 deaths).*
[b] *Latest official figures.*
[c] *Rates are deaths per 100,000 population.*

UNINTENTIONAL-INJURY DEATHS BY STATE AND TYPE OF EVENT, UNITED STATES, 1998

State	Population (000)	Total Deaths[a]	Motor-Vehicle[b]	Falls	Poison (Solid, Liquid)	Drowning[c]	Ingest. of Food, Object	Fires and Burns	Medical Misadventures[d]	Natural, Envir. Factors
Total U.S.	**270,248**	**97,835**	**43,501**	**16,274**	**10,255**	**4,406**	**3,515**	**3,255**	**3,228**	**1,521**
Alabama	4,351	2,181	1,088	197	85	112	103	92	69	54
Alaska	615	267	79	25	31	49	5	19	1	8
Arizona	4,667	2,314	985	371	380	107	55	37	68	83
Arkansas	2,538	1,197	632	150	24	57	56	70	44	20
California	32,683	9,132	3,665	1,267	2,067	532	139	227	248	93
Colorado	3,969	1,542	674	296	152	58	68	19	50	34
Connecticut	3,273	1,063	336	215	179	26	74	34	63	12
Delaware	744	292	119	38	49	15	9	4	9	2
Dist. of Columbia	521	309	84	48	80	7	12	22	16	5
Florida	14,908	5,976	2,977	833	633	441	209	123	83	94
Georgia	7,637	3,140	1,660	468	194	130	126	125	109	51
Hawaii	1,190	319	124	66	35	43	9	4	6	1
Idaho	1,231	585	289	92	27	33	11	9	13	15
Illinois	12,070	3,668	1,398	614	618	119	146	130	143	45
Indiana	5,908	2,165	1,022	360	69	80	101	88	95	22
Iowa	2,861	1,068	455	283	23	32	40	38	28	22
Kansas	2,639	1,086	509	199	49	49	50	39	36	22
Kentucky	3,934	1,728	863	225	132	77	64	51	57	20
Louisiana	4,363	1,955	975	192	112	134	77	99	61	55
Maine	1,248	452	186	99	32	31	18	13	17	5
Maryland	5,130	1,334	639	250	18	56	58	54	77	20
Massachusetts	6,144	1,311	453	374	25	63	91	52	44	13
Michigan	9,820	3,059	1,434	460	210	146	92	141	78	29
Minnesota	4,726	1,747	675	514	65	66	51	40	52	35
Mississippi	2,751	1,697	980	182	43	93	86	100	46	34
Missouri	5,438	2,645	1,266	499	142	98	108	75	84	39
Montana	880	495	244	109	12	21	7	13	10	21
Nebraska	1,661	679	341	135	24	19	36	16	16	8
Nevada	1,744	777	414	71	99	29	26	15	20	6
New Hampshire	1,186	349	141	71	38	13	17	8	5	7
New Jersey	8,096	2,133	769	412	341	58	80	62	77	18
New Mexico	1,734	1,065	444	146	230	31	22	25	26	32
New York	18,159	4,520	1,569	990	854	120	119	177	176	30
North Carolina	7,546	3,332	1,701	515	223	118	127	117	100	38
North Dakota	638	303	113	94	8	10	8	6	8	9
Ohio	11,238	3,463	1,402	708	249	91	161	113	189	32
Oklahoma	3,339	1,565	760	237	91	80	54	58	44	39
Oregon	3,282	1,411	554	282	204	81	28	25	36	15
Pennsylvania	12,002	4,563	1,614	882	657	98	241	186	318	38
Rhode Island	988	252	89	79	1	27	16	1	5	2
South Carolina	3,840	1,841	1,026	188	107	96	87	66	43	31
South Dakota	731	369	179	72	14	18	7	7	7	10
Tennessee	5,433	2,914	1,387	377	195	110	119	128	117	44
Texas	19,712	7,426	3,772	941	732	385	194	259	181	170
Utah	2,101	720	389	115	15	24	23	9	25	25
Vermont	591	223	91	45	12	12	6	11	8	3
Virginia	6,789	2,295	935	414	199	96	95	93	94	38
Washington	5,688	1,893	694	381	312	97	77	55	41	31
West Virginia	1,812	842	397	155	26	32	43	35	30	10
Wisconsin	5,222	1,914	750	516	124	74	57	63	50	23
Wyoming	480	259	159	22	14	12	7	2	5	8

See footnotes on page 157.

UNINTENTIONAL-INJURY DEATHS BY STATE AND TYPE OF EVENT, UNITED STATES, 1998, Cont.

State	Mechanical Suffocation	Machinery	Firearms	Falling Objects	Air Transport	Electric Current	Poison (Gas, Vapor)	Railway	Struck By/Against	All Other Accidents[a]
Total U.S.	1,070	1,018	866	723	692	548	546	515	336	5,566
Alabama	15	23	43	18	6	22	9	12	15	218
Alaska	2	3	5	1	23	0	0	1	0	15
Arizona	27	8	22	10	11	6	11	11	2	120
Arkansas	9	16	11	14	11	12	4	7	6	54
California	73	53	54	77	95	55	29	72	46	340
Colorado	20	10	9	16	23	6	15	8	9	75
Connecticut	11	6	6	5	4	7	4	2	5	74
Delaware	8	1	3	0	1	1	0	2	0	31
Dist. of Columbia	3	0	2	2	0	2	0	1	2	23
Florida	61	36	23	22	45	48	39	24	10	275
Georgia	32	28	31	25	12	12	9	11	4	113
Hawaii	3	0	2	0	7	1	0	0	0	18
Idaho	13	6	9	5	18	4	3	3	3	32
Illinois	60	25	26	21	16	19	29	41	10	208
Indiana	49	25	26	16	9	9	14	9	1	170
Iowa	14	28	11	12	10	8	9	3	1	51
Kansas	12	11	12	7	8	8	11	3	6	55
Kentucky	18	39	27	15	1	13	10	6	2	108
Louisiana	20	17	34	17	15	9	14	13	1	110
Maine	3	4	4	6	2	1	3	0	4	24
Maryland	12	16	8	3	9	4	3	2	1	104
Massachusetts	19	5	2	3	16	5	5	5	3	133
Michigan	49	35	18	31	16	25	16	9	21	249
Minnesota	30	21	3	17	4	6	10	4	0	154
Mississippi	13	23	15	9	6	9	9	4	3	42
Missouri	30	37	17	17	14	20	12	17	3	167
Montana	2	6	3	3	12	2	4	3	4	19
Nebraska	7	14	9	4	4	4	6	3	2	31
Nevada	7	4	6	6	30	0	6	4	1	33
New Hampshire	4	5	0	2	3	4	4	0	2	25
New Jersey	23	11	7	8	3	8	12	22	3	219
New Mexico	9	7	11	8	14	6	6	7	1	40
New York	40	46	15	35	14	16	17	38	10	254
North Carolina	21	43	43	22	10	12	15	28	5	194
North Dakota	6	11	1	0	5	1	5	1	1	16
Ohio	47	47	50	27	7	8	37	16	7	272
Oklahoma	12	15	13	10	16	13	11	6	7	99
Oregon	25	20	7	14	10	8	9	11	7	75
Pennsylvania	45	58	26	18	15	13	28	12	12	302
Rhode Island	2	2	0	2	2	1	0	3	0	20
South Carolina	18	14	27	14	12	10	10	18	6	68
South Dakota	3	11	4	11	9	3	7	0	0	7
Tennessee	23	47	69	27	15	21	12	15	49	159
Texas	71	69	76	55	54	63	39	27	24	314
Utah	10	7	4	6	12	5	7	1	1	42
Vermont	0	2	2	7	3	1	2	1	2	15
Virginia	24	31	32	20	10	9	4	9	6	186
Washington	21	19	12	15	20	8	14	11	4	81
West Virginia	8	16	5	20	5	7	2	2	4	45
Wisconsin	33	34	17	15	22	12	19	6	19	80
Wyoming	3	3	4	5	3	1	2	1	1	7

Source: National Safety Council tabulations of National Center for Health Statistics mortality data.
[a] *Deaths are by place of occurrence and exclude nonresident aliens. See also page 25.*
[b] *See page 102 for motor-vehicle deaths by place of residence.*
[c] *Includes water transport drownings.*
[d] *Complications and misadventures of surgical and medical care.*
[e] *Includes water transportation (except drowning), other transportation, adverse effects of drugs in therapeutic use, and other manners of injury.*

TECHNICAL APPENDIX

This appendix gives a brief explanation of some of the sources and methods used by the National Safety Council (NSC) Research and Statistics Department in preparing the estimates of deaths, injuries, and costs presented in this book. Because many of the estimates depend on death certificate data provided by the states or the National Center for Health Statistics (NCHS), it begins with a brief introduction to the certification and classification of deaths.

Certification and classification. The medical certification of death involves entering information on the death certificate about the disease or condition directly leading to death, antecedent causes, and other significant conditions. The death certificate is then registered with the appropriate authority and a nosologist assigns a code for the underlying cause of death. The underlying cause is defined as "(a) the disease or injury which initiated the train of morbid events leading directly to death, or (b) the circumstances of the accident or violence which produced the fatal injury" (World Health Organization [WHO], 1993). Deaths are classified and coded on the basis of a WHO standard, the *International Statistical Classification of Diseases and Related Health Problems,* commonly known as the International Classification of Diseases or ICD (WHO, 1993). For deaths due to injury and poisoning, the ICD provides a system of "external cause" codes, or E-codes, to which the underlying cause of death is assigned. (See pages 16–17 of *Injury Facts®* for a condensed list of E-codes.)

Comparability across ICD revisions. The ICD is revised periodically and these revisions can affect comparability from year to year. The sixth revision (1948) substantially expanded the list of external causes and provided for classifying the place of occurrence. Changes in the classification procedures for the sixth revision as well as the seventh (1958) and eighth (1968) revisions classified as diseases some deaths previously classified as injuries. The eighth revision also expanded and reorganized some external cause sections. The ninth revision (1979) provides more detail on the agency involved, the victim's activity, and the place of occurrence. The tenth revision, which was adopted in the United States in 1999, completely revised the transportation-related categories. Specific external cause categories affected by the revisions are noted in the historical tables.

Beginning with 1970 data, tabulations published by the NCHS no longer include deaths of nonresident aliens. In 1998, there were 649 such unintentional-injury deaths, of which 296 were motor-vehicle related.

Fatality estimates. The Council uses four classes to categorize unintentional injuries: Motor Vehicle, Work, Home, and Public. Each class represents an environment and an intervention route for injury prevention through a responsible authority such as a police department, an employer, a home owner, or public health department.

Motor vehicle. The Motor-Vehicle class can be identified by the underlying cause of death (ICD-9 codes E810–E825).

Work. The National Safety Council adopted the Bureau of Labor Statistics' Census of Fatal Occupational Injuries (CFOI) figure, beginning with the 1992 data year, as the authoritative count of unintentional work-related deaths. The CFOI system is described in detail in Toscano and Windau (1994).

The 2-Way Split. After subtracting the Motor-Vehicle and Work figures from the unintentional-injury total (ICD-9 codes E800–E949), the remainder belong to the Home and Public classes. The Home class can be identified by the "place of occurrence" subclassification (code .0) used with most nontransport deaths; the Public class is the remainder. Missing "place of occurrence" information, however, prevents the direct determination of the Home and Public class totals. Because of this, the Council allocates nonmotor-vehicle, nonwork deaths into the Home and Public classes based on the external cause, age group, and cases with specified "place of occurrence." This procedure, known as the 2-Way Split, uses the most recent death certificate data available from the NCHS and the CFOI data for the same calendar year. For each E-code group and age group combination, the Motor-Vehicle (ICD-9 E810–E825) and Work (CFOI) deaths are subtracted and the remainder, including those with "place of occurrence" unspecified, are allocated to Home and Public in the same proportion as those with "place of occurrence" specified.

The table on page 165 shows the ICD-9 E-codes and CFOI event codes for the most common causes of unintentional-injury death. The CFOI event codes (BLS, 1992) do not match exactly with ICD-9 E-codes, so there is some error in the allocation of deaths among the classes.

State reporting system. The Council operates a reporting system through which participating states send monthly tabulations of unintentional-injury death data by age group, class, and type of event or industry. This is known as the Injury Mortality Tabulation reporting system. These data are used to make current year estimates based on the most recent 2-Way Split and CFOI data, and to make monthly estimates published in *Injury Insights.*

Linking up to current year. The benchmark data published by NCHS are usually two years old and the CFOI data are usually one year old. The link-relative technique is used to make current year estimates from these data using the state vital statistics data. This method assumes that the change in deaths from one year to the next in states reporting for both years reflects the change in deaths for the entire nation. The ratio is calculated and multiplied times the benchmark figure resulting in an estimate for the next year. It may be necessary to repeat the process, depending on the reference year of the benchmark. For example, the 1998 NCHS and CFOI data were used this year for a 2-Way Split and state data were used to make estimates for 1999 and 2000 Home and Public classes using the link-relative technique. CFOI data for 1999 were also available so it was necessary only to make 2000 Work estimates.

Revisions of prior years. When the figures for a given year are published by NCHS, the 2-Way Split based on those figures and the CFOI become the final

estimate of unintentional-injury deaths by class, age group, and type of event or industry. Subsequent years are revised by repeating the link-relative process described above. For example, in the 2001 edition of *Injury Facts®*, the 1998 NCHS and CFOI data were used to produce final estimates using the 2-Way Split, the 1999 estimates were revised using more complete state data and 1999 CFOI figures, and the new 2000 estimates were made with the state data available in the spring of 2001.

Nonfatal injury estimates. The Council uses the concept of "disabling injury" to define the kinds of injuries included in its estimates. See page 21 for the definition of disabling injury and the National Health Interview Survey (NHIS) injury definitions.

Injury to death ratios. There is no national injury surveillance system that provides disabling injury estimates on a current basis. The National Health Interview Survey, a household survey conducted by the NCHS (see page 21), produces national estimates using its own definition of injury, but the data are not published until well after the reference year (Adams, Hendershot, & Marano, 1999). For this reason, the Council uses injury-to-death ratios to estimate nonfatal disabling injuries for the current year. Complete documentation of the background and new procedure, effective with the 1993 edition, may be found in Landes, Ginsburg, Hoskin, and Miller (1990).

The ratios, one for each class, are a 3-year moving average of the NHIS injury data and the corresponding Council estimates of deaths. Because the NHIS does not use the Council's definition of disabling injury, the NHIS data are adjusted to approximate the disabling concept. The adjustment involves counting only injuries that result in two or more days of restricted activity. (The NHIS counts only whole days of restricted activity even though the definition is stated in terms of half days. One day counted includes from one-half day up to one and one-half days of actual restriction. Two days counted includes from one and one-half up to two and one-half.)

Comparability over time. Even though the injury to death ratios are updated each time a new NHIS is released, the resulting estimates are not direct measures of nonfatal injuries and should not be compared with prior years.

Population sources. All population figures used in computing rates are taken from various reports in the P-25 series published by the Bureau of the Census, U.S. Department of Commerce. *Resident* population is used for computing rates.

Costs (pp. 4–7). The procedures for estimating the economic losses due to fatal and nonfatal unintentional injuries were extensively revised for the 1993 edition of *Accident Facts®*. New components were added, new benchmarks adopted, and a new discount rate assumed. All of these changes resulted in significantly higher cost estimates. For this reason, it must be re-emphasized that the cost estimates should not be compared to those in earlier editions of the book.

The Council's general philosophy underlying its cost estimates is that the figures represent income not received or expenses incurred because of fatal and nonfatal unintentional injuries. Stated this way, the Council's cost estimates are a measure of the economic impact of unintentional injuries and may be compared to other economic measures such as gross domestic product, per capita income, or personal consumption expenditures. (See page 87 and "lost quality of life" [p. 163] for a discussion of injury costs for cost-benefit analysis.)

The general approach followed was to identify a benchmark unit cost for each component, adjust the benchmark to the current year using an appropriate inflator, estimate the number of cases to which the component applied, and compute the product. Where possible, benchmarks were obtained for each class: Motor Vehicle, Work, Home, and Public.

Wage and productivity losses include the value of wages, fringe benefits, and household production for all classes, and travel delay for the Motor Vehicle class.

For fatalities, the present value of after-tax wages, fringe benefits, and household production was computed using the human capital method. The procedure incorporates data on life expectancy from the NCHS life tables, employment likelihood from the Bureau of Labor Statistics household survey, and mean earnings from the Bureau of the Census money income survey. The discount rate used was 4%, reduced from 6% used in earlier years. The present value obtained is highly sensitive to the discount rate; the lower the rate, the greater the present value.

For permanent partial disabilities, an average of 17% of earning power is lost (Berkowitz & Burton, 1987). The incidence of permanent disabilities, adjusted to remove intentional injuries, was computed from data on hospitalized cases from the National Hospital Discharge Survey (NHDS) and nonhospitalized cases from the National Health Interview Survey and National Council on Compensation Insurance (NCCI) data on probabilities of disability by nature of injury and part of body injured.

For temporary disabilities, an average daily wage, fringe benefit, and household production loss was calculated and this was multiplied by the number of days of restricted activity from the NHIS.

Travel delay costs were obtained from the Council's estimates of the number of fatal, injury, and property damage crashes and an average delay cost per crash from Miller et al. (1991).

Medical expenses, including ambulance and helicopter transport costs, were estimated for fatalities, hospitalized cases, and nonhospitalized cases in each class.

The incidence of hospitalized cases was derived from the NHDS data adjusted to eliminate intentional injuries. Average length of stay was benchmarked from Miller, Pindus, Douglass, and Rossman (1993b) and adjusted to estimate lifetime length of stay. The cost per hospital day was benchmarked to the National Medical Expenditure Survey (NMES).

Nonhospitalized cases were estimated by taking the difference between total NHIS injuries and hospitalized cases. Average cost per case was based on NMES data adjusted for inflation and lifetime costs.

Medical cost of fatalities was benchmarked to data from the National Council on Compensation Insurance (1989) to which was added the cost of a premature funeral and coroner costs (Miller et al., 1991).

Cost per ambulance transport was benchmarked to NMES data and cost per helicopter transport was benchmarked to data in Miller et al. (1993a). The number of cases transported was based on data from Rice and MacKenzie (1989) and the National Electronic Injury Surveillance System.

Administrative expenses include the administrative cost of private and public insurance, which represents the cost of having insurance, and police and legal costs.

The administrative cost of motor-vehicle insurance was the difference between premiums earned (adjusted to remove fire, theft, and casualty premiums) and pure losses incurred, based on data from A. M. Best. Workers' compensation insurance administration was based on A. M. Best data for private carriers and regression estimates using Social Security Administration data for state funds and the self-insured. Administrative costs of public insurance (mainly Medicaid and Medicare) amount to about 4% of the medical expenses paid by public insurance, which were determined from Rice and MacKenzie (1989) and Hensler et al. (1991).

Average police costs for motor-vehicle crashes were taken from Miller et al. (1991) and multiplied by the Council's estimates of the number of fatal, injury, and property damage crashes.

Legal expenses include court costs, and plaintiff's and defendant's time and expenses. Hensler et al. (1991) provided data on the proportion of injured persons who hire a lawyer, file a claim, and get compensation. Kakalik and Pace (1986) provided data on costs per case.

Fire losses were based on data published by the National Fire Protection Association in the *NFPA Journal.* The allocation into the classes was based on the property use for structure fires and other NFPA data for nonstructure fires.

Motor-vehicle damage costs were benchmarked to Blincoe and Faigin (1992) and multiplied by the Council's estimates of crash incidence.

Employer costs for work injuries is an estimate of the productivity costs incurred by employers. It assumes each fatality or permanent injury resulted in 4 person-months of disruption, serious injuries 1 person-month, and minor to moderate injuries 2 person-days. All injuries to nonworkers were assumed to involve 2 days of worker productivity loss. Average hourly earnings for supervisors and nonsupervisory workers were computed and then multiplied by the incidence and hours lost per case. Property damage and production delays (except motor-vehicle related) are not included in the estimates but can be substantial.

Lost quality of life is the difference between the value of a statistical fatality or statistical injury and the value of after-tax wages, fringe benefits, and household production. Because this does not represent real income not received or expenses incurred, it is not included in the total economic cost figure. If included, the resulting *comprehensive costs* can be used in cost-benefit analysis because the total costs then represent the maximum amount society should spend to prevent a statistical death or injury.

Work deaths and injuries (p. 46). The method for estimating total work-related deaths and injuries is discussed above. The breakdown of deaths by industry division for the current year is obtained from the CFOI and state Injury Mortality Tabulation figures using the link-relative technique (also discussed above).

The estimate of nonfatal disabling injuries by industry division is made by multiplying the estimate of employment for each industry division by the BLS estimate of the incidence rate of cases involving days away from work for each division (e.g., BLS, 2000) and then adjusting the results so that they add to the work-injury total previously established. The "private sector" average incidence rate is used for the government division, which is not covered in the BLS survey.

Employment. The employment estimates for 1992 to the present were changed for the 1998 edition. Estimates for these years in prior editions are not comparable. The total employment figure used by the Council represents the number of persons in the civilian labor force, aged 16 and older, who were wage or salary workers, self-employed, or unpaid family workers, plus active duty military personnel resident in the U.S. The total employment estimate is a combination of three figures—total civilian employment from the Current Population Survey (CPS) as published in *Employment and Earnings*, plus the difference between total resident population and total civilian population, which represents active duty military personnel.

Employment by industry division is obtained from an unpublished Bureau of Labor Statistics table titled "Employed and experienced unemployed persons by detailed industry and class of worker, Annual Average [year] (based on CPS)."

Time lost (p. 49) is the product of the number of cases and the average time lost per case. Deaths average 150 workdays lost in the current year and 5,850 in future years; permanent disabilities involve 75 and 565 days lost in current and future years, respectively; temporary disabilities involve 17 days lost in the current year only. Off-the-job injuries to workers are assumed to result in similar lost time.

Off-the-job (p. 50) deaths and injuries are estimated by assuming that employed persons incur injuries at the same rate as the entire population.

Motor-Vehicle section (pp. 82–115). Estimates of miles traveled, registered vehicles, and licensed drivers are published by the Federal Highway Administration in *Highway Statistics and Traffic Volume Trends*.

In addition to the death certificate data from NCHS and state registrars, the Council receives annual summary reports of traffic crash characteristics from about 15 states. Most national estimates are made using various ratios and percent distributions from the state crash data.

Beginning with the 1998 edition of *Accident Facts*, national estimates of crashes by manner of collision (p. 86) and motor-vehicles involved in crashes by type of vehicle (p. 96) are made using the percent changes from the previous year to the current year as reported by the states. This percent change is then applied to benchmark figures obtained from the National Highway Traffic Safety Administration (NHTSA), Fatality Analysis Reporting System (FARS), and General Estimates System (GES) data for the previous year, which yields the current year estimates. These current year estimates are then adjusted to add to the Council's overall number of deaths, injuries and fatal, injury, and property damage-only crashes that are listed on page 82. Because of these changes, comparisons to previous years should not be made.

Fleet accident rates (p. 107) represents the experience of motor fleets that participated in the Council's National Fleet Safety Contest. For the purposes of the contest all death and injury accidents were included as well as *all* accidents (preventable or not preventable) resulting in property damage except when the vehicle was properly parked. Because of the nature of the reporting system, these accident rates cannot be considered representative of the national experience of motor fleets.

REFERENCES

Adams, P.F., Hendershot, G.E., & Marano, M.A. (1999). *Current estimates from the National Health Interview Survey, 1996.* Vital and Health Statistics 10*(200).* Hyattsville, MD: National Center for Health Statistics.

Berkowitz, M., & Burton, J.F., Jr. (1987). *Permanent Disability Benefits in Workers' Compensation.* Kalamazoo, MI: W.E. Upjohn Institute for Employment Research.

Blincoe, L.J., & Faigin, B.M. (1992). *Economic Cost of Motor Vehicle Crashes, 1990. Springfield, VA: National Technical Information Service.*

Bureau of Labor Statistics [BLS]. (1992). *Occupational Injury & Illness Classification Manual. Itasca, IL: National Safety Council.*

Bureau of Labor Statistics [BLS]. (2000, December 12). *Workplace Injuries and Illnesses in 1999. Press release USDL-00-357.*

Hensler, D.R., Marquis, M.S., Abrahamse, A.F., Berry, S.H., Ebener, P.A., Lewis, E.D., Lind, E.A., MacCoun, R.J., Manning, W.G., Rogowski, J.A., & Vaiana, M.E. (1991). *Compensation for Accidental Injuries in the United States. Santa Monica, CA: The RAND Corporation.*

Kakalik, J.S., & Pace, N. (1986). *Costs and Compensation Paid in Tort Litigation. R-3391-ICJ. Santa Monica, CA: The RAND Corporation.*

Landes, S.R., Ginsburg, K.M., Hoskin, A.F., & Miller, T.A. (1990). *Estimating Nonfatal Injuries. Itasca, IL: Statistics Department, National Safety Council.*

Miller, T., Viner, J., Rossman, S., Pindus, N., Gellert, W., Douglass, J., Dillingham, A., & Blomquist, G. (1991). *The Costs of Highway Crashes. Springfield, VA: National Technical Information Service.*

Miller, T.R., Brigham, P.A., Cohen, M.A., Douglass, J.B., Galbraith, M.S., Lestina, D.C., Nelkin, V.S., Pindus, N.M., & Smith-Regojo, P. (1993a). Estimating the costs to society of cigarette fire injuries. Report to Congress in Response to the Fire Safe Cigarette Act of 1990. *Washington, DC: U.S. Consumer Product Safety Commission.*

Miller, T.R., Pindus, N.M., Douglass, J.B., & Rossman, S.B. (1993b). *Nonfatal Injury Incidence, Costs, and Consequences: A Data Book. Washington, DC: The Urban Institute Press.*

Rice, D.P., & MacKenzie, E.J. (1989). *Cost of Injury in the United States: A Report to Congress. Atlanta, GA: Centers for Disease Control and Prevention.*

Toscano, G., & Windau, J. (1994). *The changing character of fatal work injuries.* Monthly Labor Review, 117*(10), 17-28.*

World Health Organization. (1977). *Manual of the International Statistical Classification of Diseases, Injuries, and Causes of Death. Geneva, Switzerland: Author.*

World Health Organization. (1993). *International Statistical Classification of Diseases and Related Health Problems–Tenth Revision. Geneva, Switzerland: Author.*

SELECTED UNINTENTIONAL-INJURY CODE GROUPINGS

Manner of Injury	ICD-9 E-Codes[a]	OI&ICM[b] Event Codes
Air transport accident	E840–E845	46
Drowning	E910	381
Falls	E880–E888	1
Firearms	E922	0220, 0222, 0229 with source = 911[c]
Fires and burns	E890–E899	51
Mechanical suffocation	E913	383, 384, 389
Motor-vehicle accident	E810–E825	41, 42, 43
Poisoning by gases and vapors	E867–E869	341
Poisoning by solids & liquids	E850–E858, E860–E866	344
Railway accident	E800–E807	44
Suffocation by ingestion	E911–E912	382
Water transport accident	E830–E838	45

Source: National Safety Council.
[a] International Classification of Diseases, *9th Revision, external cause codes,* WHO (1977).
[b] Occupational Injury & Illness Classification Manual, *BLS (1992).*
[c] Struck by flying object where the source of injury was a bullet.

OTHER SOURCES

The following organizations may be useful for obtaining more current data or more detailed information on various subjects in *Injury Facts®*.

Visit the National Safety Council's web site at www.nsc.org for links to these and other sources.

Federal Highway Administration
400 7th Street, SW, Washington, DC 20590
(202) 366-0660   www.fhwa.dot.gov

Federal Railroad Administration
400 7th Street, SW, Washington, DC 20590
(202) 366-2760   www.fra.dot.gov

Insurance Information Institute
110 William Street, New York, NY 10038
(212) 669-9200   www.iii.org

Insurance Institute for Highway Safety
1005 N. Glebe Road, Suite 800, Arlington, VA 22201
(703) 247-1500   www.highwaysafety.org

International Hunter Education Association
P.O. Box 490, Wellington, CO 80549-0490
(970) 568-7954   www.ihea.com

International Labour Office
4, rue des Morillons
CH-1211 Geneva 22
Switzerland
Phone: +41-22-799-6111
Fax: +41-22-798-8685   www.ilo.org

Mine Safety and Health Administration
Health & Safety Analysis Center
Division of Mining Information
P.O. Box 25367, Denver, CO 80225
(303) 231-5445   www.msha.gov

Motorcycle Safety Foundation
2 Jenner St., Suite 150, Irvine, CA 92718-3812
(714) 727-3227   www.msf-usa.org

National Academy of Social Insurance
1776 Massachusetts Avenue, NW, Suite 615
Washington, DC 20036-1904
(202) 452-8097   www.nasi.org

National Center for Health Statistics
6525 Belcrest Road, Hyattsville, MD 20782
(301) 458-4636   www.cdc.gov/nchs

National Center for Injury Prevention and Control
Office Of Communication Resources
4770 Buford Hwy., NE, Mail Stop K65, Atlanta, GA 30341-3724
(770) 488-1506   www.cdc.gov/ncipc

National Clearinghouse for Alcohol and Drug Information
P.O. Box 2345, Rockville, MD 20847-2345
(301) 468-2600 or 1-800-729-6686   www.health.org

National Collegiate Athletic Association
6201 College Boulevard, Overland Park, KS 66211-2422
(913) 339-1906   www.ncaa.org

National Council on Compensation Insurance
750 Park of Commerce Drive, Boca Raton, FL 33487
1-800-NCCI-123 (1-800-622-4123)   www.ncci.com

National Fire Protection Association
P.O. Box 9101, Batterymarch Park, Quincy, MA 02269-0910
(617) 770-3000 or 1-800-344-3555   www.nfpa.org

National Head Injury Foundation
1776 Massachusetts Ave., NW, Suite 100, Washington, DC 20036
(202) 296-6443

National Highway Traffic Safety Administration
400 7th Street, SW, Washington, DC 20590
(202) 366-0123 or 1-800-424-9393   www.nhtsa.dot.gov

National Center for Statistics and Analysis (NRD-31)
400 7th Street, SW, Washington, DC 20590
1-800-934-8517

National Institute for Occupational Safety and Health
Clearinghouse for Occupational Safety and Health Information
4676 Columbia Parkway, Cincinnati, OH 45226
1-800-356-4674   www.cdc.gov/niosh

National Spinal Cord Injury Association
600 W. Cummings Park, Suite 2000, Woburn, MA 01801
1-800-962-9629 (Hotline) or (617) 935-2722   www.spinalcord.org

National Sporting Goods Association
1699 Wall Street, Mt. Prospect, IL 60056-5780
(847) 296-6742

National Transportation Safety Board
490 L'Enfant Plaza East, SW, Washington, DC 20594
(202) 382-6735   www.ntsb.gov

Prevent Blindness America
500 E. Remington Road, Schaumburg, IL 60173
(847) 843-2020   www.preventblindness.org

Transportation Research Board
2101 Constitution Avenue, NW, Washington, DC 20418
(202) 334-2935   www.nas.edu/trb

U.S. Coast Guard
2100 2nd Street, SW, Washington, DC 20593-0001
(202) 267-2229   www.uscgboating.org

U.S. Consumer Product Safety Commission
National Injury Information Clearinghouse
4330 East West Highway, Washington, DC 20207
(301) 504-0424   www.cpsc.gov

U.S. Department of Commerce
Bureau of the Census, Public Information Office
Washington, DC 20233-8200
(301) 457-2794   www.census.gov

U.S. Department of Labor
Bureau of Labor Statistics
2 Massachusetts Ave., NE, Washington, DC 20212
(202) 691-7828   stats.bls.gov/oshhome.htm
OSHA Office of Statistics, Room N-3507
200 Constitution Ave., NW, Washington, DC 20210
(202) 693-1702

World Health Organization
20, ave. Appia
CH-1211 Geneva 27
Switzerland
Phone: +41-22-791-2111   www.who.int
Fax: +41-22-791-0746

Accident is that occurrence in a sequence of events that produces unintended injury, death or property damage. *Accident* refers to the event, not the result of the event (see *unintentional injury*).

Cases without lost workdays are cases that do not involve lost workdays but result in medical treatment other than first aid, restriction of work or motion, loss of consciousness, transfer to another job, or diagnosis of occupational illness.

Death from accident is a death that occurs within one year of the accident.

Disabling injury is an injury causing death, permanent disability, or any degree of temporary total disability beyond the day of the injury.

Fatal accident is an accident that results in one or more deaths within one year.

Home is a dwelling and its premises within the property lines including single-family dwellings and apartment houses, duplex dwellings, boarding and rooming houses and seasonal cottages. Excluded from Home are barracks, dormitories and resident institutions.

Incidence rate, as defined by OSHA, is the number of occupational injuries and/or illnesses or lost workdays per 100 full-time employees. See formula on page 59.

Injury is physical harm or damage to the body resulting from an exchange, usually acute, of mechanical, chemical, thermal, or other environmental energy that exceeds the body's tolerance.

Lost workdays are those days on which, because of occupational injury or illness, the employee was away from work or limited to restricted work activity. *Days away from work* are those days on which the employee would have worked but could not. *Days of restricted work* activity are those days on which the employee was assigned to a temporary job, worked at a permanent job less than full time, or worked at a permanent job but could not perform all duties normally connected with it. The number of lost workdays (consecutive or not) does not include the day of injury or onset of illness or any days on which the employee would not have worked even though able to work.

Lost workday cases are cases that involve days away from work, days of restricted work activity, or both.

Motor vehicle is any mechanically or electrically powered device not operated on rails, upon which or by which any person or property may be transported upon a land highway. The load on a motor vehicle or trailer attached to it is considered part of the vehicle. Tractors and motorized machinery are included while self-propelled in transit or used for transportation. *Nonmotor vehicle* is any road vehicle other than a motor vehicle, such as a bicycle or animal-drawn vehicle, **except** a coaster wagon, child's sled, child's tricycle, child's carriage, and similar means of transportation; persons using these latter means of transportation are considered pedestrians.

Motor-vehicle accident is an unstabilized situation that includes at least one harmful event (injury or property damage) involving a motor vehicle in transport (in motion, in readiness for motion, or on a roadway but not parked in a designated parking area) that does not result from discharge of a firearm or explosive device and does not directly result from a cataclysm. [See Committee on Motor Vehicle Traffic Accident Classification (1997), *Manual on Classification of Motor Vehicle Traffic Accidents,* ANSI D16.1-1996, Itasca, IL: National Safety Council.]

Motor-vehicle traffic accident is a motor-vehicle accident that occurs on a trafficway—a way or place, any part of which is open to the use of the public for the purposes of vehicular traffic. *Motor-vehicle nontraffic accident* is any motor-vehicle accident that occurs entirely in any place other than a trafficway.

Nonfatal injury accident is an accident in which at least one person is injured and no injury results in death.

Occupational illness is any abnormal condition or disorder other than one resulting from an occupational injury caused by exposure to environmental factors associated with employment. It includes acute and chronic illnesses or diseases that may be caused by inhalation, absorption, ingestion, or direct contact. See also page 59.

Occupational injury is any injury such as a cut, fracture, sprain, amputation, etc., which results from a work accident or from a single instantaneous exposure in the work environment. See also page 59.

Pedalcycle is a vehicle propelled by human power and operated solely by pedals; excludes mopeds.

Pedestrian is any person involved in a motor-vehicle accident who is not in or upon a motor vehicle or nonmotor vehicle. Includes persons injured while using a coaster wagon, child's tricycle, roller skates, etc. Excludes persons boarding, alighting, jumping, or falling from a motor vehicle in transport who are considered occupants of the vehicle.

Permanent disability (or permanent impairment) includes any degree of permanent nonfatal injury. It includes any injury that results in the loss or complete loss of use of any part of the body or in any permanent impairment of functions of the body or a part thereof.

Property damage accident is an accident that results in property damage but in which no person is injured.

Public accident is any accident other than motor-vehicle that occurs in the public use of any premises. Includes deaths in recreation (swimming, hunting, etc.), in transportation except motor-vehicle, public buildings, etc., and from widespread natural disasters even though some may have happened on home premises. Excludes accidents to persons in the course of gainful employment.

Source of injury is the principal object such as tool, machine, or equipment involved in the accident and is usually the object inflicting injury or property damage. Also called agency or agent.

Temporary total disability is an injury that does not result in death or permanent disability but that renders the injured person unable to perform regular duties or activities on one or more full calendar days after the day of the injury.

Total cases include all work-related deaths and illnesses and those work-related injuries that result in loss of consciousness, restriction of work or motion, transfer to another job, or require medical treatment other than first aid.

Unintentional injury is the preferred term for accidental injury in the public health community. It refers to the *result* of an accident.

Work hours are the total number of hours worked by all employees. They are usually compiled for various levels, such as an establishment, a company, or an industry. A work hour is the equivalent of one employee working one hour.

Work injuries (including occupational illnesses) are those that arise out of and in the course of gainful employment regardless of where the accident or exposure occurs. Excluded are work injuries to private household workers and injuries occurring in connection with farm chores that are classified as home injuries.

Workers are all persons gainfully employed, including owners, managers, other paid employees, the self-employed, and unpaid family workers but excluding private household workers.

Work/Motor-vehicle duplication includes *work injuries* that occur in *motor-vehicle accidents* (see definitions for work injuries and motor-vehicle accident on this page).

INDEX